GODS OF THE ANCIENT NORTHMEN

PUBLISHED UNDER THE AUSPICES OF THE CENTER FOR THE STUDY OF COMPARATIVE FOLKLORE AND MYTHOLOGY, UNIVERSITY OF CALIFORNIA, LOS ANGELES

PUBLICATIONS OF THE UCLA CENTER FOR THE STUDY OF COMPARATIVE FOLKLORE AND MYTHOLOGY

1. Jaan Puhvel (ed.), *Myth and Law among the Indo-Europeans*, 1970.
2. Wayland D. Hand (ed.), *American Folk Legend*, 1971.
3. Georges Dumézil, *Gods of the Ancient Northmen*, 1973.

Gods of the Ancient Northmen

by GEORGES DUMÉZIL

edited by EINAR HAUGEN
introduction by C. Scott Littleton and Udo Strutynski

UNIVERSITY OF CALIFORNIA PRESS
Berkeley Los Angeles London

UCLA CENTER FOR THE STUDY OF
COMPARATIVE FOLKLORE AND MYTHOLOGY

Publications: III

University of California Press
Berkeley and Los Angeles, California

University of California Press, Ltd.
London, England

The Gods of the Ancient Northmen is translated from
Georges Dumézil, *Les Dieux des Germains,* Presses Universitaires de France

First Paperback Edition, 1977

ISBN: 0—520—02044—8
Library of Congress Catalog Card Number: 74—157819

Printed in the United States of America

1 2 3 4 5 6 7 8 9 0

Contents

Editor's Preface vii
Introduction, Part I, by C. Scott Littleton ix
Introduction, Part II, by Udo Strutynski xix
Author's Preface xlv

Part One: Gods of the Ancient Northmen

1. The Gods: Æsir and Vanir 3
   Translated by John Lindow
2. Magic, War, and Justice: Odin and Tyr 26
   Translated by John Lindow
3. The Drama of the World: Balder, Hoder, Loki 49
   Translated by Alan Toth
4. From Storm to Pleasure: Thor, Njord, Frey, Freya 66
   Translated by Alan Toth

Bibliographical Notes (Chapters 1–4) 80

Part Two: Minor Scandinavian Gods

5. Two Minor Scandinavian Gods: Byggvir and Beyla (1952) 89
   Translated by John Lindow
6. The *Rigsþula* and Indo-European Social Structure (1958) 118
   Translated by John Lindow
7. Comparative Remarks on the Scandinavian God Heimdall (1959) 126
   Translated by Francis Charat
8. Notes on the Cosmic Bestiary of the *Edda* and the *Rig Veda* (1959) 141
   Translated by George Gopen

Index 151

Editor's Preface

EINAR HAUGEN

This volume is a result of collaboration of the undersigned with students in his course in Scandinavian Mythology at Harvard University (1965–1971). The lack of an English version of Dumézil's studies left so embarrassing a lacuna in the field that I encouraged qualified students to translate a chapter or an article in lieu of a term paper. I have then carefully checked the translations against the original, revised them where necessary, and edited them into a common format. Professor Dumézil has kindly cooperated in our work of revision and translation, so that all changes in content from the originals are either proposed or authorized by him.

The names of the translators appear in the table of contents opposite each chapter or article for which they prepared the original draft. I wish to thank them here for their assistance, especially John Lindow, who has had the greatest share in the work. The others are Alan Toth, Francis Charat, and George Gopen. I am also grateful to C. Scott Littleton for his interest in the volume. For some comments on Dumézil's conceptions see my article, "The mythical structure of the ancient Scandinavians: Some thoughts on reading Dumézil," in *To Honor Roman Jakobson* (The Hague: Mouton, 1967), 855–868; reprinted in *Introduction to Structuralism*, ed. M. Lane (New York: Basic Books, 1970), 170–183.

Cambridge, Mass., 1973

Introduction, Part I

C. SCOTT LITTLETON

Several years ago, in a book[1] devoted to the remarkable scholarly achievements of Georges Dumézil, I was forced to state that as yet no English translations of his books had been attempted and that, save for a handful of specialists in the several Indo-European-speaking traditions, he was all but unknown in "le monde anglo-saxon." Since 1966, however, thanks in some small measure to that book and, more important, to the recent appearance of English translations of two of Dumézil's major works (*Archaic Roman Religion* [1970] and *The Destiny of the Warrior* [1970], both published by the University of Chicago Press), this unhappy circumstance has begun to be rectified. That Professor Haugen and his students have seen fit to render *Les dieux des Germains* into *Gods of the Ancient Northmen* is further proof that one of the most significant contributions to general knowledge yet made in this century is finally receiving the attention it deserves on this side of the Atlantic.

It would be impossible here to discuss in any detail the evolution of Dumézil's conception of the fundamental structure of the common Indo-European ideology, let alone to treat adequately its present status. Nevertheless, to put the present work into its proper context, especially for those readers otherwise unfamiliar with Dumézil, it is necessary to sketch very briefly the "grandes lignes," as it were, of this conception, to say a few words about how and why it developed, and to comment on its general significance for the human sciences.[2]

* * *

1 C. Scott Littleton, *The New Comparative Mythology*, 2d ed. (Berkeley and Los Angeles: University of California Press, 1973).

2 The following overview of Professor Dumézil's work and what I believe to be

In the early decades of the present century, thanks to the rapid demise of Max Müller's "solar mythology" at the hands of anthropologists and others, comparative mythology—especially comparative Indo-European mythology—reached a low ebb. The grand theories of the nineteenth century could no longer be supported, but no new synthesis was immediately forthcoming. Narrowly focused research into the specific Indo-European traditions—Greek, Indic, Celtic, Germanic, and the like—became the order of the day. Yet the basic problems to which Müller and his school had addressed themselves remained unresolved, and in 1924 a young Indo-Europeanist, Georges Dumézil, set out to find a new and viable theoretical framework in terms of which these problems might once more be approached; problems posed by the obvious functional, if not onomastic parallels between a great many ancient Indo-European gods and heroes.

Dumézil's first attempts (e.g. *Le festin d'immortalité* [1924], *Le problème des Centaures* [1929]) to develop a new framework, grounded as they were in Frazerian theory, proved unsuccessful. By 1938, however, he had made a major discovery and had come to draw upon a wholly different theoretical source. The discovery was that the ancient Indo-European-speaking communities, from Rome to India, were most likely characterized, at least in their earliest phases, by a tripartite social class system; one that very broadly resembled the three Aryan or "twice born" castes of medieval and modern India.[3] The new theoretical base was what might generally be termed the "French sociological school," as developed by Durkheim, Mauss, and others. Although it is certainly unfair to characterize Dumézil as an immediate disciple of this school (his fundamental training was in philology and the history of religions), he

its most important implications for the "human sciences" (the more conventional term "social sciences" somehow seems inappropriate here) necessarily reflects in some measure my own opinions as an anthropologist. It should be emphasized that Dumézil, who is not an anthropologist but a comparative philologist, does not fully agree with all of these opinions. This cordial disagreement stems in large part, I believe, from the rather considerable differences in perspective between our two fields, and it in no way affects my estimate of the soundness of his research, which, as I have already indicated, must be regarded as one of the most brilliant and fundamental scholarly achievements of our time.

[3] In recent years Dumézil has insisted that the presence of the tripartite ideology does not necessarily imply the presence of a tripartite social system (see, for example, Georges Dumézil, *Mythe et épopée* I [Paris: Gallimard, 1968], pp. 14–16). Admittedly, the evidence (outside of India) for social tripartition is far less certain than that for supernatural tripartition. Yet I do feel that, if only on the basis of general social theory—I must confess to being something of an unreconstructed Durkheimian—it *is* possible to postulate the existence of a tripartite social system among the Proto-Indo-Europeans and their immediate descendants.

nevertheless came to adopt—or adapt—several of its most important axioms, especially the one that asserts that important social and cultural realities are "collectively represented" by supernatural beings and concepts, and that there is an intimate and functional connection between social facts and religious facts.

In any event, by 1940–1941,[4] drawing upon his discovery of social tripartition, "la méthode sociologique," and the traditional methods of comparative philology, Dumézil had synthesized a comprehensive model of the common Indo-European ideology; one that, although extensively refined and modified in the years that followed, has remained fundamental to his conception of the ideology in question. As presently formulated, the salient features of this model can be summarized as follows:

The common Indo-European ideology, derived ultimately from one characteristic of the Proto-Indo-European community, was composed of three fundamental principles: (1) maintenance of cosmic and juridical order, (2) the exercise of physical prowess, and (3) the promotion of physical well-being. Each of these principles forms the basis for what Dumézil terms a *fonction*, or "function": that is, a complex whole that includes both the ideological principle itself *and* its numerous manifestations in the several ancient Indo-European social and supernatural systems.[5] The first function was thus expressed in the presence of distinct priest classes (e.g., the Indic Brahmans), which inevitably stood at the apex of their respective social systems and which were collectively represented, in the Durkheimian sense, by a pair of sovereign gods, such as Mitra and Varuṇa in Vedic India, Jupiter and Dius Fidius at Rome, and Odin and Tyr in ancient Scandinavia. Moreover, there was a clear division of labor between these two co-sovereigns: one, let us call him the "Varuṇa figure," had charge of cosmic matters, the other, who may be termed the "Mitra figure," was principally concerned with the maintenance of proper juridical relationships among men. Together they stood at the apex of the supernatural system, just as the priests were at the top of the social hierarchy.

The second function was reflected in the presence of a warrior-

---

4 Dumézil, *Mitra-Varuṇa* (Paris: Presses Universitaires de France, 1940); idem, *Jupiter, Mars, Quirinus* (Paris: Gallimard, 1941).

5 It should be pointed out this this definition of "function" differs rather sharply from that employed by most British, American, and, indeed, French sociologists and anthropologists, who ordinarily use the word to describe the effect or consequences of a behavior or institution upon the social system in which it occurs. For a more extensive discussion of this matter, see Littleton, *The New Comparative Mythology*, pp. 5–6.

ruler class, such as the Indic Kṣatriyas, whose basic role was to exercise force in defense of the society (or to further its imperialistic ambitions), as well as in the collective representations of this class, such as the great Vedic warrior divinity Indra, the Roman god Mars,[6] and the Norse war god Thor. The third function was reflected by the mass of the society, the herders and cultivators upon whom the priests and warriors depended for their sustenance (e.g. the Indic Vaiśyas); this principle was collectively represented by yet another stratum of divinities. In the majority of cases the principal occupants of this third divine stratum were conceived as a pair of closely related kinsmen, the most usual relationship being that of a set of twins[7] (e.g., the Greek Dioscuri, the Vedic Aśvins). More rarely (e.g., the Norse figures Frey and Njord) the relationship was that of father and son. In other instances, notably at Rome, where the god Quirinus embodied the essence of the third function,[8] a single divinity was the prime representative. Typically, but not universally, the third function also included a female divinity who was sometimes conceived as a close kinswoman (or bride) of the chief male representatives (or representative) of the function in question; for example, the Vedic goddess Sarasvatī, the Norse goddess Freya. These interrelated triads of social classes and divine beings served as the framework through which the ancient Indo-European speakers viewed the world. The three functions just noted were endlessly replicated—from triads of diseases[9] to three-fold conceptions of space.[10] What is more, their collective representations were not limited to purely mythic figures, but extended to many epic heroes, such as the five central figures of

---

6 To be sure, Mars cannot be linked with a distinct social class. As Dumézil rightly points out (personal communication), the same Romans devoted themselves to Mars *and* Quirinus, depending upon whether Rome was at war or at peace.

7 For a recent discussion of the extent to which the major third function divinities were conceived as a set of twins, see Donald Ward, *The Divine Twins: An Indo-European Myth in Germanic Tradition* (Berkeley and Los Angeles: University of California Press, 1968).

8 The goddess Ops is often paired with Quirinus, and the two could under certain circumstances be substituted for one another in the *Regia* cults; cf. Dumézil, *Idées romaines* (Paris: Gallimard, 1969), p. 295. As she was also paired with Consus and Mars in other contexts, however, Ops cannot be considered the canonical counterpart of Quirinus.

9 For example, Jaan Puhvel, "Mythological Reflections of Indo-European Medicine," in George Cardona, Henry M. Hoenigswald, and Alfred Senn, eds., *Indo-European and Indo-Europeans* (Philadelphia: University of Pennsylvania Press, 1970), pp. 369–382.

10 Dumézil, *Mythe et épopée*, I, 125–144; M. Mole, "Le partage du monde dans la tradition iranienne," *Journal asiatique* 239 (1952) 283–298.

the *Mahābhārata* (the Pāṇḍava, the Greek figure Herakles, and a variety of Roman and Germanic heroes.[11]

Closely associated with this tripartite model of the Indo-European ideology are several specific themes worthy of note. One involves the concept of a war pitting representatives of the first two functions against those of the third, wherein the latter are defeated[12] and brought into the system, rendering it complete. The best examples of this theme are found in the Roman account of the Sabine War—which, like most of early Roman "history," is but historicized myth—and the Norse myth of the conflict between the Æsir (Odin, Tyr, Thor, et al.) and the Vanir (Frey, Njord, et al.). In these examples the Romans and the Æsir represent the first sovereign function, while the Sabines and the Vanir, neither of whom are primarily noted for sacerdotal or warlike qualities, represent the third or herder-cultivator function and, by extension, the principle of physical well-being. (In a recent article[13] I suggested that the same theme may be found in the *Iliad,* the Achaeans representing the first two functions and the Trojans the third, although the case here is by no means as clear as that presented by the Roman and Norse traditions just described.)

A second related theme is the "three sins of the warrior."[14] As Dumézil sees it, the Indo-European warrior, divine or mortal, played an ambiguous role in the ideology. He was at once integral to the system, forming, as we have seen, the "second function" thereof, and at the same time something of an outsider, an untrustworthy fellow who might at any time turn against representatives of the other two functions. Indeed, as Dumézil has demonstrated, the Indo-European warrior figure typically commits three acts that run counter to the three ideological principles. These include defiance of the sovereign, be he god or mortal (an offense against the first function), cowardice in battle (a sin against the function of which he is the prime representative), and an assault, usually sexual or venal, upon a represen-

---

11 Cf. Dumézil, *Mythe et épopée* I, pp. 261–284; *Mythe et épopée* II (Paris: Gallimard, 1971), pp. 25–58.

12 The word "defeated" is perhaps inappropriate here, as in both the Norse and Roman contexts the third-function group is reconciled to the rest of the system, and there is an honorable peace. It is clear, however, that the dominant party in these honorable settlements is that formed by the representatives of the first two functions.

13 Littleton, "Some Possible Indo-European Themes in the 'Iliad,'" in Jaan Puhvel, ed., *Myth and Law Among the Indo-Europeans* (Berkeley and Los Angeles: University of California Press, 1970), pp. 229–246.

14 Cf. Dumézil, *The Destiny of the Warrior* (Chicago: University of Chicago Press, 1970), pp. 53–110.

tative of the third function. Even the most illustrious warriors, such as Indra, Starkad, and Hercules, were culpable; and they received progressively more severe punishments, usually involving the loss of physical vigor, as each sin was committed.

The warrior's role was not, of course, essentially antisocial; and a third theme, found in the Roman and Indic traditions, concerns the valiant defense of the community against the depredations of a three-headed monster.[15] At Rome, given the Roman tendency to historicize myths, the theme is reflected in the "historical" account by Livy and others of the three Horatii (one of whom survived) and their defeat of the three Curiatii, who may be the rationalized form of a tricephalic adversary that threatened the existence of the Roman state; in India, where myths tend to remain unhistoricized, it is reflected in the Vedic account of the slaying of the three-headed son of Tvaṣṭar by Trita Āptya, who functions in this context as an extension of Indra. Yet even here the warrior's situation is ambiguous, for, having tasted blood—even in a good cause—he is a potential danger to the peace and well-being of the rest of his society and must typically undergo a rite of purification before being readmitted to it.

A fourth theme concerns the extent to which divinities other than the prime representatives of the three functions play parts in the system.[16] For example, in the Indian tradition Mitra is closely associated with two lesser figures, Aryaman and Bhaga. The former is the patron of the community that designated itself as *Arya*; he is the patron of formalized relationships, such as marriage, and thus serves as the immediate link between human beings and the Mitra (or juridical) aspects of sovereignty. Bhaga, whose chief concern is to see that all men receive their fair "share," presides over the distributional aspects of his master's sovereign domain. At Rome, Juventas, at Jupiter's side, serves Aryaman-like functions, while Terminus, who is paired with Iuventas in a well-known tradition, appears to be a counterpart of Bhaga[17] (Terminus's Bhaga-like role is clearly evident in Ovid's *Fasti*, especially 2.642).

Finally, it should be pointed out that there are divinities in most

---

15 *Ibid.*, pp. 3–45.

16 See Dumézil, *Les dieux des Indo-Européens* (Paris: Presses Universitaires de France, 1952), pp. 40–78.

17 Some years ago de Vries suggested that the Germanic word *irmin*, which appears in the names of mythological persons and cult places, may be cognate to Indic Aryaman and therefore reflect the same Indo-European theme. There are, however, some major linguistic difficulties here, and Dumézil has never accepted this interpretation. See Jan de Vries, "La valeur religieuse du mot germanique *irmin*," *Cahiers du sud* 36 (1952), 18–27.

of the ancient Indo-European traditions who fall outside the tripartite scheme per se and who form what Dumézil once termed "l'épine du système," that is, the *whole* supernatural system.[18] Such divinities are typically concerned with beginnings and endings. Among the "introducers" can be included Vāyu in the Vedic tradition, the Roman god Janus, and the Norse Heimdall, who announces the end of the world (see chapter 7 below). At the other end of the spectrum are gods who, like the Indic Agni and the Roman Vesta, are regularly invoked at the end of a ritual and who seem to be concerned with terminations.

* * *

As the foregoing should indicate, Dumézil's model of the Indo-European ideology is indeed a many-splendored thing, and my intent is to discuss only its most essential facets. In the course of the last thirty years, however, several scholars, building upon Dumézil's pioneer research, have materially facilitated the development of the model of Indo-European ideology. Probably the most important single contribution was made in 1947 by Stig Wikander, who demonstrated that the gods of the *Rig Veda* which reflected the three functions—Mitra, Varuṇa, Indra, and others—were transposed into the heroes of the *Mahābhārata,* and thereby opened up a whole new prospect for the study of Indo-European mythology.[19] Another longtime coworker was the late Lucien Gerschel, who, in a series of studies ranging from an analysis of the Indo-European character of the Coriolanus episode[20] in early Roman history to a demonstration of the extent to which the tripartite ideology persists in contemporary Germanic folklore,[21] has added some important new dimensions to the model in question.

In addition to Wikander and Gerschel, several other scholars early and/or long associated with Dumézil's work should be mentioned: Émile Benveniste, whose 1932 demonstration of the tripartite character of the ancient Iranian social structure[22] had a profound influence on the development of Dumézil's ideas; his fellow Iranianist

18 Dumézil, "La tripartition indo-européenne," *Psyche* 2 (1947), 1348–1356.

19 Stig Wikander, "Pāṇḍava-sagan och Mahābhāratas mytiska förutsättnigar," *Religion och Bibel* 6 (1947) 27–39. See also Dumézil, *Mythe et épopée* I, pp. 31–257.

20 Lucien Gerschel, "Coriolan," in *Hommages à Lucien Febvre,* 2 (Paris, 1953), 33–50.

21 Gerschel, "Sur un schème trifonctionnel dans une famille de légendes germaniques," *Revue de l'histoire des religions* 150 (1956), 55–92.

22 Émile Benveniste, "Les classes sociales dans la tradition avestique," *Journal asiatique* 221 (1932), 117–134.

Jacques Duchesne-Guillemin; the eminent Germanist Edgar Polomé; and the late Jan de Vries and Marie-Louise Sjoestedt. More recent contributors have been Francis Vian, Françoise Le Roux, Atsuhiko Yoshida, Donald Ward, Jaan Puhvel, David Evans, Einar Haugen, and the authors of this introduction. All of the foregoing have applied Dumézil's model, or an aspect thereof, to one or several of the ancient Indo-European traditions and in doing so have contributed significantly to its further development.

These, then, are some brief observations about the origin and development of "the new comparative mythology," as practiced by Dumézil and others. As has been seen, this new approach to Indo-European mythology combines theories and methods drawn from several otherwise fairly distinct fields of inquiry—Durkheimian sociology, comparative philology and mythology, and the history of religions—and it remains for me to say something about the overall significance of Dumézil's ideas for the human sciences.

* * *

At first glance, Dumézil's theoretical framework, characterized as it is by the concept of structural replication, would appear to be almost identical to that of the eminent French anthropologist Claude Lévi-Strauss.[23] But there are some important—indeed fundamental—differences between the two. While it is perhaps fair to refer to Dumézil as a "structuralist"[24] in that he is as much concerned with the underlying patterns in myths as he is with their specific content, he does *not* suggest that the tripartite structure found among the ancient Indo-Europeans is a universal feature of the human psyche. Indeed, one of the fundamental axioms upon which his whole system rests is that, in the Old World, it is *uniquely Indo-European*; and that all of the several manifestations of social and supernatural tripartition so far discovered among the several ancient (and not so ancient) Indo-European-speaking communities are linked together into a single, genetically related tradition, one that is indeed bounded in time and space. This is not to imply that elements of this ideology have not from time to time diffused beyond the borders of the Indo-

[23] For example, Claude Lévi-Strauss, "The Structural Study of Myth," in Thomas Sebeok, ed., *Myth: A Symposium*, Bibliographic and Special Series of the American Folklore Society, 5 (1955), 50–68; idem, *Le cru et le cuit* (Paris: Plon, 1964).

[24] Lévi-Strauss has on several occasions referred to Dumézil as a pioneer structuralist; cf. "Social Structure," in A. L. Kroeber, ed., *Anthropology Today* (Chicago: University of Chicago Press, 1953), p. 535; idem, *Le cru et le cuit*, pp. 23, 300.

European-speaking domain,[25] or that communities far removed from that domain may not be possessed of a tripartite ideology predicated upon another (or indeed similar) set of structural principles. What is implied is that the Indo-European ideological tradition is but one tradition among many traditions. To put it another way, while Lévi-Strauss sees, perhaps correctly, a universal tendency to mediate between oppositions, a tendency that in one form or another will manifest itself in all human thought, Dumézil suggests that the tripartite ideology emerged among the speakers of Proto-Indo-European and was developed separately by the heirs to this community as they migrated to their several attested geographical locations, from India to Ireland. In short, the two scholars are working at quite different levels of abstraction and inclusiveness. For Lévi-Strauss, the level is one of the human mind per se; for Dumézil, the level is the much more immediate one of an historically bounded set of related traditions. As I see it, they complement rather than contradict one another, and it is perhaps possible to find supportive evidence for Lévi-Strauss's model within the Indo-European framework discovered by Dumézil; for example, the binary opposition between the two halves of the first function and the dual character of the third function.

Perhaps the most important general implication of Dumézil's research is that the phenomenon he has discovered among the ancient Indo-European speakers may not be unique. It may be that most if not all of the major linguistic communities, from the Afro-Asian to the Sino-Tibetan, are (or were at some point in their histories) also characterized by genetically related ideological structures. Elsewhere[26] I have suggested that the Siouan language family of North America seems quite clearly to share a quadripartite ideology, an ideology that, like that of the Indo-Europeans, is endlessly replicated throughout the several departments of the cultures concerned. A similar quadripartite structure, oriented around the points of the compass rather than any social hierarchy, seems to have been characteristic of most Uto-Aztecan speakers, from the Paiute of northern Nevada to the Aztecs of central Mexico. It should be emphasized of course, that more research needs to be done here. But should it become evident that genetically related ideologies are a common concomitant of the human condition, the probability that their structures will prove to be wholly different from one another would appear to be quite high.

---

25 For a discussion of the extent to which Japanese myth has been influenced by the Indo-European ideology, see A. Yoshida, "Sur quelques figures de la mythologie Japonaise," *Acta Orientalia* 29 (1965), 221–233.

26 Littleton, *The New Comparative Mythology*, pp. 232–233.

For like the one case now clearly recognized—that of the Indo-Europeans—they would be products of unique historical circumstances, and if we have learned anything from the study of history it is that it rarely if ever repeats itself.

Returning to more immediate matters, it should be emphasized that the clearest evidence for the common Indo-European ideology comes from the most ancient texts. But as we have seen, the traditional Indian social system still reflects this ideology; and in the West, certain of its basic structural features seem to have persisted until almost the modern era—the three "estates" of Medieval and later European society are suspiciously similar to the three Indo-European functions hypothesized by Dumézil.[27] Moreover, the tendency to divide phenomena into three segments, stages, or levels, which has been fundamental to Western thought since well before Aristotle, is still very much with us. Even our anecdotes are usually divided into three segments: a first incident, a second incident, and the punch line. This habit of thinking, which, as Dundes has recently demonstrated,[28] is deeply imbedded in the modern American psyche, cannot, of course, be automatically linked to the three Indo-European functions delineated by Dumézil. But I do think that, as Indo-European speakers, we Westerners are still heirs to a fundamental, linguistically-linked Weltanschauung, the earliest manifestations of which Dumézil has so convincingly explicated.[29]

In sum, the implications of Dumézil's research, both for the student of mankind in general and for the student of Germanic or any other Indo-European tradition in particular, are profound indeed. And it is against the background of these implications and the model from which they stem that this book must be read.

---

27 Indeed, Dumézil has recently suggested (personal communication) that the principal question here is whether the tripartite social organization of Medieval Europe survives primarily from the Celtic or the Germanic variant of the common Indo-European structure. On this point see Jean Batany, "Des 'trois fonctions' aux 'trois états'?" *Annales economiques societiés civilizations* 18 (1963), 933–938.

28 Alan Dundes, "The Number Three in American Culture," in Alan Dundes, ed., *Every Man His Way* (Englewood Cliffs, N.J.: Prentice-Hall, 1968), pp. 401–423. See also Littleton, *The New Comparative Mythology*, pp. 231–232.

29 It should be emphasized that Professor Dumézil himself does *not* suggest that there is any necessary connection between the tripartite ideology of the ancient Indo-Europeans and the widespread tendency among contemporary Indo-European speakers to structure their thinking along tripartite lines. It is an anthropological implication for which I must take sole responsibility.

Introduction, Part II

UDO STRUTYNSKI

Georges Dumézil's writings in the field of Germanic mythology span a period of more than three decades. Beginning in 1939 with the publication of *Mythes et dieux des Germains: Essai d' interprétation comparative,* which launched his career as a comparativist along the lines outlined by Scott Littleton above, his works in this area to date number more than twenty books, articles, and parts of books, and measure nearly a fourth of his total output.

Einar Haugen's present English translation offers the reader a sampling of some of the most important and most representative of these writings. This translation is divided into two parts. The first part comprises a fully revised version of *Mythes et dieux des Germains,* published in 1959 under the title *Les dieux des Germains: Essai sur la formation de la religion scandinave.* The second part of the translation consists of four articles written between 1952 and 1959, which cover a range of deities and themes either not directly dealt with in the book or only briefly touched upon therein. There is a major difference in form as well as in intent between this book and the appended articles. Dumézil wrote *Les dieux des Germains* as an extended balance sheet, that is, as a schematic presentation of his discoveries and thoughts on the subject of Germanic myth, covering a period of over twenty years. The scope of such a compendium did not, however, leave Dumézil room for adequate arguments to establish or defend the fruits of his research. If the reader wishes to see demonstrations of proof, he must look to the articles where such arguments can be found.

The importance of the present works cannot be appreciated without some knowledge of their place in the context of Germanic mythological studies. Dumézil's canon in general, and his Germanic writings in particular. These Germanic writings play a significant role in the development of Dumézil's Indo-European canon, for they helped to establish the basic ideological structure of Indo-European mythology. At the same time they also defined Germanic myth as essentially Indo-European in character. In the words of Einar Haugen, Dumézil's writings "have restored to Scandinavian and to other Indo-European mythologies their backward perspective, revealing them as indigenous products with roots going back to the parent society of the Indo-Europeans."[1]

The implications of viewing Germanic myth through such a "backward perspective" are far reaching: if Dumézil's conclusions are valid for the Indo-European comparativist, they must also be valid for the specialist of Germanic antiquities. In the end, Dumézil's discoveries required nothing less than a complete reinterpretation of Germanic mythology, as a look at the history of scholarship will reveal.

* * *

Comparative mythology has its roots in nineteenth century Germany that saw the emergence of two important movements, both concerned primarily with the question of origins: the "discovery of language" and the birth of Romanticism. While the Romantics called attention to the myths of a common Germanic past, the philologists developed a comparative method that established once and for all the basic historical identity of the Indo-European language family. These two movements joined forces in the persons of the Brothers Grimm whose influence in turn spawned two complementary schools of thought. The first of these is the school of "solar mythology"—also called "nature mythology"—which saw reflected in the tradition of the Germanic peoples the myths of their Indo-European ancestors. This school tried to do for myth what the philologists had done for language, but its central hypothesis—that myth is, in Max Müller's words, a "disease of language"—led to the establishment of fantastic etymologies, and its main thesis, based on themes found in the Indic *Vedas* and the Iranian *Avesta*, that all

[1] Einar Haugen, "The Mythical Structure of the Ancient Scandinavians: Some thoughts on reading Dumézil," *To Honor Roman Jakobson: Essays on the Occasion of his Seventieth Birthday, 11 October 1966* (The Hague, 1967), II, 856.

Indo-European myth essentially reflects the primeval struggle of light against darkness, was simply not acceptable.[2]

The second school turned its attention to the comparative study of epics, sagas, histories, legends, and folktales and, as a result of its investigations, were able to claim that certain motifs—if not whole episodes—could be traced back to India, and thus possibly to a common Indo-European heritage.[3]

With the demise of solar mythology, studies of Germanic myth turned in the direction of positivism. Scholars such as the Dane Vilhelm Grönbech, whose first study appeared over sixty years ago,[4] abandoned the quest for origins to concentrate on reconstructing the psychological world of the ancient Germans. He endowed ethical concepts such as honor with magical force, thereby introducing a strict creed of predestination which led to the widely accepted notion of "germanischer Schicksalsglaube."

Another school of thought dealt with the notion of ecstasy. Although in 1927 Bernhard Kummer's book *Midgards Untergang* presented an antiecstatic picture of an ancient Germanic religion without any "tremendum"—a religion in which men and gods coexisted in a relationship of mutual trust—the contrary and prevailing opinion was expressed in Otto Höfler's *Kultische Geheimbünde der Germanen* (Part I of which appeared in 1934) and was taken to its extreme in Martin Ninck's 1935 *Wodan und germanischer Schicksalsglaube,* a work in which the god Wodan/Odin is interpreted as the incarnation of the berserk's fury.[5] Closely allied with these views was the Vienna School of Anthropology whose basic thesis—that religious patterns develop in conformity with levels of culture—led to a discussion of what could be retrieved of ancient Germanic ritual.

2 See Richard M. Dorson, "The Eclipse of Solar Mythology," in Thomas A. Sebeok, ed. *Myth: A Symposium* (Bloomington, 1968), pp. 25–63; cf. also Holger Pedersen, *The Discovery of Language: Linguistic Science in the Nineteenth Century,* trans. John Webster Spargo (Bloomington, 1962).

3 Wilhelm Grimm in his postscript to *Grimm's Household Tales,* trans. and ed. Margaret Hunt (London, 1892), II, 575–583, suggests three possibilities to explain the presence of such motifs in Germanic folk literature: independent invention, transmission along trade routes or borrowing from other cultures, and inheritance from the time of Indo-European unity (the famous "indogermanische Erbgutthese"). Grimm argues against the exclusivity of any one of these theories, suggesting rather that they cover the entire range of possibilities, and advises the scholar to study each individual tale or motif carefully to determine which explanation is the most applicable.

4 Vilhelm Grönbech, *Kultur und Religion der Germanen* (Hamburg, 1937). This is the edition most often cited.

5 See below, chap. 2.

The question of origins was also revived by Alois Closs, a prominent member of this school, who resurrected the theory of H. Güntert that the ancient Germanic people came into being as a result of the mixture of two populations: the "megalithic" pre-Indo-European agriculturalists and the Indo-European invaders.[6]

The folklorists who had followed the lead of the Grimms also felt the effects of the decline of Max Müller's grand system. After the formation of the Folklore Fellows (also known as the Finnish School) comparative historical and geographical research continued with even more fervor than before. But, interest in the origin of individual tales underwent a subtle methodological shift in emphasis whose implications, like the lines of even the most acute angle, led farther away from the specific question of Indo-European origins the more they were extended. What had happened was that folklorists, despairing of ever finding ultimate origins, either arranged the material in their collections according to "types" or atomized this material into constitutive elements called "motifs." In either case the cause for Indo-European comparativism was lost, for whole Indo-European structures were either embedded in larger non-Indo-European units or, as was more often true, they were broken up into individual motifs or even parts of motifs, so that both their form and their origin became unrecognizable.

The study of Germanic antiquities at the time of Dumézil's first publication in the field had fallen victim to the hazards of introspection which accompany the lack of a broad comparative historical and cultural base. This is especially true in the case of the dominant school of the day, the school of historical evolutionism.

The main contention of the historical-evolutionist school is based on the Darwinian premise that higher and more complex forms of life necessarily evolve from lower and less complex forms. By applying this principle to mythology, the historicists saw the "evolution" of primitive animistic demons to the level of gods, one of which in time came to be the "high god." An equally important source for the theoretical groundwork of this school was the positivist philosophy of Auguste Comte, whose main tenets can be summed up in the French proverb, "Il n'y a que les détails qui comptent"—only the details are really important. Thus armed, the adherents of this school turned their attention to the oldest Germanic texts and found that there was no documentary evidence of the state of Germanic religion

[6] See Edgar Polomé, "The Indo-European Component in Germanic Religion," in Jaan Puhvel, ed., *Myth and Law among the Indo-Europeans* (Berkeley and Los Angeles: University of California Press, 1970), p. 57.

dating back to the time of Germanic unity—if indeed there ever was such a time or such a common religion. The only extant documents were scanty and desultory and revealed a fragmentation of worship not only between the major groups of Scandinavians and Continental Germans—with practically no evidence of the activities of the latter group—but also a fragmentation within these groups. As early as the time of the Brothers Grimm Ludwig Uhland had pointed out that while Sweden worshipped Frey as its chief god, Norway paid homage to Thor. The god Odin he saw as a later importation from Saxaland to Scandinavia where he took hold mainly among the members of courtly society, owing chiefly to the proselytizing efforts of the court poets, the scalds. Uhland therefore concluded that the "Germanic" pantheon, as described in what is considered to be the major source for our knowledge of Germanic myth, the two Icelandic Eddas, was a late and exclusively Scandinavian development.

Eugen Mogk echoed these ideas in works published in 1923 and 1932 and further developed them in his critique of the *Prose Edda* of Snorri Sturluson.[7] He contended that this thirteenth-century Icelander—easily one of the most learned Europeans of his day—had less knowledge of Germanic mythology than we today possess. Thus most of the mythological data that Snorri added to the already extant lays or scaldic poems were either his own inventions or wandering folk motifs that he synthesized, creating thereby a new literary genre, the mythological tale, which also bears the unmistakable influence of its author's conversion to Christianity.

Research along these lines was also carried on by Wilhelm Mannhardt. In his 1877 *Antike Wald- und Feldkulten* he posited that the accounts describing the struggle between two groups of gods called Æsir and Vanir represented history in the garb of myth. Mannhardt based this conclusion on the hypothesis that the Vanir cults of the deities Njord, Frey, and Freya belonged to an earlier level of common European-Scandinavian vegetation religion than did the myths of the warlike Æsir gods Odin and Thor. Thus the struggle between these two groups of gods represents the actual struggle of the indigenous, sedentary, agricultural population against a band of migratory invaders. Generous in victory, the invaders allowed the worship of the old gods to continue. Or, as the myth would have it, the Æsir opened the doors of their pantheon to the Vanir, who themselves subsequently came to be called Æsir. In this manner the "Germanic pantheon" evolved.

---

[7] Cf. E. O. G. Turville-Petre, "Professor Dumézil and the Literature of Iceland," *Hommages à Georges Dumézil* (Brussels, 1960), p. 210.

The most distinguished exponent of this school of thought is the late Marburg philologist Karl Helm. His now classic 1925 essay "Spaltung, Schichtung und Mischung im germanischen Heidentum,"[8] serves as a microcosm for his monumental *Altgermanische Religionsgeschichte,* a work that occupied more than forty years of his life. Perhaps most representative of Helm's work is his 1946 study *Wodan / Ausbreitung und Wanderung seines Kultes,* in which he traces the "evolution" of this god—known in Scandinavia as Odin—from the Continental demon Wode, leader of the Wild Hunt and of the spirits of the dead, to Wodan, god of war and magic, and finally ends with Odin, the Scandinavian god of poets and kings. Helm's position is thus the inverse of that taken by Jacob Grimm who saw Odin as the archetype and in the demon Wode a dim reflection of this "sunken" high god.

With the comparativism that had served as the basis for Grimm's interpretation long since discredited, no possibility existed of properly evaluating the relative stands taken by either scholar. On the question of Odin—as well as on similar points—Germanic evidence alone proved inconclusive. To paraphrase Turville-Petre's assessment of this impasse: as long as Germanic mythology was studied solely by those who studied nothing else, the road was blocked.[9] An "objective correlative" was needed, and it took a scholar of the caliber of Georges Dumézil to provide it.

* * *

When Georges Dumézil entered the Germanic arena his primary concern was to place his comparativism on a firm footing. As an Indo-Europeanist he had already replaced the etymological approach of Max Müller with a more solidly grounded structural approach that took into account the social, religious, and ideological facets of the Indo-European heritage. The task he then set himself was to establish that he had found the correct structure of the parent Indo-European society and to show that the link between Indo-European and the various national traditions was not merely typological but genetic.

Dumézil's central discovery regarding the culture of the Indo-Europeans was his recognition of the pervasive role that the tripartite structure played in their lives. He had struck upon the tripartite formula as early as 1930 when he observed social tripartition in the

[8] Karl Helm, "Spaltung, Schichtung und Mischung im germanischen Heidentum," *Vom Werden des deutschen Geistes, Festgabe für G. Ehrismann* (Berlin, 1925), pp. 1–20.

[9] Turville-Petre, "Iceland," p. 210.

remnants of the Indo-Iranian caste system.[10] By 1938 he had adduced parallels from the Roman pantheon (and some hints from Celtic tradition) whose implications elevated that discovery to the level of an "ideology of the three functions."[11] That same year Dumézil began the research that led to the publication of *Mythes et dieux des Germains*. To confirm this ideology as a legacy that the daughter cultures had preserved from the time of Indo-European unity, he needed an independent corroborative *tertium comparationis*. Next to Indo-Iranian and Italic, and by contrast with Slavic, Baltic, or even Celtic, Germanic tradition had preserved more texts of its myths and religious history than any other Indo-European speaking tradition. (From the Indo-European comparative perspective, Greek tradition may for all intents and purposes be discounted.) Furthermore, the Germanic homeland represented the third point of a geographical triangle describing the territories over which the Indo-Europeans had dispersed, and as the northernmost outpost by virtue of its isolation—which precluded the likelihood of borrowing, especially from other Indo-European cultures—it could be legitimately expected to manifest what folklorists have called the "archaism of the fringe."[12]

Germanic evidence proved to hold true to expectations. With the publication of *Mythes et dieux des Germains* Dumézil established the presence of not merely fragmentary survivals of a common Indo-European past—as he had done for Greece—but a reasonably well articulated tripartite ideology in the magico-religious Odin, a legislative-ordering figure of equal rank termed variously Tyr, Ullr, Mithothyn, or *Tiwaz, the warrior god Thor, and such third function divinities as Njord and Frey. Dumézil saw in the detailed correspondences between accounts of the dethronement and subsequent restoration of Odin and the dynastic conflicts of the Greek Ouranos and his successors, in the similarities between Thor and Indra as thunder wielders, and in such other parallels as the Germanic and Indic accounts of obtaining the vessel to hold the intoxicating drink

---

10 Georges Dumézil, "La préhistoire indo-iranienne des castes," *Journal asiatique* 216 (1930), 109–130.

11 Georges Dumézil, "La préhistoire des flamines majeurs," *Revue de l'histoire des religions* 118 (1938), 188–200. See C. Scott Littleton, *The New Comparative Mythology: An Anthropological Assessment of the Theories of Georges Dumézil* (Berkeley and Los Angeles: University of California Press, 1966), p. 5, where he explains the terms "ideology" and "function." See also the beginning of his introduction, above.

12 Certainly this theory holds true for Iceland, that most centrifugal of outposts of the Germanic-speaking world, where most of the oldest documents such as sagas, histories, and the *Eddas* can be found.

not the mere duplication of motifs but the preservation of core mythologems, most basic to an understanding of the pantheon. The studies of Otto Höfler and other anthropologically oriented scholars helped Dumézil's investigations by providing a link to the social life of the ancient Germans which led Dumézil to the discovery of corroborative religious structures in Germanic cult and ritual practices. Dumézil in fact extended the area of his search to include folklore, literature, and early "history." By these means Dumézil was able to adduce further correspondences between initiation rituals, connected to the Germanic bands of wild warriors such as the *Berserks,* and their counterparts the Indo-Iranian *Gandharvas* and the Greek *Kentauroi,* and between Germanic and Indo-Iranian tales of the killing of the great bear, boar, or giant. Significant is the presence of structural parallels and the lack of etymological parallels, for the presence of the latter might weaken the argument for inheritance and strengthen the argument for borrowing.[13] Thus what originally began as an attempt to determine to what degree the Indo-European component was preserved in Germanic tradition turned out to also open the door to an assessment of the extent of the role the Indo-European heritage played in the total framework of Germanic antiquities.

Reflexively, Dumézil gained from the Indo-European perspective as well. Along with the addition of the ancient Germanic peoples to the Indo-European fold and the rapid crystallization of his structural interpretation of their myths, Germanic evidence allowed Dumézil to refine his structure and thereby better to understand the dynamics of Indo-European thought. The split in the sovereign function between its magico-religious and juridical aspects which Dumézil had observed in its representative gods Odin and Tyr respectively became the subject of an investigation centered primarily on Indic tradition where Dumézil found a clearly enunciated and structurally significant concept of joint sovereignty in the gods Varuṇa and Mitra, with their respective parallels in the Roman Jupiter and Dius Fidius.[14] From this comparative evidence Dumézil was able to state that this first function bifurcation was an essential part of the original Indo-European conception of sovereignty. All in all, Dumézil's successful test of his comparative scheme in the Germanic area proved to be pivotal and determined the direction his thought was to take for the next several decades.

---

[13] Cf. Haugen, "Structure," p. 858 on Tyr as a possible sky-god.

[14] Georges Dumézil, *Mitra-Varuṇa: Essai sur deux représentations indo-européennes de la souveraineté* (Paris, 1940; 2d ed., 1948).

The relative richness of Germanic tradition made it impossible for Dumézil to avoid a clash with the specialists. In the preface to *Mythes et dieux des Germains* Dumézil raises and answers two general points of contention: 1) While his thesis might appear revolutionary, it in no way opposes the historical analysis, philological criticism, or internal consistency of the Germanic data as outlined by Jan de Vries in his *Altgermanische Religionsgeschichte*;[15] 2) Dumézil feels justified in ignoring the traditional division between Scandinavian and Continental Germanic because the lack of substantial evidence from the Continent neither proves nor disproves that there were essential differences between the religions of these two areas. In Dumézil's mind, the differences that do occur are the result of more recent historical developments. His comparative interests lead him to sacrifice local color for form and detail for structural principles.[16]

Of course Dumézil's main bone of contention was with the historicists, not so much because he had provided the Germanic pantheon with a structure—that would have been allowable, if fanciful, speculation—but because Dumézil had insisted on two cardinal points: 1) that Germanic religion is, *mutatis mutandis*, the religion of the Indo-Europeans rather than the religion of the indigenous preinvasion inhabitants of the Germanic lands; and 2) that this religion of the Indo-Europeans was historically far more sophisticated and complex than anything later found preserved or altered in Germanic tradition. In short, Dumézil could not admit to the evolution of something that had existed already in its mature state prior to the very emergence of the tradition, *qua* tradition, out of which it was supposed to have evolved.[17]

In the years between *Mythes et dieux des Germains* and the revision that serves as the core of this book, Dumézil continued his

---

15 Jan de Vries, *Altgermanische Religionsgeschichte* I, 2 vols. (Berlin, 1935–1937).

16 Georges Dumézil, *Mythes et dieux des Germains: Essai d'interprétation comparative* (Paris, 1939), p. x.

17 Cf. Karl Helm, "Mythologie auf alten und neuen Wegen," (Paul-Braunes' *Beiträge zur Geschichte der deutschen Sprache und Literatur*, Tübingen) [*PBB* (*T*)] 77 (1955), 333–365, esp. 365 where to Dumézil's insistence that Germanic religion is *mutatis mutandis* in essence the religion of the Indo-Europeans, Helm answers: "Germanic religion is in the least part Indo-European; its basis is the religion of the indigenous inhabitants of the territories that were later settled by Germanic-speaking tribes, that is, the religion of a cultural substratum of such antiquity that it quite possibly antedated even the formation of the proto-Indo-European community" (my translation). Cf. Dumézil's rejoinder to Helm, "L'étude comparée des religions des peuples indo-européennes," *PBB(T)* 78 (1956), 173–180.

argument with the historicists. At the same time he managed to uncover new comparative evidence, to modify and refine his thought, and to delve deeper into the "local color" of Germanic tradition he had eschewed in his 1939 study.

In 1948 Dumézil tackled the Germanic trickster-god Loki,[18] and at the same time he was forced to consider Balder, a god he had failed to discuss in *Mythes et dieux des Germains*, by his own admission because he presented too much of a problem for the comparativist. Dumézil contends that Loki represents the same Indo-European divinity as is represented by the evil demon Aṇra Mainyu of the Iranian *Avesta* and by Syrdon of Ossetic popular tradition. A significant portion of *Loki* is devoted to rehabilitating the major source of the Loki data, Snorri, against the earlier attacks of Eugen Mogk (see above, at note 7). Here Dumézil stresses the importance of oral tradition as a source for Snorri's knowledge and criticizes the tendency of philologists in general to regard "explication de texte" as merely the fitting together of so many pieces of a jigsaw puzzle. Written texts are, after all, merely the tip of the iceberg that comprises the whole of Germanic tradition.[19]

Dumézil's third and, discounting revisions, final book-length study of Germanic tradition is his 1953 *La saga de Hadingus*. Here Dumézil delves further into the problem of the transposition of myth to epic. His subject is the account of the career of the hero Hadingus, which is found in chapters five to eight of the first book of the *Gesta Danorum* of Saxo Grammaticus. After a defense of Saxo's reliability, similar to that undertaken for Snorri, Dumézil argues convincingly that the heroes Hadding and Frotho represent the gods Njord and Frey respectively, and that these in turn parallel the "divine twins"

18 Dumézil, *Loki* (Paris, 1948).

19 Dumézil quotes de Vries' *The Problem of Loki* (Helsinki, 1933), p. 288 in his revised German edition of *Loki* (Darmstadt, 1959), pp. 56–57, n. 5: Still it would be unwise to reject Snorri's testimony altogether. This is impossible in those cases where he gives the only information about a myth. Moreover he may have had access to far better and richer sources of old lore than is possible for us, who live so many centuries afterwards. His interpretations, sometimes betraying the narrow-minded conceptions of mediaeval learning, may in other cases be founded on a better understanding of the heathen traditions, which may be ascribed to the fact that he was an Icelander himself and that he lived only a couple of centuries after the breakdown of paganism. . . . It may be preferable to involve a certain amount of spurious traditions in our investigations to preclude the wasting of the slightest piece of useful evidence. Here I am inclined to place the largest part of the later material on the same level of trust-worthiness as the most venerable traditions of pagan times . . . because even later literary inventions will follow generally the same paths trodden by heathen poets."

of Indic tradition, the Vedic Nāsatya. Here "epic history" provides evidence of the third-function Dioscuri that Germanic mythological tradition had failed to preserve.[20]

The last important work of this intervening period also concerns itself with Saxo's transposition of myth to history. In this instance it is books six to eight of the *Gesta Danorum* which recount the three sins of the warrior hero Starcatherus.[21] Dumézil shows how this account (and similar evidence from other sources) parallels accounts of the three sins of the god Indra and the panhellenic hero Herakles. Starcatherus sins against the first function when, by means of a ruse, he strangles the Norwegian king Wicarus in a sacrilegious parody of the hanging sacrifice to Odin. His second sin involves cowardice in battle: he deserts the Swedish troops in whose service he is fighting and thus causes the war to be lost. As his last sin Starcatherus kills the Danish king Olo while the latter is bathing and unable to defend himself. The state of being unarmed and bathing suggests the physical well-being governed by the third function; Starcatherus' venal motive for the killing confirms this third sin as an offense against that specific function. The punishments Starcatherus receives for each of his three sins also correspond generally to those inflicted on Indra and Hercules. When Starcatherus was born Odin blessed him with three lives. After each offense he loses one of these lives, and after killing Olo he commits suicide. While Indra, being a god, is allowed to be purified of his crimes, Starcatherus' heroic counterpart Herakles must share the Norse hero's fate by putting a voluntary end to his mortal existence.

The results of these studies provide a good index of what a comparativist can accomplish when he is freed from the vice of seeking etymological parallels, when he has a firm grasp on the structure of his data, and when he is able to range over the entire fund of a national tradition rather than forced to restrict himself to religious or mythological documents.

* * *

By 1958 Dumézil was ready to begin a summing-up of his contributions to the study of Germanic mythology. Supported by the inter-

---

20 Georges Dumézil, *La Saga de Hadingus (Saxo Grammaticus I, v–viii): Du mythe au roman* (Paris, 1953). Cf. also Donald Ward, *The Divine Twins: An Indo-European Myth in Germanic Tradition* (Berkeley and Los Angeles: University of California Press, 1968), pp. 75–76.

21 Georges Dumézil, *Aspects de la fonction guerrière chez les Indo-européens* (Paris, 1956). Cf. also Littleton's introduction, above.

vening studies of Jan de Vries, Werner Betz, and Otto Höfler old arguments had been thoroughly rethought and new evidence—both Germanic and comparative—had been adduced. Dumézil's plan was to incorporate all these into a coherent picture of the Indo-European core of Germanic religious tradition. Thus in 1959 Dumézil published a major revision of *Mythes et dieux des Germains* under the title: *Les dieux des Germains: Essai sur la formation de la religion scandinave.* The new work contained such significant additions to the old edition as discussions of the Æsir-Vanir conflict, the mutilations suffered by the sovereign gods Odin and Tyr, and the role of Balder in Germanic eschatology.[22] Absent are several specific comparisons from the 1939 edition which Dumézil in retrospect found tenuous or not pan-Indo-European. Absent also are certain points regarding the Germanic warrior which Dumézil included in a later work dealing exclusively with the second function.[23]

Dumézil also signaled a significant change in emphasis in the title of the revised edition. The word "myths" was dropped; the focus is on the "gods." The difference between the subtitles is even more illustrative. The 1959 edition is still an "interprétation comparative," but here again the focus is on achieving a better understanding of *Germanic* tradition *qua Germanic,* where the Indo-European heritage has undergone certain unique alterations. Nor has Dumézil capitulated to the specialists on the issue of Scandinavian versus Continental Germanic. He simply concentrates on that area where evidence is well enough preserved to allow him to discuss the "formation de la religion." Thus, on the whole, the basic structure and the main thrust of *Mythes et dieux des Germains* remained unchanged.

Not included within the scope of *Les dieux des Germains* are sev-

---

22 Dumézil's position owes a great deal to Jan de Vries, "Der Mythos von Balders Tod," *Arkiv för nordisk filologi* 70 (1955), 41–60, esp. 44–45, which once and for all laid to rest the Mannhardtian-Frazerian interpretation of Balder as a vegetation deity. Dumézil, however, did not agree with de Vries's new interpretation that Balder was a reflection of Odin's warrior aspect and, in the German edition of *Loki* (also published in 1959) he linked Balder to Odin's aspect of sovereignty. On the eschatological problem in general, Dumézil owes much to the insights of Stig Wikander, especially his "Pāṇḍava-sagan och Mahābhāratas mytiska förutsättningar," *Religion och Bibel* 6 (1947), 27–39. But when Wikander attempted to relate Germanic eschatology to that of the Indo-Iranian continuum ("Från Bråvalla till Kurukshetra," *Arkiv för nordisk filologi* 75 [1960], 183–193 and idem, "Germanische und indo-iranische Eschatologie," *Kairos* 2 [1960], 83–88) by structurally comparing the Scandinavian Bravellir and Indic Kurukshetra battles and their attendant circumstances, Dumézil was not entirely convinced.

23 Georges Dumézil, *Heur et malheur du guerrier: Aspects mythiques de la fonction guerrière chez les Indo-Européens* (Paris, 1969); translated as *The Destiny of the Warrior* (Chicago, 1970).

eral themes worthy of note. These are the god Heimdall and, with the exception of Freya, the entire chorus of goddesses. The very important issue of the reliability of the sources for Germanic myth, notably Snorri and Saxo, is touched upon but briefly, most notably in the first chapter where Dumézil defends his use of Snorri's account of the Æsir-Vanir war.[24] Since the original plan of the book was to deal only with Scandinavian gods, Dumézil also leaves off discussing the epic hero Starkad, whose exploits Dumézil has related to the Indo-European theme of the "three sins of the warrior."[25]

To some degree Einar Haugen has rectified these omissions to the original "étroite embarcation" by including translations of several Dumézil articles on Germanic mythology, especially an important paper on the survival of the tripartite Indo-European social structure as reflected in the Eddic poem *Rígsþula. The Rígsþula* article is the only one dealing with tripartition.[26] Of the remaining articles, "Byggvir and Beyla" shows a side of Dumézil that is more Germanist than comparativist, while "Heimdall"[27] and "Notes on the Cosmic Bestiary of the Edda and the Rig Veda" represent two of Dumézil's few excursions into the realm of Indo-European cosmology.

---

24 A full analysis of this problem and a response to the critics, esp. E. Mogk, can be found in *Loki* (German ed.) where Dumézil discusses Snorri and in *La Saga de Hadingus* (recently reissued as Dumézil, *Du mythe au roman*: *La Saga de Hadingus* [*Saxo Grammaticus I, v–viii*] *et autres essais* [Paris, 1970], with revisions and a number of appended articles) where Saxo's basic reliability is established.

25 See Littleton above. A fuller discussion of this can be found in Dumézil, *Aspects*, and idem, *Aspekte der Kriegerfunktion bei den Indogermanen*, trans. Inge Köck (Darmstadt, 1964)—a slightly revised translation of the 1956 *Aspects*. In 1971 Dumézil devoted Part II and Appendix II of his *Mythe et épopée: Types épiques indo-européens, un héros, un sorcier, un roi* (= *Mythe et épopée II*) (Paris, 1971) to an even more detailed discussion of the accounts regarding this figure.

26 In an earlier paper ("Tripertita fonctionnels chez divers peuples indo-européens," *Revue de l'histoire des religions* 131 [1946], 53–72) Dumézil pointed to a similar parallel of tripartite survival in the Icelandic *Grettissaga Ásmundarsonar* in which the free landholders (the *goðar*, lit. "priests") and the warriors are distinguished from the rest of the people. In another section of this same paper he reported that each of the functions had its own color: black, blue, or green for the third function; red for the warrior; and white for the priestly class. Cf. Polomé, "Component," p. 60 for confirmation of Dumézil's view of Germanic social tripartition from a source generally antipathetic to Dumézil, R. Derolez. Please note also that the Germanic king, who was both priest and warrior, has a functional reflex in ancient India where the king was chosen from the *rājanya*, an elite segment of the warrior class—but once he was king, he assumed total sovereignty for all the functions.

27 See Dumézil, *Les dieux des Indo-europeens* (Paris, 1952), where he compares Heimdall with the Roman Janus, and discusses the corresponding roles these gods play in the "épine du système" of tripartition. See also Haugen, "Structure," p. 862.

* * *

Reaction to Dumézil's work has, on the whole, been favorable. The reviews of *Les dieux des Germains* were laudatory. Still, there exists a noticeable difference between German and Scandinavian scholars in their response to Dumézil's theories. This can be seen by examining which "Dumézilian" works have appeared in their respective languages.

In Germany, with the exception of Jan de Vries's "Dumézilian" revision of his 1935–1937 two-volume *Altgermanische Religionsgeschichte* which appeared in 1956–1957 as number 12 of H. Paul's *Grundriss der germanischen Philologie* (Berlin), the works that have appeared deal with matters less centripetal to the tripartite structure of the Germanic pantheon than is the case in Scandinavia. Thus in 1959 the Wissenschaftliche Buchgesellschaft of Darmstadt published a revised German edition of Dumézil's 1948 *Loki*, and in 1964 they issued a similarly revised version of Dumézil's 1956 *Aspects de la fonction guerrière chez les indo-européens* under the German title *Aspekte der Kriegerfunktion bei den Indogermanen.* These two titles remain the only works of Dumézil on Germanic myth which have been translated into German. *Loki* has consistently been one of Dumézil's most popular books, even with his critics, and the latter book is more of general interest, since a good two-thirds of it deals with traditions other than Germanic. About 1963 the series *Religionen der Menschheit* commissioned Dumézil to write a book—but the subject was to be Roman religion. As it turned out, that book was never published in German.[28] It may be of interest that this same series, under the general editorship of Christel Matthias Schröder, has published a "Dumézilian" study of Celtic religion by Jan de Vries[29] and has announced plans to publish a study of Germanic religion, to be written by Werner Betz whose 1962 encyclopedia article "Die altgermanische Religion"[30] represents essentially Dumézil's point of view.

While in Germany *Les dieux des Germains* remained untranslated, in Scandinavia it was translated twice: into Swedish as *De nordiska gudarna: En undersökning av den skandinaviska religionen,* by Åke Ohlmarks (Stockholm, 1962); and into Danish as *De nordiske Guder*

---

[28] It appeared in French as Dumézil, *La religion romaine archaïque* (Paris, 1966), and was recently translated into English as *Archaic Roman Religion* (Chicago, 1970).

[29] Jan de Vries, *Keltische Religion* (Stuttgart, 1961).

[30] Werner Betz, "Die altgermanische Religion," in Wolfgang Stammler, ed., *Deutsche Philologie im Aufriss,* 2d ed., Vol. III (Berlin, 1962), cols. 1547–1646.

(Copenhagen, 1969). England, which to some extent shares the Scandinavian heritage, has also shown signs of recognizing Dumézil's work. While Dumézil has remained untranslated,[31] the two currently standard handbooks on Scandinavian mythology, E. O. G. Turville-Petre's philologically oriented *Myth and Religion of the North* (New York, 1964) and H. R. Ellis Davidson's anthropologically oriented *Gods and Myths of Northern Europe* (Penguin Books, 1964)[32] display a rather wholesome open-mindedness toward Dumézil.

In discussing the reaction to Dumézil's work, mention should be made of his influence on other scholars. The first to be won over was the Dutch philologist and folklorist Jan de Vries, the first edition of whose *Altgermanische Religionsgeschichte* served as an important source for Dumézil's 1939 *Mythes et dieux des Germains.* Before 1940 de Vries began revising his work along Dumézilian lines and after 1940 he wrote several books and articles supporting Dumézil in both the Celtic and Germanic areas. The most noteworthy of these in the latter field are—in addition to those already discussed—an introduction of Dumézil's theory and methods to a German audience,[33] a paper reconstructing a Germanic god *Irmin* as cognate to Dumézil's "troisième souverain," the Indic Aryaman,[34] and a contribution to the Dumézil festschrift which suggests that apparent functional overlapping between the gods Odin and Tyr might have been influenced by specific social conditions prevailing among certain individual Germanic tribes, notably the Saxons and Franks.[35]

While in addition to historical primacy de Vries deserves to be accorded a primacy of honor among the Germanists who came to accept Dumézil, his is an exceptional case. In the years following 1939 scholars of Germanic antiquities largely ignored Dumézil's contributions to their field. In fact, the historicist Karl Helm, writing in 1955, states that distinguished Germanists had admitted to him never having heard the name Georges Dumézil.[36] A possible explanation

31 Professor Rodney Needham, the Oxford University anthropologist, is presently preparing a translation of Dumézil's 1948 edition of *Mitra-Varuṇa.*

32 Cf. also her later work: H. R. Ellis Davidson, *Scandinavian Mythology* (London, 1969).

33 Jan De Vries, "Der heutige Stand der germanischen Religionsforschung," *Germanisch-romanische Monatsschrift* 33 (1951), 1–11; idem, "Über das Wort 'Jarl' und seine Verwandten," *La nouvelle Clio* 4 (1954), 461–469.

34 Jan de Vries, "La valeur religieuse du mot germanique *irmin,*" *Cahiers du Sud* 36 (1952), 18–27. Cf. Littleton above, n. 17, where he points out that Dumézil has indicated some reluctance in accepting de Vries's conclusions.

35 Jan de Vries, "Sur certain glissements fonctionnels de divinités dans la religion germanique," *Hommages à Georges Dumézil* (Brussels, 1960), pp. 83–95.

36 Helm, "Mythologie," p. 358.

for this might be what Helm playfully calls "Spaltung, Schichtung und Mischung"[37] in Dumézil's writings—that is, the change of direction Dumézil's thought took from 1924 to 1939.[38] Dumézil in a rejoinder to Helm[39] quickly set this confusion aright by providing a list of those of his works on Germanic that bear his ideological imprimatur.

A change came after 1955 as the influence of the historical school began to wane. Comparativism had never fully died out as an ideal—witness the popularity of the historical-geographical method among German folklorists. And with the rise of universal structuralism based on the phonological principles of the Prague school of linguistics as applied to folktales by V. Propp as early as 1928[40] and later to anthropological data by C. Lévi-Strauss, or based on typological analysis such as the concept of archetypes coined by C. G. Jung and applied to religious studies by Carl Kerényi and Mircea Eliade, scholars in Germany and elsewhere have very quietly allowed some of Dumézil's insights to shape or modify their own points of view.

Dumézil's opposition to the historicists is not comparable to the opposition between diachronic and synchronic linguists. In the first place, Dumézil's concerns are far more historical (as opposed to historicist) than those of the synchronists with whom he has been identified. In the second place, even synchronic linguistics is divided by a controversy that echoes the medieval scholastic struggle between realism and nominalism. There is the "God's Truth" school of linguistics versus the "Hocus-Pocus" school; the former aims at reconstructing patterns that once truly existed *as such*, while the latter defines structure as "what you do to the data." Dumézil's discovery of *historical* patterns that are found replicated throughout the Indo-European continuum biases him toward the school of realism. Once this is realized, the so-called conflict between Dumézil's structuralism and historical analysis can be seen for the false issue that it is.[41]

---

37 An obvious reference to Helm's earlier article of the same title; cf. n. 8 above.

38 De Vries in the first edition of *Altgermanische Religionsgeschichte* (Berlin, 1935), I, 93 mentions Dumézil only in connection with his first book, *Le festin d'immortalité: Étude de mythologie comparée indo-européenne* (Paris, 1924), and comments that the new Indo-European comparativism will hopefully be able to avoid the pitfalls that caused the eclipse of Solar Mythology. Cf. Dorson, "Eclipse."

39 Cf. Dumézil, "L'étude," p. 180.

40 Vladimir Propp, *Morphology of the Folktale*, 2d ed., rev. (Austin, 1968).

41 For a discussion of the differences between Dumézil's structuralism and that of Lévi-Strauss, see Littleton above. See also Otto Höfler, "Zur Einführung," in Dumézil, *Loki* (Darmstadt, 1959), pp. xiv–xv; Helm, "Mythologie," p. 356; Betz,

In the German-speaking lands the list of scholars "subliminally" influenced by Dumézil includes the anthropologists Otto Höfler[42] and Alois Closs[43] and the Germanist Franz Rolf Schröder whose comparative studies on the warrior figures Indra, Thor, and Herakles[44] and on the god Heimdall[45] bear unmistakable traces of Dumézil's framework, even though they do not proceed along "Dumézilian" lines.

Turning to France, prominent mention should go to Lucien Gerschel, Dumézil's faithful student and friend, whose studies on the survival of Indo-European tripartition in Germanic saga and legend aided significantly in establishing the validity of later tradition as a source for even the oldest Indo-European themes.[46] Gerschel's study of Germanic legends is also important for another reason. By relating various motif clusters to their underlying Indo-European ideological pattern, Gerschel was not only able to establish the origin and meaning of these legends, he also provided an implicit but concrete argument against the motif-splitting tendency of many major folklorists.[47]

The last significant area to be treated remains the United States where, thanks primarily to the efforts of Jaan Puhvel, who established a program of comparative Indo-European studies at the University of California, Los Angeles in 1959 and to his former student C. Scott Littleton who first introduced Dumézil's theories to the American scholarly world, Dumézilian scholarship has begun to flourish.[48] With

---

"Religion," col. 1558; and Haugen, "Structure," pp. 856 ff. for further discussion of this supposed antinomy.

42 Otto Höfler, *Kultische Geheimbünde der Germanen* (Frankfurt a.M., 1934); idem, "Das Opfer im Semnonenhain und die Edda," *Edda, Skalden, Saga: Festschrift zum 70. Geburtstag von Felix Genzmer*, herausgegeben von Hermann Schneider (Heidelberg, 1952), pp. 1–67; idem, *Germanisches Sakralkönigtum* I (Münster-Cologne, 1952).

43 Alois Closs, "Die Heiligkeit des Herrschers," *Anthropos* 56 (1961), 469–480.

44 Franz Rolf Schröder, "Indra, Thor und Herakles," *Zeitschrift für deutsche Philologie* 76 (1957), 1–41.

45 Franz Rolf Schröder, "Heimdall," *PBB(T)* 89 (1967), 1–41; cf. also idem, "Die Göttin des Urmeeres und ihr männlicher Partner," *PBB(T)* 82 (1960), 221–264, esp. pp. 236–241 on Indic and Norse parallel notions that "offspring of the sea" is a kenning for "fire"; also pp. 249–264 on various Indic parallels to Heimdall.

46 Lucien Gerschel, "Un épisode trifonctionnel dans la saga de Hrólfr Kraki," *Hommages à Georges Dumézil* (Brussels, 1960), pp. 104–116; idem, "Sur un schème trifonctionnel dans une famille de légendes germaniques," *Revue de l'histoire des religions* 150 (1956), 55–92.

47 Lucien Gerschel, "Georges Dumézil's Comparative Studies in Tales and Traditions," *Midwest Folklore* 7 (1957), 141–147.

48 Littleton, "The Comparative Indo-European Mythology of Georges Dumézil," *Journal of the Folklore Institute* 1 (1964), 147–166; idem, *New Comparative Mythology*; the papers in Jaan Puhvel, ed. *Myth and Law* were originally delivered at a symposium held at UCLA in Spring 1967; a similar volume, *Myth in Indo-*

the exception of Edgar Polomé whose acquaintance with Dumézil's work goes back at least to 1953 and on whose writings[49] Dumézil has had only a marginal influence, most of the affirmative reactions to Dumézil can be traced back to the efforts of Puhvel and Littleton.[50]

The most interesting work in the area of Germanic mythology has been that of another former student of Puhvel, the Germanist and folklorist Donald Ward. In a series of studies dealing with themes related to the "Divine Twins" who comprise the most striking exponent of Dumézil's third function, Ward has been able to show how the Indo-European mythical account of their rescue of the "sun maiden" has been preserved in such disparate sources as Baltic folksongs and the Middle High German epic *Kudrun*.[51] Ward's primarily folkloric investigations of this body of material have also yielded comparative evidence to suggest that there existed an Indo-European trifunctional human sacrifice among the Germanic peoples which could be broken down as follows: victims to Odin were hung, those dedicated to the warrior divinity were presumably killed by a weapon, and third function sacrifices to Njord or Nerthus were drowned. While Ward admits that the evidence for the second function sacrifice is meager, his suggestion of the overall pattern is nonetheless valuable.[52] In another paper[53] Ward speculates that the historicized

European Antiquity, is planned for the papers given at a symposium held in honor of Georges Dumézil at the University of California, Santa Barbara, in Spring, 1971, edited by Gerald J. Larson, C. Scott Littleton, and Jaan Puhvel. Interest in this Santa Barbara volume has spread to Europe where Professor Matthias Vereno of the Forschungskreis für Symbolik of Heidelberg University, Germany, plans to issue a German translation.

49 Edgar Polomé, "L'étymologie du terme germanique **ansuz* 'dieu souverain,'" *Études germaniques* 8 (1953) 36–44; idem, "À propos de la déesse Nerthus," *Latomus* 13 (1954) 167–200; idem, "La religion germanique primitive, reflet d'une structure sociale," *Le Flambeau* 37 (1954) 427–463; idem, "Notes critiques sur les concordances germano-celtiques," *Ogam* 6 (1954) 145–164; idem, "Some Comments on *Vǫluspá*, Stanzas 17–18," in E. C. Polomé, ed., *Old Norse Literature and Mythology* (Austin, 1969), pp. 265–290.

50 Of course Dumézil has also received due recognition and friendly support from Mircea Eliade, who is an illustrious figure in religious studies in his own right; cf. his Foreword to Dumézil's *Archaic Roman Religion*, pp. xi–xiv.

51 Donald Ward, "The Rescue of Kudrun: A Dioscuric Myth?" *Classica et Mediaevalia* 26 (1965), 334–353; idem, "Solar Mythology and Baltic Folksongs," *Folklore International: Essays in Traditional Literature, Belief, and Custom in Honor of Wayland Debs Hand* (Hatboro, Pa., 1967), pp. 233–242; idem, "An Indo-European Mythological Theme in Germanic Tradition," in *Indo-European and Indo-Europeans* (Philadelphia, 1970), pp. 405–420; idem, *Divine Twins*, esp. pp. 30–91.

52 Donald Ward, "The Threefold Death: An Indo-European Trifunctional Sacrifice?" *Myth and Law*, pp. 123–142.

53 Donald Ward, "The Separate Functions of the Indo-European Divine Twins," *Myth and Law*, pp. 193–202.

mythical twins Hengist and Horsa, who reportedly led the Anglo-Saxon invasion of the British Isles, could be distinguished from each other in that Hengist was the more warlike of the pair. By adducing comparative evidence from other Indo-European traditions in which this distinction is also noticeable, Ward suggests that at some early point in time Indo-European tradition took one twin out of the third function and placed him in the second function.[54]

Concluding this discussion of Dumézil's reception in the United States, some mention must be made of Dumézil's most persistent critic, the University of Illinois Germanist Ernst Alfred Philippson. On the whole, Philippson's criticism is based on the historicist viewpoint of Karl Helm and thus raises no issues nor offers any insights that have not appeared earlier. Philippson's opinions continue to influence Germanists, however, so in the interests of "equal time" it might be profitable to take a closer look at his main objections.[55]

Philippson sees in Tyr an ancient sky and war god, in Thor a god of fertility, and objects to Dumézil's "invention" of Irmin to correspond to the Indic Aryaman. Philippson may be answered on the first two counts by saying that he is confusing function with feature. Dumézil has already pointed out that Tyr's warrior feature was a later development (below chap. 2) and that Thor's importance to farmers was derived from his warrior function which gave him control over the atmosphere (below, chap. 4). Thus there is no reason to maintain that these features belong to a pre-Indo-European stratum of Germanic society. As regards Irmin, the reconstruction was

[54] Structurally speaking, this suggestion would be quite seductive, were it not for the fact that each function, no matter which Indo-European tradition one is speaking of, at some time reflects aspects of the other two functions. But these aspects are always subordinated to the function they modify. Thus Odin may be characterized as a "warlike sovereign," but not as a "sovereign warrior"; and in Rome the theology recognized a martial aspect to the third function god Quirinus in the "arma Quirini."

[55] These objections can be found in E. A. Philippson, "Phänomenologie, vergleichende Mythologie und germanische Religionsgeschichte," *PMLA*, 77 (1962). Philippson's criticism in print of Dumézil begins, however, with his review of the second edition of de Vries's *Altgermanische Religionsgeschichte*, in the *Journal of English and Germanic Philology* 56 (1957), 309–316. Comparing the revised edition with the earlier edition, Philippson finds that de Vries has abandoned the old distinction between West and North Germanic and comments that any bridges gapping these two must rest on uncertain foundations. Philippson also objects to the Indo-Europeanization of proto-Germanic religion, especially with respect to the Æsir-Vanir conflict and the figure of Odin/Wodan. In 1962 Philippson again wrote a critical review of another "Dumézilian" work, Betz's "Religion," in the *Journal of English and Germanic Philology* 62 (1962), 826–828. Here Philippson unjustifiably lends his authority to support those who have criticized Dumézil's work in other Indo-European areas, notably India, Iran, and Rome. His position as a biased observer is thereby clearly established.

not made by Dumézil but by de Vries, and Dumézil has not subscribed to it.

Another of Philippson's objections deals with the cult of Odin, which even de Vries admits could have undergone evolutionary changes.[56] This quotation is rather out of context and de Vries makes it clear that he does not regard such changes as a threat to Odin's first function status.

Philippson further objects that the Vanir gods Njord and Frey do not form a dioscuric pair engaged in the rescue and wooing of the sun maiden. Donald Ward has shown, however, that this very myth was preserved in later Germanic heroic and folk tradition.

Philippson brings up the point that there was no tripartite social structure in early Germanic society. The priestly function was assumed by the king, the keepers of the temple, or the paterfamilias. Yet even such anti-Dumézilian scholars as Derolez have admitted that the facts still tend to confirm the presence of a *sovereign* function whose jurisdiction included the maintenance of religious worship. Philippson also points out that there was no social distinction between the second and third functions: there were only farmers who became warriors when hostilities broke out. Here again Derolez offers evidence to the contrary. But even if such evidence did not exist, Rome still presents a favorable parallel for the preservation of the ideological structure despite changes in the social structure. As Dumézil has pointed out (see Littleton above, n. 6), the same Romans were devoted to Mars or to Quirinus, depending on whether Rome was at war or at peace.

On one point Philippson and Dumézil do agree. Philippson recognizes the importance of regarding myths as whole entities and of going beyond the motif analysis of folklorists who all too often are unable to see the forest for the trees. In this regard he is fully convinced by Dumézil's analysis of the Hadingus episode in Saxo, which shows that heroic legends are often derived from myths. Thus only by knowing the structure of the whole mythologem can myths be salvaged from the folk tradition into which they have sunk.

* * *

From 1959 to the present Dumézil has added little to his canon of Germanic studies. These years have mostly been spent in consolidating and refining his position, preparatory to a final "summing up." Two themes dominate Dumézil's comparative work of this

---

56 De Vries, *Altgermanische Religionsgeschichte*, 2d ed., II, 91.

period: the transposition of myth into epic literature and the role of the epic hero as representative of the warrior function, with specific emphasis placed on the "three sins of the warrior."

In Germanic tradition the material for Dumézil's treatment of the first theme is restricted to two authors: the Icelander Snorri Sturluson and the Seeland monk Saxo Grammaticus. Specifically, Dumézil has found myth in the guise of history in the first chapters of Snorri's *Ynglingasaga* and in numerous passages scattered throughout the first several books of Saxo's *Gesta Danorum.* The results of Dumézil's earlier investigations of these authors and their sources can be found in *Loki* and *La Saga de Hadingus.* Dumézil's purpose in these works was twofold: to demonstrate how "early history" can serve as a repository for sunken myth and to prove the reliability of Snorri and Saxo as recorders rather than inventors of the stories they wrote down.

These last years have seen a significant change of emphasis on Dumézil's part. Concentrating his attention on Saxo, Dumézil in 1970 issued a revised edition of *La Saga de Hadingus* under the title *Du mythe au roman.* There, in addition to restating his earlier thesis, Dumézil also displays a newfound interest in the personality of Saxo. As a result, Dumézil has altered his earlier supposition that the differences between the myth of Njord and the account of Hadingus can be attributed directly to Saxo's lost Icelandic source. Now Dumézil recognizes that Saxo himself must bear the responsibility for most of these alterations.

Appended to *Du mythe au roman* are several articles—some of them new—dealing either more closely with particular issues raised in connection with Hadingus (specifically the hanging and drowning episode) or with similar transpositions of myth to epic in other parts of Saxo's writings, where Dumézil is able to show that Saxo took more liberties with his source than had been previously supposed. Finally, there are two articles that discuss the problem of the relationship of folklore to myth.[57] In the first of these, Dumézil identifies Saxo's three "Frothones" with Frodi, the Danish analogue of Frey. The closest parallel to Frey is Frotho III, who, after his death is carried about in state for three years. Similar to Frotho's *gestatio* is Frey's burial within a mound that becomes his habitat. Dumézil concludes (from this and other evidence) that the mound of Frey/

[57] These are Dumézil, "La *Gestatio* de Frotho III et le folklore du Frodebjerg, *Études germaniques* 7 (1952), 156–160, and idem, "Njǫrðr, Nerthus et le folklore scandinave des génies de la mer," *Revue de l'histoire des religions* 147 (1955), 210–226.

Frodi is in all probability a vestige of an ancient ritual involving the *gestatio*: the passing of the god through the villages in order to ensure the benefits of the earth to the people. In the second, Dumézil investigates a particular aspect of the Njord-Nerthus complex by relating these divinities to the mermen and mermaids of later folk tradition.

The new articles—that is, those appearing after 1959—include a previously unpublished paper "Gram" that outlines the title hero's role in the Hadingus episode; a 1961 article "Balderus et Høtherus"[58] in which Dumézil shows that Saxo's Høtherus is in many respects a variant of Balder rather than Hoder, and that Saxo's Balderus represents a transposition of the god Frey as he appears in the *Skírnismál*; and "Horwendillus," also published as a separate article in 1970[59] where Dumézil again brings evidence to demonstrate that the differences between Saxo's account and all the other accounts are the result of Saxo's literary inventiveness.

Dumézil's investigation of the warrior hero Starkad links his interest in Saxo to his other major concern, the phenomenology of the warrior function. *Du mythe au roman* contained, in Dumézil's words, his "final evaluation" of Saxo's writings—with one major exception. That exception concerns the career of the trifunctional sinner Starkad (= Starkaðr), and Dumézil's discussion of this figure can be found in the second volume of a series whose title, *Mythe et épopée*, attests Dumézil's preoccupation with epicized myth throughout the Indo-European continuum.

Dumézil's study of Starkad in *Mythe et épopée* is by far the most complete treatment he has accorded this figure. In earlier studies[60] Dumézil concentrated on the sins that Starkad commits against each of the functions. In *Mythe et épopée* Dumézil examines the whole career of this Scandinavian hero (including of course an "explication" of all the pertinent texts, particularly Saxo) and compares it with not only the career of the Greek hero Herakles, as he had done in earlier works, but also with the career of a new discovery, the Indic hero Śiśupāla whose life and deeds are recorded in the *Mahābhārata*. Śiśupāla replaces the god Indra who had served as the *tertium comparationis* in the earlier studies and thus allows Dumézil to compare

---

[58] Georges Dumézil, "Høtherus et Balderus," *PBB(T)* 83 (1961), 259–270.

[59] Georges Dumézil, "Horwendillus et Aurvandill," *Echanges et Communications: Mélanges offerts à Claude Lévi-Strauss à l'occasion de son 60ème anniversaire*, ed. by Jean Pouillon and Pierre Maranda (The Hague and Paris, 1970), II, 1171–1179.

[60] Dumézil, *Aspects* (1956) and the slightly revised German 1964 *Aspekte*; Dumézil, *Destiny of the Warrior*, p. 83 n. 1, for an explanation of the revision.

a triad of entirely epic heroes. The parallels brought to light by this comparison are numerous and convincing. They show not only that a common Indo-European conception of the warrior role can exist in epic guise, but also that certain traditions preserved in epic literature contain elements that are of even greater antiquity than those preserved in myth.

In addition to the works outlined above, this period also saw Dumézil publish two other new articles on Germanic. The first of these, "Le dieu scandinave Víðarr,"[61] appeared in 1965 and compares Vidar, who in Norse eschatology destroys the wolf Fenrir, with the post-Vedic Viṣṇu who acts decisively in Indic eschatology. Dumézil describes not only their respective connections to the warrior gods Thor and Indra but links Vidar and Viṣṇu to each other etymologically, inasmuch as the stem meaning "wide" is at the root of both names. The second article was delivered as a lecture in Spring 1971 at a symposium given in Dumézil's honor by the University of California, Santa Barbara.[62] Entitled simply " 'Le Borgne' and 'le Manchot,' " it discusses the state of the problem of the one-eyed and one-handed figures in Indo-European tradition. Dumézil admits that he is dissatisfied with the parallels adduced for the mutilations of the gods Odin and Tyr. His main purpose seems to be that ritual, as well as "legendary" survivals of "borgne" and "manchot" are found at Rome.[63] After also introducing new evidence pertaining to one-handedness from Iran, Dumézil concludes that the problem deserves further study.

---

[61] Dumézil, "Le dieu scandinave Víðarr," *Revue de l'histoire des religions* 168 (1965), 1–13.

[62] Cf. n. 48, above.

[63] Dumézil adduced comparative evidence from Rome where the warrior Horatius Cocles casts an almost magic spell on the enemy by closing one eye and opening the other to superhuman dimensions and where Mucius Scaevola loses his right hand in affirming an untruth. Cf. Dumézil, *Mitra-Varuṇa* (1940 ed.); idem, "Mythes romains," *Revue de Paris* 58 (Dec., 1951) 105–115; de Vries' discussion of the one-eyed Lug and the one-armed Nuadu in Celtic tradition in "L'aspect magique de la religion celtique," *Ogam* 10 (1958), 273–284; Ward, *Divine Twins*, p. 101 n. 11 for a possible parallel in the epic *Waltharius* where Hagen loses an eye, Walther his right arm, and Gunther loses a leg. Philippson, "Phänomenologie," p. 191 n. 21 draws a facetious parallel to two figures from German history who have found a place in literature: the one-eyed poet Oswald von Wolkenstein and the one-armed rebel Gottfried (Götz) von Berlichingen. Dumézil in "La transposition des dieux souverains mineurs en héros dans le *Mahābhārata*," *Indo-Iranian Journal* 3 (1959), 1–16 retracts his position that Odin and Tyr are paralleled by the Indic Bhaga and Savitar (cf. idem, *Mitra-Varuṇa* 2d ed., last chapter) and sees the Aryaman-Bhaga pair reflected in the Norse brothers Balder (peaceful) and Hoder (blind) as well as in the Roman Iuventas and Terminus. Littleton, *Mythology*, pp. 45–52, criticizes Dumézil for not having been able to adduce ritual evidence.

* * *

In closing this introduction to Dumézil's work in the field of Germanic mythology, it seems appropriate to turn to the future and ask what further contributions one can expect to come from his pen and what kind of contributions these will be. In his introduction to *Du mythe au roman* Dumézil announced that a revision of *Loki* was in preparation, a revision that would presumably do for Snorri what *Du mythe au roman* had done for Saxo: examine the author more closely and thus gain a deeper insight into the living significance enjoyed by the Indo-European heritage in Scandinavia.

This new emphasis evidences a growing concern on Dumézil's part for the uniqueness of each of the national traditions he has examined. Of course, such a concern had been growing for a long time. Anyone familiar with even Dumézil's early works could not fail to have been impressed with the painstaking research and careful attention paid to details. It seems to have been consistently in the forefront of Dumézil's mind that to speak to the specialists he would have to know as much as the specialists, even though he was speaking from the Indo-European comparative perspective. And, as Dumézil's work in Germanic mythology progressed over the years, he came ever closer to enlarging his perspective to include the specialists' point of view. All the revisions that occurred between *Mythes et dieux des Germains* and *Les dieux des Germains* bear the mark of this tendency toward a more precise grasp of the particular.

While Dumézil's appreciation of the uniqueness of his sources gained in importance, however, his Indo-European perspective and his comparativism did not diminish. No major shift in Dumézil's viewpoint occurred until 1966 when *La religion romaine archaïque* appeared. And even then the changes Dumézil signaled in the preface to *La religion* were at once consistent as well as striking. First, Dumézil drew the boundaries of the comparative method: "As my work proceeded, I gained a clearer awareness of the possibilities, but also of the limits, of the comparative method, in particular of what should be its Golden Rule, namely, that it permits one to explore and clarify structures of thought but not to reconstruct events, to 'fabricate history,' or even prehistory, a temptation to which the comparatist is no less exposed, and with the same gloomy prognosis, than the philologist, the archaeologist, and of course the historian" (p. xvi).

Then Dumézil joined the specialists and stole what was left of their thunder:

> It is not enough to extract from early Roman religion the pieces which can be explained by the religions of other Indo-European peoples. It is not enough to recognize and to present the ideological and theological structures which are shown by the interrelations of these blocks of prehistoric tradition. One must put them back in place, or rather leave them *in situ,* in the total picture and observe how they behaved in the different periods of Roman religion, how they survived, or perished, or became changed. In other words, one must establish and reestablish the continuity between the Indo-European "heritage" and the Roman reality. At a very early stage I had understood that the only means of obtaining this solidarity, if it can be obtained, was to change one's viewpoint, to join those whom one had to convince. Without surrendering the advantages of the comparative method, or the results of Indo-European research, but by adding to this new apparatus, in no order of preference, the other traditional ways of knowing, one must consider Rome and its religion in themselves, for themselves, as a whole. Stated differently, the time had come to write a general history of the religion of the Roman Republic, after so many others, from the Roman point of view (pp. xvi–xvii).

Later in the same preface Dumézil makes clear the relevance of this announcement for the studies presently under discussion: "If the labors of Werner Betz exempt me from making a reevaluation similar to the present work for the Germanic world . . ." (p. xix). Thus Dumézil plans a study of the total Germanic tradition, a synthesis in which the Indo-European heritage is only one of many elements, in harmony with the others. It will be interesting to see which of the two scholars will actually write this study, and to what degree it will be more than an updating of de Vries's still excellent second edition of *Altgermanische Religionsgeschichte*. Yet, one thing is certain. Having established the existence of an umbilical cord manifested in the ethnographic presence of a parent Indo-European ideology in Germanic tradition, Dumézil has seen fit to cut that cord and in so doing he has come full circle. No genotype can fully explain the mature phenotype. Germanic mythology must once again be viewed as *Germanic* mythology, for only in this way can the demands of theory and reality, history and structure be equitably met. Many issues still remain to be resolved, but Dumézil has at last defined the limits of the question and provided a language in which the answer can be expressed. For this reason, the student of Germanic tradition not only has much to be grateful for but also a great deal to look forward to.

Author's Preface

GEORGES DUMÉZIL

The first edition of this book, which through the kindness of Dr. Paul-Louis Couchoud was issued as the first volume of this excellent series (*Mythes et Religions*), was composed at the very beginning of my active period in comparative research. Not until the spring of 1938, after three lustra of painful groping, did I discover the great correspondences that require us to attribute to the Indo-Europeans (before their dispersion) a complex theology based on the structure of the three functions of sovereignty, force, and fecundity. Prepared in the autumn of 1938 and published in 1939, the book therefore conformed to the tripartite division. But in order to make this first of a long series of essays intelligible, I had to take it for granted that the Germanic documentation as well as the comparative documentation that should clarify it, had been rethought in the new framework. The date and the haste sufficiently explain, I believe, the unevenness of a disquisition that was outdated as quickly as it went out of print.

After twenty years it seems desirable to present a firmer and more organized demonstration under a similar title, built on my own further researches and on those of my colleagues. Here I am thinking above all of Jan de Vries of Leyden and Werner Betz of Bonn, who have made important researches and discoveries in the same spirit as mine. I refer the student once and for all to the new edition of *Altgermanische Religionsgeschichte* by de Vries (Volume I, 1956; II, 1957), which constitutes the twelfth section of *Grundriss der germanischen Philologie*, founded at the beginning of the century by Hermann Paul; and to the account "Die altgermanische Religion"

(1957), which occupies columns 2467–2556 of the great collection *Deutsche Philologie im Aufriss* by Professor W. Stammler.

The three first chapters are an expansion of lectures given at Oxford in May, 1956, on the friendly initiative of Professor C. Turville-Petre. The third, however, has been considerably revised: It proposes a solution of "the problem of Balder" which was not made precise until 1957. The fourth chapter rapidly completes the description of the form taken in the Scandinavian countries by the theology of the three functions. The considerable remainder of religious representations, especially of a god as problematic as Heimdall and the whole band of goddesses beside Freya, could not find space in this limited enterprise. Nor have I returned to the question of rehabilitating the sources, a topic I believe I have considered sufficiently for Snorri in my book *Loki* (1948), German edition revised in 1958; and for Saxo in *La saga de Hadingus* (1953).

Paris, October, 1958

Part One: Gods of the Ancient Northmen

CHAPTER 1

The Gods: Aesir and Vanir

In Scandinavian mythology—the best described, or rather the only one of the Germanic mythologies which is described—the leading roles are divided among two groups, the Æsir (ON *æsir,* sg. *áss*), and the Vanir (ON *vanir,* sg. *vanr*). Certain other divine types are mentioned, such as the Elves (ON *alfar,* sg. *alfr*), but no important or even specifically named gods are found among such groups. The meaning to be attributed to this coexistence of Æsir and Vanir constitutes our fundamental problem. In the analysis of *altnordische,* and consequently in that of *altgermanische, Religionsgeschichte* (see Bibliographical Notes), everything depends on which solution one proposes to this problem. All new attempts at interpretation must immediately come to grips with it, even to establish the very setting of the mythology.

No text provides a general and differentiating definition of the two divine groups. They are easily characterized, however, by examining their principal representatives. The distinction is so clear that, at least with regard to their leading traits, interpreters of all schools are in agreement. The two outstanding Æsir are Odin (Óðinn)[1] and Thor (þórr), along with Tyr (Týr), clearly somewhat faded, while the three most typical Vanir are Njord (Njǫrðr), Frey (Freyr), and Freya (Freyja). Even if it exceptionally occurs that they must be or do something else, the latter three are first and foremost rich and givers of riches; they are patrons of fecundity and of pleasure (Frey, Freya), also of peace (Frey); and they are associated, topographically and

[1] Old Norse names are anglicized according to the principles usually followed in English and American writings on Scandinavian mythology. If the Old Norse form differs significantly, it will be given in parentheses on its first occurrence.

economically, with the earth that produces crops (Njord, Frey), and with the sea that enriches its sailors (Njord). Odin and Thor have other cares. Neither is of course uninterested in riches or in the products of the soil, but, at the time when Scandinavian religion is known to us, they have other centers of gravity. Odin is the supreme magician, master of runes, head of all divine society, patron of heroes, living or dead. Thor is the god of the hammer, enemy of the giants, whom he occasionally resembles in his fury. His name means "the god who thunders," and, if he helps the peasant in his work with the earth, it is in some violent fashion, even according to modern folklore, and as a mere byproduct of his atmospheric battle. In the course of the following chapters, we shall expand these brief descriptions; but they will suffice to show how the homogeneous Vanir stand in opposition to the Æsir, who are much more varied in their vocations.

With regard to their affinities, they are of two kinds, depending on whether one contemplates the cult practice and the divine state of things that maintains it, or the traditions concerning the remote origins of this state of things, what might be called the divine prehistory.

In the religious present, Æsir and Vanir live in perfect accord, without quarrel or jealousy, and this harmony permits men, in prayer and more generally in cult, to associate them without wariness. It also permits poets to forget occasionally that the Vanir indeed *are* Vanir and to designate with the name Æsir a divine community that is noted for its unity. Their association is often expressed in a three-term enumeration that brings out a clear hierarchy, with the Æsir coming first, superior to the Vanir: Odin, Thor, Frey (occasionally, in the third position, Frey and Njord; more rarely the god Frey gives his place to the goddess Freya). This formula so frequently sums up the needs and imaginations of men, in such different circumstances, and in such different parts of the Scandinavian world, that it must be significant.

Here are the principal examples of it. When Adam of Bremen, toward the end of the pagan period, reported on the religion practiced at the temple of Uppsala by the Swedes in Uppland, it was physically symbolized by the three idols standing side by side in the temple, presenting to the believers a semicircle of devotions:

> In this temple, entirely covered with gold, there are the statues of three gods, which the people worship, so arranged that the mightiest of them, Thor, occupies a throne in the middle of the chamber, while Wodan and Fricco have places on either side. The significance of these gods is as

follows: Thor, they say, rules in the air, governing the thunder and lightning, the winds and rains, fair weather and crops. The other, Wodan —that is, "Frenzy" (*furor*)—wages war and grants man courage against his enemies. The third is Fricco, who bestows peace and pleasure to mortals. His likeness, too, they fashion with an immense phallus.

For all their gods there are appointed priests to offer sacrifices for the people. If plague and famine threaten, a libation is poured to the idol Thor; if war, to Wodan; if marriages are to be celebrated, to Fricco.[2]

These notices pose problems of detail which we shall examine later, both with regard to the boundaries of divine specialties and to the place of honor accorded to Thor. What is important now is simply that these idols attest to, and excellently describe, a tripartite theological structure.

We know very little about the Scandinavian form of cult and liturgies, but two points of agreement show that the same triad at least presided over the most solemn maledictions. In the saga that bears his name, Egill Skallagrímsson, on the verge of leaving Norway for Iceland, curses the king who has stripped him of his goods and consigned him to this exile. After a general appeal to the gods under the names of *bǫnd* and *goð*, he continues:

. . . reið sé rǫgn ok Óðinn!	. . . may the gods and Odin grow angry (at him)!
. . . folkmýgi lát flýja, Freyr ok Njǫrðr, af jǫrðum!	. . . may Frey and Njord make the oppressor of the people flee his lands!
Leiðisk lofða stríði	May Thor ("God of the land") loathe
landǫss, þanns vé grandar![3]	the scourge who defiles the sanctuaries!

In his commentary, Finnur Jónsson analyzes the action of this stanza well: "The poet first invokes the gods in general; then individually the all-powerful Odin, Thor, the vigorous God-of-the-land, then Frey and Njord, as gods of fecundity and dispensers of riches."[4] In the still earlier Eddic poem *Skírnismál*, Frey's servant, relinquishing his attempts to convince Gerd, object of his master's love, menaces her in these terms (str. 33):

---

2 *Gesta Hammaburgensis Ecclesiae Pontificum*, IV, 26–27; here from Adam of Bremen, *History of the Archbishops of Hamburg-Bremen*, trans. Francis J. Tschan (New York: Columbia University Press, 1959), pp. 207–208.

3 *Egils saga Skalla-Grímssonar*, chap. 56; ed. S. Nordal, *Islenzk fornrit* 2 (Reykjavík, 1933), 163.

4 F. Jónsson, *Altnordische Sagabibliothek* 3 (1894), 180.

Reiðr er þér Óðinn, reiðr er þér ásabragr,
þik scal Freyr fiásc,
in fyrinilla mær, enn þú fengit hefir
gambanreiði goða.[5]

Angry is Odin at you, angry is the foremost god (=Thor) at you,
Frey shall hate you,
monstrous maid, and you have won
the wrath of the gods.[6]

At the beginning of the eleventh century, in the poem about his conversion, Hallfreðr Vandræðaskáld, before giving himself over to Christ, the Father, and "God," defies the same heathen divinities (str. 9):

mér skyli Freyr ok Freyja,	Let Frey and Freya rage,
fjǫrð létk af dul Njarðar,	and Thor the thunderer too;
líknisk grǫm við Grímni,	let wretches worship Odin:
gramr ok þórr enn rammi.[7]	I forsook the folly of Njord.

In magic such tripartite formulas against sickness or evil were possibly maintained for a long time: " 'In the name of Odin, Thor, and Frigg' alternates there [Norway] with the Christian trinity."[8]

Finally, mythology frequently joins the same characters in a triad. Among them alone are divided the three treasures forged by the dwarfs after losing a bet with the malicious Loki: Odin gets the magic ring, Thor the hammer that is to be the instrument of his battles, and Frey the wild boar with the golden bristles.[9] It is they, and only they, whom the *Vǫluspá* (strs. 53–56) describes as being joined in the supreme duels and deaths of the eschatological battle.[10] More generally, it is they—and the goddess Freya, closely associated

---

[5] Here and elsewhere the Old Norse text of poems from the *Poetic Edda* is cited from *Edda: die Lieder des Codex Regius*, ed. Hans Kuhn (Heidelberg: Carl Winter, 1962). Abbreviated: *Edda* (Kuhn).

[6] Most of the translations of poems from the *Poetic Edda* are cited from *The Poetic Edda*, trans. H. A. Bellows (New York: The American-Scandinavian Foundation, 1923 and later). Abbreviated: *Edda* (Bellows). Some strophes have been done by the translator for greater precision.

[7] E. A. Kock, *Den norsk-isländska skaldediktningen* (Lund, 1946), I, 86.

[8] A. Bang, *Norske hexeformularer og magiske opskrifter* (Christiania, 1901), pp. 21, 127 (nos. 40, 127).

[9] *Edda Snorra Sturlusonar*, ed. Finnur Jónsson (Copenhagen, 1931), p. 123 (*Skáldskaparmál*, chap. 44). References to Snorri's *Edda* (also known as *The Prose Edda*) are to this edition. Abbreviated: *Snorra Edda* (Jónsson). *The Prose Edda* is divided into parts with separate chapter numbering: *Gylfaginning*, *Bragarœður*, *Skaldskaparmál*, *Háttatal*.

[10] *Edda* (Kuhn), pp. 12–13; *Edda* (Bellows), pp. 22–23. References to individual poems of the *Edda* are frequent in the text and are not separately footnoted except for direct quotations.

with Freyr and Njord—who dominate, who indeed monopolize almost all the mythological material. It is no less significant that the three gods who split the property of the dead—the last two under rather obscure conditions—are Odin, who consigns to himself the nobles or "half the dead" from the battlefield, Thor, to whom go the thralls (more correctly, no doubt, the nonnobles), and Freya, who according to one text[11] takes the other half of those killed in battle and according to another text takes the dead women.[12]

Such is the present situation. But this union and this happy harmony, founded on a clear analysis of human wishes, have not always existed, according to the legend. In a far distant past the two divine groups lived at first separately, as neighbors; then they fought a fierce war, after which the most distinguished Vanir were associated with the Æsir, with the rest of their "people" living somewhere away from the struggle and the cares of their cult. Four strophes from that breathless poem, the *Vǫluspá,* in which the sibyl relates quite allusively the entire history of the gods; two texts of the erudite Snorri; and finally an unadroit plagiarism by his contemporary Saxo Grammaticus—these inform us of this initial crisis of the gods, which is presupposed also in several passages from other Eddic poems. These documents are not homogeneous: two present the event in mythological terms, two transpose it into historical and geographical terms. The first group includes strophes 21–24 of the *Vǫluspá* and a passage in Snorri's mythological manual written for the use of poets, the *Skáldskaparmál* (chap. 4); the second includes chapters 1, 2, 4, and 5 of the *Ynglingasaga,* discussing the *Ynglingar,* supposed descendants of Frey, and chapter 7 of the first book of Saxo's *Gesta Danorum,* a fragment of the "saga of Hadingus" which fills chapters 5 through 8 of that book.

a) *Vǫluspá* 21–24. I have elsewhere[13] made an extended analysis of this passage, which the hypercritical Eugen Mogk[14] sought to eliminate from the dossier on the Æsir and Vanir. The order of events—described as "the first war of armies in the world"—seems somewhat confused in these rapid and discontinuous strophes, which do not narrate, but content themselves with evoking episodes already known to the listeners. There is extensive reference to a female being called

---

[11] *Grímnismál,* str. 14: *Edda* (Kuhn), p. 60; *Edda* (Bellows), pp. 90–91.

[12] *Egils saga,* chap. 78.

[13] Dumézil, *Tarpeia* (Paris: Gallimard, 1947), pp. 249–291.

[14] Mogk, E., *Die Gigantomachie in der Völuspá. Folklore Fellows Communications* 58 (Helsinki, 1924).

Gullveig, literally, "gold-drink, gold-drunkenness," sent by the Vanir to the Æsir, who, despite metallurgical treatment, cannot rid themselves of her. A sorceress, she sows corruption, particularly among women. There is also reference (24) to a spear, apparently magic, thrown by Odin against an enemy army, which does not prevent that "broken was the wall of the stronghold of the Æsir" and that "the warlike (?) Vanir were able to trample the plains." But nothing decisive results from these contrary movements, because (23) the gods hold an assembly for peace where they discuss eventual compensation.[15]

b) *Skáldskaparmál* (chap. 5, *Prose Edda*) (The response of Bragi to the question "Whence comes the art called poetry?"):

> The beginning of it was that the gods were at war with the people known as the Vanir and they arranged for a peace meeting between them and made a truce in this way: they both went up to a crock and spat into it. When they were going away, the gods took the truce token and would not allow it to be lost, and made of it a man. He was called Kvasir. He is so wise that nobody asks him any question he is unable to answer. He travelled far and wide over the world to teach men wisdom and came once to feast with some dwarfs, Fjalar and Galar. These called him aside for a word in private and killed him, letting his blood run into two crocks and one kettle. The kettle was called Óðrörir, but the crocks were known as Són and Boðn. They mixed his blood with honey, and it became the mead which makes whoever drinks of it a poet or a scholar. The dwarfs told the Æsir that Kvasir had choked with learning, because there was no one sufficiently well-informed to compete with him in knowledge.[16]

(There follows the story of the acquisition of the mead by Odin, who is to be its greatest beneficiary).

c) *Ynglingasaga* (the beginning of the *Heimskringla*) (chaps. 1, 2, 4, 5):

> 1. Of the Three Continents. –The earth's round, on which mankind lives, is much indented. Great seas cut into the land from the ocean. We know that a sea goes from the Norva Sound [the Strait of Gibraltar] all the way to Jórsalaland ["Jerusalem Land," Palestine]. From this sea a long arm extends to the northeast which is called the Black Sea. It separates the three parts of the world. The part to the eastward is called Asia; but that which lies to the west of it is called by some Europe, by others Eneá. North of the Black Sea lies Svíthjóth the Great or the Cold.

[15] *Edda* (Kuhn), p. 5; *Edda* (Bellows), pp. 10–11.

[16] *The Prose Edda of Snorri Sturluson*, trans. Jean I. Young (Berkeley and Los Angeles: University of California Press, 1964), p. 100. Translations from the *Snorra Edda* are taken from this version, abbreviated *Prose Edda* (Young).

Some men consider Svíthjóth the Great not less in size than Serkland the Great ["Saracen Land," North Africa], and some think it is equal in size to Bláland ["Blackman's Land," Africa]. The northern part of Svíthjóth is uncultivated on account of frost and cold, just as the southern part of Bláland is a desert because of the heat of the sun. In Svíthjóth there are many large provinces. There are also many tribes and many tongues. There are giants and dwarfs; there are black men and many kinds of strange tribes. Also there are animals and dragons of marvellous size. Out of the north, from the mountains which are beyond all inhabited districts, a river runs through Svíthjóth whose correct name is Tanais [the Don River]. In olden times it was called Tana Fork or Vana Fork. Its mouth is in the Black Sea. The land around the Vana Fork was then called Vana Home or the Home of the Vanir. This river divides the three continents. East of it is Asia, west of it Europe.

2. Of Ásgarth and Óthin. —The land east of the Tana Fork was called the Land or Home of the Æsir, and the capital of that country they called Ásgarth. In this capital the chieftain ruled whose name was Óthin. This was a great place for sacrifices. The rule prevailed there that twelve temple priests were highest in rank. They were to have charge of sacrifices and to judge between men. They are called *díar* or chiefs. All the people were to serve them and show them reverence.

Óthin was a great warrior and fared widely, conquering many countries. He was so victorious that he won the upper hand in every battle; as a result, his men believed that it was granted to him to be victorious in every battle. It was his habit that, before sending his men to battle or on other errands, he would lay his hands on their heads and give them a *bjannak* [benediction]. Then they believed they would succeed. It was also noted that wherever his men were sore bestead, on sea or on land, they would call on his name, and they would get help from so doing. They put all their trust in him. Often he was away so long as to be gone for many years.

4. The War between the Æsir and the Vanir. —Óthin made war on the Vanir, but they resisted stoutly and defended their land; now the one, now the other was victorious, and both devastated the land of their opponents, doing each other damage. But when both wearied of that, they agreed on a peace meeting and concluded a peace, giving each other hostages. The Vanir gave their most outstanding men, Njorth the Wealthy and his son Frey; but the Æsir, in their turn, furnished one whose name was Hœnir, declaring him to be well fitted to be a chieftain. He was a large man and exceedingly handsome. Together wth him the Æsir sent one called Mímir, a very wise man; and the Vanir in return sent the one who was the cleverest among them. His name was Kvasir. Now when Hœnir arrived in Vanaheim he was at once made a chieftain. Mímir advised him in all things. But when Hœnir was present at meetings or assemblies without having Mímir at his side and was asked for his opinion on a difficult matter, he would always answer in the same way, saying, "Let others decide." Then the Vanir suspected that the Æsir had defrauded them in the exchange of hostages. Then they seized Mímir and beheaded him and sent the head to the Æsir. Óthin took it and embalmed it with

herbs so that it would not rot, and spoke charms over it, giving it magic power so that it would answer him and tell him many occult things.

Óthin appointed Njorth and Frey to be priests for the sacrificial offerings, and they were *díar* [gods] among the Æsir. Freya was the daughter of Njorth. She was the priestess at the sacrifices. It was she who first taught the Æsir magic such as was practiced among the Vanir. While Njorth lived with the Vanir he had his sister as wife, because that was the custom among them. Their children were Frey and Freya. But among the Æsir it was forbidden to marry so near a kin.

5. Gefjon Ploughs Zeeland Out of Lake Mælaren. —A great mountain chain runs from the northeast to the southwest. It divides Svíthjóth the Great from other realms. South of the mountains it is not far to Turkey. There Óthin had large possessions. At that time the generals of the Romans moved about far and wide, subjugating all peoples, and many chieftains fled from their possessions because of these hostilities. And because Óthin had the gift of prophecy and was skilled in magic, he knew that his offspring would inhabit the northern part of the world. Then he set his brothers Vé and Víli over Ásgarth, but he himself and all *díar*, and many other people, departed. First he journeyed west to Garthríki [Russia], and then south, to Saxland [northwestern Germany]. He had many sons. He took possession of lands far and wide in Saxland and set his sons to defend these lands. Then he journeyed north to the sea and fixed his abode on an island. That place is now called Óthinsey [Óthin's Island], on the island of Funen.

Thereupon he sent Gefjon north over the sound to seek for land. She came to King Gylfi, and he gave her a ploughland. Then she went to Giantland and there bore four sons to some giant. She transformed them into oxen and attached them to the plough and drew the land westward into the sea, opposite Óthin's Island, and that is [now] called Selund [Zeeland], and there she dwelled afterwards. Skjold, a son of Óthin married her. They lived at Hleithrar. A lake was left [where the land was taken] which is called Logrin. The bays in that lake correspond to the nesses of Selund. Thus says Bragi the Old:

> Gefjon, glad in mind, from
> Gylfi drew the good land,
> Denmark's increase, from the
> oxen so the sweat ran.
> Did four beasts of burden—
> with brow-moons eight in foreheads—
> walk before the wide isle
> won by her from Sweden.

But when Óthin learned that there was good land east in Gylfi's kingdom he journeyed there; and Gylfi came to an agreement with him, because he did not consider himself strong enough to withstand the Æsir. Óthin and Gylfi vied much with each other in magic and spells, but the Æsir always had the better of it.

Óthin settled by Lake Logrin, at a place which formerly was called Sigtúnir. There he erected a large temple and made sacrifices according to the custom of the Æsir. He took possession of the land as far as he had

called it Sigtúnir. He gave dwelling places to the temple priests. Njorth dwelled at Nóatún, Frey at Uppsala, Heimdall at Himinbjorg, Thór at Thrúthvang, Baldr at Breithablik. To all he gave good estates.[17]

d) Saxo Grammaticus, *Gesta Danorum,* I, 7.[18] This brief passage is clarified by the texts of the *Voluspá* and of Snorri, but in itself clarifies nothing. It gathers and alters radically several features of the legend of the war and of the reconciliation of the Æsir and the Vanir, notably the gold statue (*Vǫluspá*), the beheading of Mímir (*Ynglingasaga*), and the murder of Kvasir (*Skáldskaparmál*). "Othinus" here too is a king, whose capital is "Byzantium," but who willingly spends time *apud Upsalam.*[19]

I have quoted these texts at length, first to make the reader feel, on the basis of a precise example, in what state, or rather in what diverse states, Scandinavian mythology has been transmitted to us, but also so that he may refer back to them constantly during the discussion that follows.

* * *

In 1903 Bernhard Salin (1861–1931) proposed a literal interpretation of the "invasion of the Æsir" which has remained the model accepted (at least until recently) by most historians of Scandinavian religion.[20] Salin was a great man, as learned as he was modest, and the fine *Nordiska Museet* in Stockholm owes a great deal to him. Salin's theory was that Snorri's narrative, including the episode of the war between the Æsir and the Vanir and their reconciliation, contains in corrupted form the memory of great, historical, authentic events: a long *migration* of a people according to a precise itinerary from north of the Black Sea to Scandinavia, and a *struggle* between two peoples, one worshipping the Æsir and the other the Vanir. This struggle, according to the tradition that transposed men into gods or rather confused the gods with their worshippers, ended in a compromise, a fusion. Certain critics, such as H. Schück and E. Mogk, have thought of a religious war, which in itself is quite improbable. The majority, like H. Güntert and more recently E. A. Philippson, think

17 *Heimskringla: History of the Kings of Norway,* trans. Lee M. Hollander (Austin, Texas: University of Texas Press, 1964), pp. 6–10. Abbreviated: *Heimskringla* (Hollander).

18 Cited from the edition of J. Olrik and H. Ræder (Copenhagen, 1931).

19 Dumézil, *La saga de Hadingus* (Paris: Presses Universitaires de France, 1953).

20 For references see the Bibliographical Notes at the end of Chapter 4.

of a purely ethnic and political war, a war of conquest, a type more assuredly present in the ancient history of Europe. According to some writers, who follow B. Salin closely, these events would have occurred around the fourth century; according to others, they might even represent the Indo-European invasion into the Germanic area, clearly far earlier. It would appear that this second opinion is in greater favor. In archaeological language—for archaeology is often appealed to in such a debate—the combatants in this great duel, first historic, later legendary and mythic, would be the representatives of two cultures that the excavations in northern Europe make it possible to identify: the Megalith people and the Battle Axe people (or *Schnurkeramiker*). Here, for example, is how E. A. Philippson explains it:

> The difference between the religion of the Vanir and the religion of the Æsir is a fundamental one. The religion of the Vanir was older, autochthonous, the product of an agricultural civilization. The religion of the Æsir was younger, the expression of a virile, warlike, but also more spiritual epoch. The gap between these religions, which was missed by Roman observers, was obvious to the pagans: the legend of the Scandinavians relating to the war of the Vanir confirms it.[21]

Other interpreters, few in number but growing, such as O. Höfler, J. de Vries, W. Betz, and myself, resist this historicizing view, this idea of transcription, in mythic language, of historical events. We do not deny, of course, the material changes, the invasions, the fusions of peoples, or the duality of civilization which is observable, archaeologically, on Germanic soil, between what was there before the Indo-Europeans and what followed their invasion. Nor do we contest that Germanic religions, especially the Scandinavian, evolved during the course of centuries. But we do believe that the duality of the Æsir and the Vanir is not a reflection of these events, nor an effect of that evolution. We believe rather that it is a question here of two complementary terms in a unitary religious and ideological structure, one of which presupposes the other. These were brought, fully articulated, by those Indo-European invaders who became the Germanic peoples; we believe that the initial war between the Æsir and the Vanir is only a spectacular manifestation, as is the function of a myth, in the form of a violent conflict, of the distinction, the conceptual opposition, which justifies their coexistence. Finally, we suggest that the unbreakable association that follows the war, and which the war only prepares for, signifies that the opposition is also a complementarity, a solidarity, and that the Æsir and Vanir adjust

21 E. A. Philippson, *Die Genealogie der Götter* (Urbana, Illinois, 1953), p. 19.

and balance themselves for the greatest good of a human society that feels an equal need for protectors of both kinds.

I propose to show briefly the fragility and the internal contradictions of the historical thesis, and then to indicate the principal positive reasons that support the structural thesis.

1. Among the three principal documents relating to the war between the Æsir and the Vanir just cited (that of Saxo being without interest here), the historical thesis is founded only on the third. Neither the *Vǫluspá* nor the *Skáldskaparmál*—where Snorri has no other concern than to recount the divine stories—localizes the two groups of adversaries; nor does either imply any migration. On the contrary, they present the divine beings and their actions in the same tone and in the same perspective as, for example, the combats between the gods and giants, that is in the imprecise time and space of myth. Only the beginning of Snorri's second work is expressed in terms of geography and history, multiplying its precisions, going to the point of a Roman synchronization. But these terms, even these precisions, are suspect: Snorri, this time, sees himself as historian and genealogist, and he acts like the Irish monks of the high Middle Ages who joyously historicized information inherited from the druids and the pagan *filid*. They inserted it into their Latin erudition, drawing their principal arguments from word play, from the consonance of indigenous proper names with biblical or classical names, deriving the *Scots* from *Scythia*, supposing a great migration of *Picts* with, naturally, a stop in France, at Poitiers, capital of the *Pictaui*. Snorri proceeds no differently. He not only reduces the gods to kings now dead, who have succeeded one another and who, during their lifetimes, moved, emigrated, and invaded. He also localizes on the map of the known world the divine races thus humanized, and for that, depends on puns, some of them excellent (*Æsir—Asia*), others less successful (*Vanir—*Vana-kvísl-Tanaïs*, "River Don"). If he places the Æsir and the Vanir, initially, on the banks of the Black Sea, at the mouth of the Don, it is not from an obscure memory of some migration, Gothic or otherwise, nor even from knowledge of a great commercial route going from the Crimea to Scandinavia, but simply from the allure of a play of sounds, during an epoch when such quasi-etymological word play was acceptable as a historical argument.

2. Those who, despite this a priori improbability, wish to utilize the chapters from the *Ynglingasaga* to found a historical interpretation of the war between the Æsir and the Vanir, fall—have fallen—now into contradiction, now into arbitrariness. Snorri, in fact, lo-

calizes the war before all migration, at the very place of the primitive home which he attributes to the two peoples, that is the frontier of "Asia," at the mouth of the Don. It is only after the postwar reconciliation that Odin, gathering up his new subjects, the three great Vanir, with the same privileges as his older subjects, the Æsir, starts off on the expedition which is finally to lead them to Uppland in Sweden. To credit this text, the formation of a unified religion would have taken place far from Scandinavia, far from Germania, previous to any encounter on Germanic soil between an agricultural culture and a more virile, warlike one, one more spiritual, too, as E. A. Philippson generously suggests. But it is in Scandinavia and northern Germany that archaeological traces of a duality and succession of cultures appear. If one wishes to justify the duality of divine types by the duality of cultures, it is in these Germanic lands that the contact, struggle, and fusion of the two peoples must be located, and not somewhere around the mouth of the Don. If in order to escape contradiction, one retains from Snorri, as is usual, only the *idea* of the conflict and of the reconciliation, reserving the right not to situate everything where Snorri does, on the Black Sea, during the initial period, but on the contrary, near the terminus, at a northern point in the Germanic regions, one is clearly being arbitrary, for what objective criteria permit one to decide that one part of a text is truly remembered, hence useful as a historical document, and that some other part is fantasy?

3. A third criticism of the historicizing thesis leads us directly to our own task. Even in this text of the *Ynglingasaga* which claims to be historical with more reason than the other two purely mythological texts, which contain no attempt whatsoever at spatial or temporal localization, one is struck by an abundance of details of another order. These details concern the phases of the war (*Vǫluspá*) and the terms of the peace (*Skáldskaparmál, Ynglingasaga*), notably the gods exchanged as security, their characters and their adventures. These minute and picturesque details cannot be even greatly deformed history; they cannot possibly represent any trace of the customs of peoples supposedly in conflict. The historicizers must therefore ignore them completely and consider them only secondary devices to make the text more lively. It is, however, these very details that are the essence of the stories, and which clearly interested the Icelandic writer Snorri most when he was not absorbed in word play, as they did the *Vǫluspá* poet and no doubt the listeners or readers of both.

An important question of principle is here raised: is it sound, when using a mythological text, thus to abstract away all the rich detail of its contents? In my view, it certainly is not. The historian of religions must, like all historians, treat his documents with respect. Before asking which features, great or small, he can extract from them to support his thesis, he must read and reread them, immerse himself in them passively and receptively, being extremely careful to leave all features in their places, both those that support him and those that resist him. If one submits to this regimen, one soon learns that there is more to be done with such texts than to destroy them in order to insert a few relics drawn from the debris into other constructions. First one must understand their internal structure, which justifies the ordering of their elements, even the strangest and most bizarre. What might thus be lost from the realm of history is regained in that of theology, in knowledge of the religious thought embedded in the documents.

It is occasionally argued that this structural view also leads to arbitrariness or even to a mirage. What is related by Snorri and suggested by the *Vǫluspá* is after all picturesque and strange, and does not at first glance have an air of containing or even wishing to express a religious concept. To reject the localization of the Æsir on the threshold of Asia, as some historians do, or to retain the "idea" of the conflict between the two peoples, as the more moderate do, is well and good. But does one not show equal credulity in seeking, indeed discovering, any sense in the mass of details that after all might be just as artificial, literary, or late—in a word, useless—as the onomastic puns?

It is here that comparative considerations may [and must] intervene to assure us that our texts do in fact have meaning, and to determine what that meaning is. Let us be very precise: we are concerned here with comparative Indo-European considerations, implying a common genetic relationship (filiation), not simply typological or universal considerations. The latter are by no means negligible: it may happen that a trait or group of traits which seems strange and meaningless on a page of Snorri may be found in the folklore of peoples far removed from the Scandinavians, and may there be understood, commented on, and justified by these people in terms valid also for the Icelandic documents. But our efforts shall not advance in that direction: we shall employ a more delicate instrument of comparison.

The Scandinavians and all Germanic peoples spoke Indo-European languages, curiously deformed phonetically, but in which the non-Indo-European residue of the vocabulary is negligible compared to what can be observed in certain southern languages within the Indo-European family. If the concepts of language, nation, and race, even of civilization, are not interchangeable, it is no less true, especially for very ancient times, that community of language implies a rather considerable minimum of community in concepts and in their mode of organization, in short "ideology," for which religion has long been the principal expression. It is thus legitimate and even methodologically necessary, before denying significance or antiquity to a "theologeme" or myth among the Scandinavians, to ask if the religions of the most conservative Indo-European peoples, the speakers of Sanskrit, Italic, and Celtic, do not present a similar belief or story. This is sometimes the case, and it happens that in its Indic version for example, which is attested earlier in books written directly by the keepers of divine knowledge, the structure of a formula or the meaning of a story appears more clearly, more obviously linked to religious and social life, than in the literary works of the Christian Snorri. And if this kind of comparative observation is applied to a complex tradition, that is, one articulating a fairly large number of ideological elements, and which is furthermore truly singular, seldom found throughout the world, it becomes less likely that the Scandinavian-Indic concordance should be fortuitous and not to be explained by common prehistoric heritage. It happens that the problems of the Æsir and the Vanir are of the kind that lend themselves to such a method.

* * *

In Vedic religion, in fact in pre-Vedic religion—this we know from the list of Aryan gods by Mitani, preserved in epigraphic documents from the fourteenth century B.C.—and already in Indo-Iranian religion—this we know from the transplantation of it into the hierarchy of Zoroastrian archangels—a small number of gods were regularly associated in invocations, rituals, and hierarchical lists, in order to sum up the totality of the invisible society. These divinities were distributed, with regard to their functions, into the three levels of an already well-known structure: the one that later, in classical India, gave rise to the rigid social classification of the *varṇa*, namely *brāhmaṇa* or priests, *kṣatriya* or warriors, and *vaiśya* or breeder-farmers—so parallel to that which ancient Ireland exhibited in more supple fashion with its corps of druids, its military class of *flaith*, and its freemen, the cattle-owning *bō airig*. The briefest form of this list, that of Mitani, enumerates first two sovereign gods, *Mitra* and *Varuṇa*, then the god essentially representing strength and war, *Ind(a)ra*, and then the twin gods who give health, youth, fertility, and happiness, the *Nāsatya* or *Aśvin*. The Zoroastrian transposition rests on the same list with one additional entry, also known in India, a goddess found linked to the twins of the third level. In the mythology, not of the Vedas but of Indian epic, the gods of the first level are quite diminished, and although they have not completely vanished, it is Indra who figures as king of the gods, which no doubt reflects a social evolution favorable to the warrior class. In 1938 it was possible to demonstrate that the pre-Capitoline triad, which presided over the oldest Roman religion, rested on the same analysis of the needs of man and of divine services: the *Jupiter* of the *flamen dialis,* so narrowly associated with the *rex,* brought to the Romans all the forms of sovereign and celestial protection; *Mars* gave them physical force and victory in combat against both visible and invisible enemies; *Quirinus,* judging by the offices of his Flamen, by the ritual of his festival, by the gods regularly associated with him, even by his name, and finally by the definitions conserved down to a late commentary in the *Æneid,* supervised the good harvest and the conservation of grains, the social masses which were the substance of Rome, and civil life (cf. Lat. *quirites*) during a vigilant peace. The historicizing hypotheses that have attempted to explain this triad as a secondary feature, the effect of historical accident, the cooperation of peoples in the founding of Rome, are a priori condemned because among other Italic peoples, the Umbrians of Iguvium—at a time when Roman influence was out of the question—the ritual of the famous *Tables* honors within the same hierarchy a very similar triad composed of a *Juu-*, a *Mart-*, and a *Vofiono-*.

The concordance of Indo-Iranian and Italic religious features guarantees that the tripartite theological structure and the practice of summarizing it in a brief list of gods characteristic of each level dates back to the time of the Indo-European community. The exact parallel of Scandinavian mythology, expressed in the formula Odin-Thor-Frey, may not therefore be an innovation, but a faithfully conserved archaism. No more than that of Jupiter-Mars-Quirinus does the grouping of the three Scandinavian gods justify an explanation through chance or compromise in the prehistory of the great peninsula or in northern Germany. Each has a meaning, the same meaning, and each of the three terms requires its complements. If we recall, furthermore, the precise analogies long noticed between Thor and Indra (red hair; hammer and *vajra,* etc.), if we note that the third level in Scandinavia is sometimes occupied not only by Frey but also by the pair Njord and Frey, who, not being twins but father and son, are no less closely associated than the two Nāsatya, if we recall too that on this same third level the goddess Freya is often honored beside the gods Njord and Frey, just as a goddess is usually associated with the Indo-Iranian Nāsatya, then we begin to discern not only the parallelism of the entire structure but also important correspondences of individual terms which simply could not have been accumulated by chance. Finally, Vedic ideology—and we already have good reasons to call it Indo-Iranian—displayed a firm solidarity between the first two levels in opposition to the third, as occurred later in human society, between the Brahmins and the kṣatriya, called the two forces, *ubhe vīrye,* in opposition to the vaiśya. Completely parallel is the union of Odin and Thor in Scandinavia in a single divine race, the Æsir, in opposition to the Vanir, Njord, Frey, and Freya.

It has been objected that this comparative procedure takes into account from all Germanic religion only its Scandinavian form, and in the relatively late state in which we know it, that is, that nothing establishes this tripartite division among other Germanic peoples, such as the Goths or those of the West Germanic group. Further, it has been noted that while the name of the Æsir is to be found elsewhere, that of the Vanir is found nowhere outside of Scandinavia, and finally that the oldest archaeological material in Scandinavia seems to show that the god of the hammer and the ithyphallic god preceded the Indo-European invasion.

These objections are not as considerable as they appear at first glance. As for the last one, we admit perfectly willingly that the Indo-European gods of the second and third levels, Thor and Frey, probably annexed to themselves certain conceptions of another origin, already popular among the conquered indigenous population. Again we must not interpret too generously the famous rock carvings of Sweden, where the archaeologists have a tendency to call all the silhouettes armed with hammers Thor and all the obscene silhouettes Frey. As for the objection about the names, I believe that it rests on an unjustified, unreasonable claim, for the proper names are not of such great importance. The name *vanir,* of obscure etymology (of the eight which have been proposed, the best is still that which equates it with Lat. *Venus, venerari,* etc.), may well be limited to Old Norse, but the type, the class of gods which it designates could have existed elsewhere under another name or without any generic name. The Scandinavian Njord (ON *Njǫrðr* ← **Nerþu-*), one of the principal Vanir, must be the one described by Tacitus under the name Nerthus, with feminine sex and clear characteristics of the third function (fecundity, peace, etc.) in northern Germany. Furthermore it is not quite true that the triad or other very similar triads are not attested in other areas of the ancient Germanic world.

One can not argue on this point from the silence of the Goths: we know almost nothing of their mythology. As for the West Germanic peoples, our oldest explicit source, Tacitus,[22] enumerates to the contrary—and in terms that prove that there was a structure—gods who are clearly distributed into the three levels, and in the expected hierarchical order. The most honored god, whom Tacitus calls *Mercurius*, is surely the equivalent of Odin. Then came Hercules and Mars, that is the two warrior gods who are surely the Scandinavian Thor and Tyr (we shall take up the latter in the next chapter). Finally, at least for a part of the Suevians, a goddess is joined to these two gods. Tacitus calls her Isis; there is no reason (especially that which he gives: the cult boat) to consider her of foreign origin, *advectam religionem*. It is even possible that before Tacitus Caesar, in his short and inexact account of the Germanic gods, may have attempted to interpret summarily a comparable triad:

> To the number of the Gods they admit only those whom they see and whose good deeds they enjoy, the *Sun, Vulcan*, and the *Moon*; they have not even heard the others spoken of.[23]

Even if the term "sun" is indeed inadequate to describe a god of the sovereign type such as Odin, in return Vulcan, god of the hammer, may be a translation, certainly functionally improper, but obviously explicable, of the continental counterpart of Thor, and, for a goddess of fertility seen by a Roman, the lunary label would be no more bizarre than for many maternal or nourishing goddesses of the Mediterranean world who have received it too, from Oriental Isis and Semele to that Roman Anna Perenna who figures in the speculations of Ovid. Finally, more recently, among the Saxons, who were converted by Charlemagne even before the Eddic poems we have were composed in Scandinavia, a triad is attested which must, term for term, be the same as that of the Scandinavians. The formula of abjuration imposed on them, which is conserved in the Vatican in a ninth-century manuscript, contains in fact these words: "I renounce all works and words of the devil, *Thunar, Uuōten*, and *Saxnot* and all the demons who are their companions (*hira genōtas*)." The first two of these divine names are the cognates of Thor and Odin. The third name, whose second element corresponds to modern Germanic *(Ge)noss* "companion," means nothing more than "companion of the Saxons." We have to do with a Saxon god who actually appears only in Old English, where it has the form *Seaxnēat*. This reminds us that,

---

22 C. Tacitus, *Germania*, chap. 9.

23 G. Caesar, *The Gallic Wars*, VI, 21, 2.

just as in Rome Quirinus (probably **co-uirīno-*) was the god of the *quirites* collectivity, so the Scandinavian Frey is distinctly, among the gods, the *folkvaldi* "captain, lit. leader of men or of the folk" (*Skírnismál* 3: *folkvaldi goða*). Also, in the cult he is the *veraldar goð*, that is the god of that complex Germanic notion (Ger. *Welt*, Eng. *world*, Swed. *värld*, etc.), which designates etymologically men (*ver-*) through the ages (*ǫld*). These indications compel us not to interpret silence as absence in other Germanic realms where our information has even more lacunae.

* * *

Indo-European parallels help to explain not only the formula of the composition of the triad, but also the legend of the initial separation and war, as well as the reconciliation and fusion of the Æsir with the Vanir. To be sure, the Vedic hymns say nothing about this, oriented as they are toward eulogy and prayer: they are hardly proper for recalling the delicate episodes of divine history. The later literature, the epic, knows that the gods Indra and the Nāsatya, whose association is so necessary and so close, were nevertheless not always joined in one unified society. By chance an Iranian legend confirms that several essential traits of the material in this story, which probably comes from the "fifth Veda," the oral corpus of legends, were pre-Vedic, indeed Indo-Iranian. Originally the gods of the lower level, the Nāsatya or givers of health and prosperity, were apart from the other gods. The gods, headed by Indra (for such is the state of the divine hierarchy in the epic), whose weapon is the lightning, refused them what is the privilege and practically part of the credentials of divinity, participation in benefits of the oblations, under the pretext that they were not "proper" gods, but rather some kind of artisans or warriors who were too much mixed in with men. On the day when the Nāsatya raised their claims and tried to enter into divine society, a bitter conflict ensued.

We see how this entrance is substantially parallel to the initial separation of the higher Æsir—the masters of magic and lightning—and the lower Vanir—givers of richness and fecundity. In India, let us note without delay, the heterogeneity of the two groups of gods could not be explained by the contact and conflict of religions or of different peoples, as is proposed in Scandinavia for the Æsir and Vanir: Mitra-Varuṇa and Indra on the one hand, the Nāsatya on the other, grouped together at the same time and with the same hierarchical order, were brought by the Indo-Iranian conquerors to the bend in the Euphrates as well as into the Iranian plateau and the basin of the Indus in the fourteenth century B.C. But the correspondences between Snorri and the *Mahābhārata* do not stop there. They extend to a group of rare and complex traits which permit the comparativist to be more positive.

We recall from the *Skáldskaparmál* the birth and death of Kvasir: at the moment when peace is concluded between the divine adversaries, they all spit into the same vessel. Out of this "pledge of peace" the gods fashion a man named Kvasir who has extraordinary, absolutely enormous, wisdom. He travels about the world, but two dwarfs kill him, distributing his blood among three bowls, mixing honey with it and thus concocting the "mead of poetry and wisdom." Then they tell the gods that Kvasir has choked with learning, no one having been able to compete with him in knowledge.

The name *Kvasir* in this legend has long been interpreted: since 1864 K. Simrock, then R. Heinzel (1889), and then E. Mogk (1923) have shown that it is an onomastic personification of an intoxicating drink which recalls the *kvas* of the Slavs.[24] It is natural that the precious intoxication given by the mead of poetry and wisdom should have honey as an ingredient. It is equally natural that a drink fermented from squashed vegetables (Dan. *kvas* "crushed fruits, wort of those fruits") should be made to ferment by spittle. This technique is frequently attested; it is at least conceivable, as we are here dealing with a ceremonial or communal drink, sanctioning the agreement between two social groups, that such fermentation should be caused by the spittle of all concerned. Furthermore, on this point E. Mogk has gathered sufficient ethnographic parallels.

What is less common is that the intoxicating drink prepared with the spittle and called upon to enter as a component of the other intoxicating drink, the mead of poetry, between its two stages as a drink, should take on a completely different form, that of a man or superman, and this by the will of the gods. Furthermore, this theme is not only rare (the "King Soma," and Dionysos-Zagreus, are something else again); it is inserted in a complex and precise whole, which must not be dislocated. It was not under just any circumstance, nor without design, that this man-drink was created. He was created at the conclusion of the war between the Æsir and Vanir, to seal the peace. Then he was put to death, and his blood, spread among the

24 For references see the bibliography in Jan de Vries, *Altgermanische Religionsgeschichte*, 2d ed., 2 vols. (Berlin: Walter de Gruyter, 1956–1957), pp. ix–xlix. Abbreviated: *AGR* 2 (the first edition, Berlin 1935–1937, is *AGR* 1).

three recipients, served to make another drink, more durable in that it still inebriates Odin, poets, and visionaries.

Let us return now from Scandinavia to India, where we have left the higher gods and the Nāsatya in a great conflict, Indra already brandishing his thunderbolts against the latter. How does this crisis turn out? An ascetic allied with the Nāsatya who, as part of their usual services, have restored his youth to him, creates, through the force of his asceticism—the great weapon of Indian penitents—a gigantic man, who threatens to swallow the world, including the recalcitrant gods. This enormous monster's name is *Mada* "Drunkenness": he is drunkenness personified. Even Indra gives in, peace is made, the Nāsatya definitely join the divine community, and no allusion will ever be made to the distinction among gods or to the initial conflict. But what to do with this character, Drunkenness, whose task is finished and who is now only dangerous? The one who created him, this time with the accord of the gods, cuts him into four pieces and his unitary essence is split up into the four things that, literally or figuratively, are indeed intoxicating: drink, women, gaming, and hunting.

Such is the story to be read in the third book of the *Mahābhārata*, sections 123–125. An Iranian legend that I called attention to in the last section of my *Naissance d'archanges*[25] and which Professor Jean de Menasce has further scrutinized,[26] that of the *Hārūt-Mārūt*, confirms the linkage of drunkenness with this affair from the beginning of Indo-Iranian mythology. The reader will not have failed to notice the analogy between the fabrications and the liquidations of Kvasir and Mada, an analogy that it is easy to delimit and define. Here is how the balance sheet was formulated in my *Loki*:

> Certainly the differences between Germanic and Indic myth are striking, but so is the analogy between their fundamental situations and results. Here are the differences: among the Germanic peoples, the character "Kvas" is formed *after* the peace is concluded, as a *symbol of that peace*, and he is made according to a precise realistic technique, fermentation with spittle, whereas the character "Drunkenness" is made as a *weapon*, *in order to* force the gods into peace, and he is made *mystically* (we are in India), by the force of ascetism, without reference to a technique of fermentation. Then, when "Kvas" is killed and his blood divided in thirds, *it is not done by the gods* who made him, but by two dwarfs, whereas in India, it is his creator who at the order of the gods dismembers "Drunken-

25 Dumézil, *Naissance d'archanges* (Paris: Gallimard, 1945), pp. 158–170.

26 Menasce, Jean de, in *Revue de la Société Suisse d'Études Asiatiques* 1 (1947), 10–18.

ness" into four parts. Further, the dismemberment of "Kvas" is simply *quantitative*, into three homogeneous parts (three vessels receiving the blood, all of the same value, though one happens to be larger than the others), whereas that of "Drunkenness" is *qualitative*, into differentiated parts (four sorts of drunkenness). In Germanic legend, it is simply as a lying explanation that the dwarfs afterwards tell the gods of an intolerable force (of a purely *intellectual* kind), out of proportion with the human world, which *would* have led to the suffocation of "Kvas," whereas in the Indian legend the excess of force (*physical*, brutal) of Drunkenness is *authentically* intolerable, incompatible with the life of the world, and as such leads authentically to his being dismembered. Finally the Germanic legend presents "Kvas" as a *benefactor* from the beginning, well disposed toward men—a sort of martyr—and his blood, properly treated, produces that most valued thing, the mead of poetry and wisdom, whereas in India "Drunkenness" is a *malefactor* from the beginning and his four fractions are the scourge of mankind.

All this is true, but it would only prove, if there were need of it, that India is not Iceland and that the two stories were told in civilizations that in content and form had developed in almost diametrically opposite directions. Notably their ideologies of insobriety had become just about inverse. There exists nevertheless a common pattern. It is at the moment when divine society is with difficulty but definitively joined by the adjunction of the representatives of fecundity and prosperity to those of sovereignty and force, it is at the moment when the two hostile groups make their peace, that a character is artificially created incarnating the force of intoxicating drink or of insobriety and is named after it. When this force proves to be excessive for the conditons of this world—for good or for evil—the person thus made is then killed and divided into three or four intoxicating parts that either aid or threaten man.

This pattern is original. It is not met with anywhere in the world but in these two cases. In addition, its principle is easily understood, if one pays attention to the social conditions and conceptions which must have existed among the Indo-European peoples. In partcular, intoxication under various names and shapes would have been of use to all three social functions. On the one hand, it is one of the fundamental stimuli in the life of a sorcerer-priest and of a hunter-warrior in this culture, and, on the other hand, it is procured through plants that the farmer must *cultivate* and *prepare*. It is thus natural that the "birth" of intoxication and all that goes with it should be situated at that moment of mythological history when society is formed through reconciliation and the union of priests and warriors on the one hand with farmers and all the powers of fecundity and nourishment on the other. There is a profound harmony between this sociomythological event and the appearance of intoxication, and it is not superfluous to remark here that neither the poets of the *Mahābhārata* nor Snorri could still have been aware of this, which lends a strange air to their tales. For the poets of the *Mahābhārata*, the Nāsatya are no longer what they were at the time of the Vedic compilation, typical canonized representatives of the third function. However well Snorri in his various treatises portrays the differing characters of Odin, Thor, and

Frey, he surely does not understand the reconciliation of the Æsir and the Vanir as a myth concerning the origin of the harmonious collaboration of the diverse social functions.[27]

This correspondence is not the only one. We have also a Roman tradition that presents a new pattern for the events of the war between the Æsir and the Vanir given by the sibyl in the *Vǫluspá*, one that confirms the meaning of the entire story. In Rome, as we know, there is no more mythology, and the earliest lore is deposited in the epic of origins. Further, the "complete society" whose creation interested the very matter-of-fact Romans could only be their own. It is in fact the tradition about the birth of the city which offers the Germanist the parallel of which we speak. Rome, says the legend, was constituted by the union of two groups of men, the purely masculine companions of the demigod Romulus, maintainers of the *promises of Jupiter* and strong in their *military valor*, and the Sabines of Titus Tatius, *rich farmers* and, through their *women*, the only ones capable of giving fecundity and durability to the nascent society. But the happy union of these two complementary groups, like that of the Æsir and Vanir, was brought about at the conclusion of a difficult and long-contested war, in the course of which each adversary in turn gained the upper hand. The union was affirmed in a scene and by means that would well illustrate its "functional specialty." The Sabines, the "rich ones," nearly won by occupying the capitol, but how did they occupy it? By bribing Tarpeia, a *woman*, with *gold*—or with *love*, according to another version. Later, in the battle of the forum, when his army fled in disorder, Romulus not only restored order, but even drove the Sabine army out of the capitol back to their camp. How did he achieve this result? With his eyes and hands to the sky, he addressed himself to the *sovereign Jupiter*, reminding him of his promises, imploring a miraculous suspension of panic; and Jupiter granted it. It is notable that the two episodes of the war of the two divine clans in the *Vǫluspá* correspond to these two, with the same functional features. The rich and voluptuous Vanir send among the Æsir as a scourge the woman called Gullveig, "insobriety (or power) of gold," who corrupts their hearts, especially those of the women. Further, Odin *throws his spear* in a gesture that the sagas know well, where it regularly has the effect of throwing the enemy army into a fatal panic. In the conflict of Indra and the Nāsatya which was treated at some length above, and which does not achieve the dignity of a war of peoples, the conduct of the two parties is no less clearly significant

27 Dumézil, *Loki* (Paris: G.-P. Maisonneuve, 1948), pp. 102–105.

of their functional levels. The Nāsatya have as their ally the ascetic *Cyavana,* whom they obtained by restoring his *youth* and *beauty* and by permitting him to keep his *wife* whom they had first intended to take for themselves. And it is with brandished thunderbolt that Indra responds to their audacity.

Even if all the picturesque details of Snorri's narrative have not found equally striking correspondences outside Scandinavia (I am thinking of the stories of Hœnir and the decapitation of Mímir), those just recited should suffice to establish that the war of the Æsir and the Vanir is indeed a myth that is *older* than the Germanic peoples, *older* than the dispersion of their ancestors and those of the Italic, Indo-Iranian, and other Indo-European peoples. It is a myth whose apparently strange elements still preserve, though not fully understood by its narrators, the complex elements and nuances of a "lesson" on the structure of Indo-European societies.

CHAPTER 2

Magic, War, and Justice: Odin and Tyr

It would be a lengthy task even to present a bare inventory of what the literary tradition tells us about the god Odin. All we can hope to do is describe the most important aspects and state the most characteristic facts. It is important to note that there is no palpable difference, in any case no contradiction, between the image of Odin formed from a reading of the various Eddic poems, and that formed from the works of Snorri. The Odin of Saxo and of the sagas, historical as well as romantic, is easily explained from this starting point.

Odin is the head of the gods: their first king, as we have seen, in the historicizing narratives that let him live and die on earth. In the mythology he is their only king until the end of time, and consequently the particular god of human kings and the protector of their power, even when they glory in being descended from someone else. He is also the god who sometimes requires their blood in sacrifice, for it is almost exclusively to him that sacrifices are made of kings whose power is no longer sufficient to make the crops prosper. In his quality as chief of the gods, it is he who experiences most profoundly the great drama of divine history, the murder of his son Balder. He foresees it, but cannot prevent it; he deplores it as a father and as master of the world, and it gives rise on his part to a confidence spoken into the ear of the corpse, a mystery the texts have respected. He is finally the father of all the gods, while his own ancestry links him to the primordial giants.

He is the clairvoyant one. This gift was assured to him and symbolically expressed by a mutilation which would seem to have been voluntary: he is one-eyed, having given his other eye in payment to the honeyed source of all wisdom. "I know," says the sorceress of the *Vǫluspá* (str. 28):

alt veit ec, Óðinn,	I know exactly, Odin,
hvar þú auga falt:	where your eye was hidden:
í inum mæra Mímis brunni.'	in the famous fountain of Mimir."
Dreccr miǫð Mímir	Mimir drinks mead each morning
morgin hverian	
af veði Valfǫðrs— . . .	from the pledge of Valfather (Odin)— . . .[1]

More generally, he is the high magician. He submitted to a severe initiation, a "near death," which has been plausibly interpreted (R. Pipping, 1927) in the light of shamanistic practices of Siberia: "I know," says Odin himself in the *Hávamál* (strs. 138–140):

Veit ec, at ec hecc vindgameiði á	I know that I hung on the wind-battered tree
nætr allar nío,	nine full nights,
geiri undaðr oc gefinn Óðni,	wounded with the spear and given to Odin,
siálfr siálfom mér,	myself to myself,
á þeim meiði, er mangi veit,	on that tree, of which none knows
hvers hann af rótom renn.	whence the roots come.
Við hleifi mic sældo	They did not comfort me with the loaf
né við hornigi,	nor with the drinking horn,
nýsta ec niðr;	I glanced down;
nam ec upp rúnar, œpandi nam,	I took up the runes, crying out their names,
fell ec aptr þaðan.	I fell back down from there.
Fimbullióð nío nam ec . . .	Nine mighty songs I took . . .[2]

The runes, the magic of letters and of the most powerful secrets, are in fact the creation of Odin. Through them, he knows more than any other being on earth—except perhaps a certain giant, whose even greater age has given him much experience, and with whom, according to an Eddic poem, Odin goes one day to test his wisdom (*Vafþrúðnismál*). But, besides the runes, Odin masters all forms of magic. It is worth recalling here, from the historicizing narrative of the *Ynglingasaga* (chaps. 6–7), the ideas formed around the end of paganism about his talents.

> Chap. 6. Of Óthin's Skills. It is said with truth that when Ása-Óthin came to the Northlands, and the *díar* wih him, they introduced and taught the skills practiced by men for a long time afterwards. Óthin was the most

---

[1] *Edda* (Kuhn), p. 7; cf. *Edda* (Bellows), p. 13.
[2] *Edda* (Kuhn), p. 40; cf. *Edda* (Bellows), pp. 60–61.

prominent among them all, and from him they learned all the skills, because he was the first to know them. Now as to why he was honored so greatly—the reasons for that are these: he was so handsome and noble to look at when he sat among his friends that it gladdened the hearts of all. But when he was engaged in warfare he showed his enemies a grim aspect. The reasons for this were that he knew the arts by which he could shift appearance and body any way he wished. For another matter, he spoke so well and so smoothly that all who heard him believed all he said was true. All he spoke was in rimes, as is now the case in what is called skaldship. He and his temple priests are called songsmiths, because that art began with them in the northern lands. Óthin was able to cause his enemies to be blind or deaf or fearful in battle, and he could cause their swords to cut no better than wands. His own men went to battle without coats of mail and acted like mad dogs or wolves. They bit their shields and were as strong as bears or bulls. They killed people, and neither fire nor iron affected them. This is called berserker rage.

Chap. 7. Óthin's Magic. Óthin could shift his appearance. When he did so his body would lie there as if he were asleep or dead; but he himself, in an instant, in the shape of a bird or animal, a fish or a serpent, went to distant countries on his or other men's errands. He was also able with mere words to extinguish fires, to calm the sea, and to turn the winds any way he pleased. He had a ship called Skíthblathnir with which he sailed over great seas. It could be folded together like a cloth.

Óthin had with him Mímir's head, which told him many tidings from other worlds; and at times he would call to life dead men out of the ground, or he would sit down under men that were hanged. On this account he was called Lord of Ghouls or of the Hanged. He had two ravens on whom he had bestowed the gift of speech. They flew far and wide over the lands and told him many tidings. By these means he became very wise in his lore. And all these skills he taught with those runes and songs which are called magic songs [charms]. For this reason the Æsir are called Workers of Magic.

Óthin had the skill which gives great power and which he practiced himself. It is called seith [sorcery], and by means of it he could know the fate of men and predict events that had not yet come to pass; and by it he could also inflict death or misfortunes or sickness, or also deprive people of their wits or strength, and give them to others. But this sorcery is attended by such wickedness that manly men considered it shameful to practice it, and so it was taught to priestesses.

Óthin knew about all hidden treasures, and he knew such magic spells as would open for him the earth and mountains and rocks and burial mounds; and with mere words he bound those who dwelled in them, and went in and took what he wanted. Exercising these arts he became very famous. His enemies feared him, and his friends had faith in him and in his power. Most of these skills he taught the sacrificial priests. They were next to him in all manner of knowledge and sorcery. Yet many others learned a great deal of it; hence sorcery spread far and wide and continued for a long time.[3]

[3] *Heimskringla* (Hollander), pp. 10–11.

We see that this mysterious wisdom of Odin's is inseparable from the no less mysterious inspiration of poetry. In the preceding chapter, the reader has seen how the mead of wisdom and poetry was produced, which, thanks to his shape changing powers, fell into the exclusive possession of Odin. In fact, poetic genius depends upon Odin: it is he for example who confers it on the hero Starkad in a rather sombre story, simultaneously with the energy of the soul: *Starcatherum . . . non solum animi fortitudine, sed etiam condendorum carminum peritia illustravit.*[4]

One part of Odin's talents as enumerated by Snorri applied especially to war: paralysis of the enemy troops, "madness" increasing by tenfold the normal powers of the favored soldiers. The sagas show him often, in addition, as arbiter of combats, snatching away with one gesture victory from those who thought they had it, condemning to death the warrior whose arms he touches with his own. The sagas also show him throwing over the doomed army a spear that marks its destiny. Some of the later sagas grant him astonishing devices, such as a kind of multiple projectile, a bowstring artillery, with which he discreetly installs himself behind the lines of those he favors. "His men" are of two kinds. First there are bands of *berserkir* warriors, who seem to share his powers of shapechanging and magic, and who in the sagas degenerate into companies of brigands, without morals and without shame, the terror of peasant men and women, and the terror, too, of the poor Lapps, who no doubt identified them with the type of one of the most feared spirits of their folklore, the *stalo* "steel men." Then there are the nobles, knightly and charming types, the "Odinic" heroes, of whom Sigurd of the Scandinavian Nibelungen cycle is the most celebrated example.

Odin does not abandon such heroes at the hour of their death. For one thing, it is often he who, on the battlefield, chooses those who are to fall—and to figure in this harvest is the opposite of misfortune. His feminine emissaries, the Valkyries (ON *valkyrjur,* those who choose, *kjósa,* the dead in battle, *val*), gather them up after the battle and transport them to a resting place—which is not underground—where they lead eternally the only life that is worth anything in their eyes, the life of battle. The *Grímnismál* (strs. 21–23) describes this residence of the god and his favorites, who are henceforth the *einherjar* "great (unique) warriors." This Valhalla is entered after crossing a large and noisy river and clearing the *valgrind,* the old gate whose lock only a few men know how to open:

---

4 Saxo Grammaticus, *Gesta Danorum,* VI, 5–6.

Fimm hundruð dura	Five hundred doors and four tens,
oc um fiórom togom,	
svá hygg ec at Valhǫllo vera:	I think there are at Valhalla;
átta hundruð einheria	eight hundred warriors
ganga ór einom durom,	go out of each door,
þá er þeir fara at vitni at vega.	when they go to fight the wolf.[5]

While awaiting the desperate final battle at the end of the world, the heroes indulge constantly in battles among themselves which are without consequence, since wounds can no longer kill them, and which they interrupt only for delicious banquets. No doubt these representations of the other world, and that of Odin riding his eight-legged mount, the demonic Sleipnir, are the basis of modern beliefs, especially attested in Denmark and southern Sweden, where "Odin" is the leader of the Fantastic Hunt. During the times that Snorri reported, hope of going to Valhalla gave rise to a ritual usage that assured this at least cost, for it could at the last minute make the most sedentary man the equal of heroes. In order to "go to Odin," it was sufficient to mark oneself before death with the sign of Odin, that is, to receive a cut from the point of a spear. Equally efficient but more worthy was another way: after the example of the chief of the gods, men could hang themselves. Among others, the hero Hadingus did this.

The character of Odin is complex and not very reassuring. His face hidden under his hood, in his somber blue cloak, he goes about the world, simultaneously master and spy. It happens that he betrays his believers and his protégés, and he sometimes seems to take pleasure in sowing the seeds of fatal discord, as at the beginning of the *Vǫlsungasaga*. In the sagas that deal with the luckless Ynglingar, or more gratuitously with King Vikarr, he is the god par excellence who receives or even requires the sacrifice of innocent men. This is an ancient trait, for Tacitus remarks that the Germans reserve human victims for Mercurius-*Wōðanaz while they appease their two other great gods, Hercules and Mars, with animal victims. Finally the few dialogue poems of the *Poetic Edda* where sarcasms are employed, such as the *Hárbarðsljóð* which pits Odin against Thor, and the *Lokasenna* where Odin, like the other gods, submits to the malicious allusions of Loki, enable us to catch sight of other less glorious or ambiguous traits of the god, notably of a lascivious order.

It is necessary to come all the way down to modern folklore to find the phantom of Odin linked with any certainty to practices or beliefs concerning rural and agricultural life, in the usage of names, for ex-

[5] *Edda* (Kuhn), pp. 61–62; cf. *Edda* (Bellows), p. 93.

ample, for the "last sheaf." Earlier there were only a few nicknames for Odin, of uncertain interpretation, a few place-names where his name is compounded with that of "field," the sacrificed kings—note, however, that they are *kings*—in case of a bad harvest, finally, the single mention of a sacrifice *til gróðrar* "for growth" to obtain good harvests. In the *Heimskringla*, Snorri states formally that in the course of solemn libations, the pagans offered toasts to different gods for different purposes: they drank to Odin "that he might grant victory and power to the king," then to Njord and Frey to obtain "good harvest and peace": the distinction between functions was precise and probably broke down only during the dissolution of paganism.[6]

* * *

Until the last quarter of the previous century, neither the ensemble nor any single element of Odin's dossier had been seriously examined. The handbooks limited themselves to taking note of his eminent position and his multiple activities. In 1876 a short account of 139 pages, the doctoral thesis of the young Dane Karl Nikolai Henry Petersen (1849–1896),[7] initiated a crisis that has subsequently only intensified. Petersen was an archaeologist. Even if he wisely devoted the rest of his career to the excavation of ruins of castles and churches and the study of medieval relics, he still had as his beginnings a revolutionary intuition that he was able to support with abundant and striking arguments. Odin, he thought, was a late comer to northern religion. From another point of view than that of Bernhard Salin later, he guessed similarly (p. 107, n. 1) that "the legends on the migration of Odin to the north may contain a kernel of truth." This thesis made a deep impression on the scholarly world, "scholars being," said Jan de Vries wittily, "particularly inclined to any hypothesis which attacked the originality of the heathen deities." Since then, with many variations, the "reduction" of Odin has become a common theme for exercises in Germanic studies, leading up to the 1946 book by Karl Helm, *Wodan, Ausbreitung und Wanderung seines Kultes*.[8] One group of radicals continues to maintain that Odin is not indigenous in Scandinavia, but that he is a late penetration there, coming from the South. The other group grants that he may be a god who is both Scandinavian and German, but maintains that his origins

---

[6] *Heimskringla* (Hollander), p. 107 ("The Saga of Hákon the Good," chap. 14).

[7] Karl Nikolai Henry Petersen, *Om Nordboernes Gudedyrkelse og Gudetro i Hedenold, en antikvarisk Undersøgelse* (Copenhagen, 1876).

[8] Karl Helm, *Wodan, Ausbreitung und Wanderung seines Kultes, Giessener Beiträge zur deutschen Philologie*, 85.

in these areas was humble, nearly insignificant. Only later, in some locality, did he reap the benefits of an astonishing promotion which would spread rapidly throughout the greater part of the Germanic world. None of the foundations of this theory would seem to be firmly established.

It is unreasonable, they say or imply, that the Germanic peoples, among whom royalty had no great span of influence and who lived divided into a great number of tribes, could have conceived on their own of a powerful god-king and of a universal sovereign. That could only have occurred as a reflection of the great kings of neighboring empires, Rome or even Byzantium. This evolution, it is alleged, had already begun in the time of Tacitus as indicated in chapter 9 of the *Germania* where Mercurius-*Wōðanaz is presented as the most honored of the gods and in chapter 39 as the *regnator omnium deus* of the Semnones. And this could refer only to strictly localized facts, along the Rhine and between the Elbe and the Oder, that is in the proximity of the Roman Empire. This reasoning is unfounded. There are numerous examples of peoples, some retarded, others highly advanced, who nevertheless conceive of one or several very powerful gods of universal competence. There is frequent disproportion between the political reality, the limited power of the local ruler, and his mythic transposition, the unlimited power of the cosmic ruler. The Vedic tribes, for example, who conceived of the universal sovereign Varuṇa and celebrated him in terms reminiscent of the God of the Psalms, were no less divided than the Germanic peoples and attributed no more power to their kings. Furthermore Odin has absolutely none of the characteristics of a Caesar or a Basilius, but is of a type *sui generis*, that of a sorcerer king. In addition, despite the ingenious comparison of Magnus Olsen, the Valhalla and its *einherjar* have nothing much in common—except the multiplicity of its portals and the bloody use of the building—with the Colosseum and its gladiators.

The point is made that the name of Odin, **Wōðanaz*, is not common Germanic, but only West and North Germanic. If this god existed among the Goths, it is argued, and held among them the same eminent position he holds in the Eddic poems and among the few West Germanic tribes where Tacitus identifies him, is it not strange that none of the authors who spoke of the Goths mentioned him? And, if the Goths were ignorant of him or gave him no great homage, is that not an indication that he did not belong, at least with this rank, to the initial structure of "the" Germanic religion? This argument exaggerates the importance of names in religious studies. Odin, who in Scandinavia has innumerable secondary appellations, some clear, others obscure, could certainly have been designated regularly among the Goths by another word than that derived from *Wut*. Furthermore, through one of his Scandinavian appellations, *Gautr*, and by the localization in the two "Götalands" of the majority of Odin place-names, the Scandinavian Odin shows himself precisely to have a particular bond with the Goths. Finally, it is certainly this *Gautr*, that is, Odin, who is to be recognized in the *Gapt* who according to Jordanes opened the mythic genealogy of the Amalians, the royal family of the Goths, as Odin in Scandinavia and Woden in England are the source of several dynasties.

Three negative facts are urged against the god: the relative rarity throughout Scandinavia, and in Iceland even the complete absence of Odin place-names; the nearly complete parallel absence of men with Odin names; and finally the absence of a correspondent to Odin (since the explanation of Rota from Odin, proposed in 1914 by W. von Unwerth,[9] has not been accepted) in the mythology that the Lapps borrowed from the Scandinavians, in which only Thor, Frey, and Njord are honored. These major facts are quite correct, but they admit other plausible justifications than the lateness either of the god or of the place he occupies in the Nordic pantheon. If Odin was at all times the god of the chieftains, of the function of chief, and the great Scandinavian sorcerer, he had no chance of being adopted by the Lapps, who, though dominated and colonized, kept their own magic, different in origin from that of their enterprising neighbors. In contrast, the beneficent god of thunder, the god of animal and vegetable fecundity, the god of wind and navigation—a skill borrowed by them from the Scandinavians—these touched on their immediate interests. In Scandinavia itself it is understandable that farms, built up areas, refuges of peasants and sailors, would more often have received their names from one of the patron gods of rural prosperity, navigation, storms, and their beneficial consequences, than from the great chief of the gods and sorcerer. As the head of social groups that would be statistically small, the god would not appear frequently in place-names. The situation in Iceland confirms this view. It is natural that those settlers who had fled Europe and founded in their new home a veritable republic of rich peasants would not have had occasion to name a single place after the god-king. Finally the extreme rarity of personal names of men containing that of Odin may be explained by the character of the god, in certain respects disquieting and terrifying. A similar reserve has caused the

[9] W. von Unwerth, "Óðinn und Rota," *Paul and Braunes Beiträge* 39 (1914), 213–223.

archives of various Indo-Iranian peoples to transmit many proper names containing the divine names *Mitra-* (*Mithra-*) and *Indra-*, but not one containing that of *Varuṇa.*

The illustrious Swedish archaeologist Oscar Montelius is the author of another oft-repeated argument. Odin, as we have said, is the great god of runes, and of the magic of runes. Now runic writing is fairly recent, no inscription being earlier than the Christian era. It was imported, from the southeast according to some, from the south according to the argument more and more generally accepted. The consequence of this, for the "god of runes," would be a terminus a quo post-dating the Christian era and the massive influence of the Roman empire on Germania. But this argument is not compelling, either. If Odin was first and always the highest magician, we realize that the runes, however recent they may be, would have fallen under his sway. New and particularly effective implements for magic works, they would become by definition and without contest a part of his domain. Furthermore, *rúnar* is an old Germanic (**rūnō-*) and Celtic word that first designated magic secrets. In Gothic *runa* had only the sense of "secret, secret decision," similar to its meaning in Old Irish (*rūn*), "secret, mystery, secret purpose." In the Finnish borrowing *runo* the word refers only to epic and magic chants. Odin could have been the patron, the possessor par excellence of this redoubtable power of secrecy and secret knowledge, before the name of that knowledge became the technical name of signs both phonetic and magic which came from the Alps or elsewhere, but did not lose its former, larger sense.

The critics would probably not have given credit to these precise but fragile arguments against the age of Odin or of his function if they had not more or less explicitly depended on two much more general considerations.

The first is provided by the very number and diversity of the domains where Odin operates, which seem to confirm that there has been a development, a growth. King of the gods and great magician, god of warriors and of one group of the dead, he is all that, not to speak of the agricultural component that is sometimes extracted from the folkloristic usages of the great winter festival. Is it not too much for a single god, especially when one takes into account that no other of the Æsir or Vanir plays so large a role in the action of the mythology? Must this not be the effect of extensions, annexations, which it ought to be possible to explore, by retracing the course of time and civilization, until one reaches, perhaps in Scandinavia itself, or in some western area of continental Germania, a humbler point of departure, from which the rest would progressively have issued, or to which the rest could have been added? Several models of such a development have been proposed: for some, the god would at first have been only a goblin or a minor sorcerer-god, for others a god of the dead, for others still a god of fecundity.

The other reason, which is complementary, stems from Indo-European considerations. In the abyss of disgrace where the studies of "comparative mythology" had sunk in reaction to the generous illusions and intelligent excesses of the school of Max Müller, one onomastic correspondence, and one only, had nevertheless been respected—and respected all the more, as its very isolation allowed scholars to declare that in matters of divine personnel, it constituted the totality of the Indo-European heritage, leaving the field open to the study of the "separate mythologies." That correspondence is the one comparing the Vedic sky god, *Dyauḥ* (gen. *Divah*), Greek *Zeus* (gen. *Divos*), Lat. *Jup-piter* (gen. *Jovis*), and the Germanic character whose name became *Týr* in Old Norse and *Zio* in Old High German. He is surely "the" most ancient god, since he was already Indo-European, and a "great god," it is added, as is proved if not by his somewhat faded Vedic heir, at least by the eminent position of his Mediterranean heirs. Now, though this god persists among the Scandinavians as among the other Germanic peoples, he has not—rather, he has "no more"—the importance, the undisputed first position, which is believed to be attributable to his prototype. Pale, without many adventures, subordinated to Odin in the same way as all the other gods, he is visibly at the end of a long retreat by the time of our documents. And is it not a precious indication of the point—the Rhenish frontier of Roman Gaul—where the substitution began, when, in chapter 9 of Tacitus's *Germania*, we see him, under the name of Mars, already very honorably in the second rank, on the level of Hercules-*Þunraz, the first rank being already occupied by Mercurius-*Wōðanaz?

These two pieces of "evidence" are at the center of the problem. But are they evidence or are they preconceived notions? The first is already suspect because of the multiple points of departure and the hypothetic wanderings from which scholars have tried to draw a precise image. These successive stages, these "stratifications," are vainly presented in terms of history, for they are only speculations that radically contradict each other, thus proving that not one is at all satisfying. On paper it is of course possible to suppose that a god of the dead, or a god of fecundity, or a minor sorcerer god was promoted to all the rest, and finally to the highest rank. But, in reality, how is this growth, especially this ending, his coronation, to be imagined? One is always reduced, finally, to imagining foreign influence, the liberation of Germanic fancies, on the Rhine or in the fjords, by the sight or the rumor of the imperial power of Rome or Byzantium. But that, as has been said above, is not at all probable, since the god of the Æsir has about him nothing of a Trajan or a Constantine, nor even of a Nero, and his omnipotence takes another form. On the contrary, if one resigns oneself to thinking that the summit of this pyramid of functions existed from the beginning, at the same height, if one admits that the solidary values of the chief of gods and men and the grand magician are fundamental and original in the god, the rest follows naturally. All the developments and details are plausible, because, in truth, the "function of sovereignty" is the only one that potentially contains all the others and can easily actualize these potentialities. Ought not terrestrial kings, humble counterparts to Odin, *as* kings, be *sigrsæll* as well as *ársæll,* that is, blessed in victory" as well as "happy in harvest?" Is not the Roman Jupiter in Capitoline practice as well as in Romulean legend—Stator, Feretrius—the giver of victory *because* he is a sovereign? And do not the Vedic dead wish to rejoin not only Yama, the specialist, if you will, of life *post mortem,* but *also* the great sovereign god, Varuṇa? "Go," says a strophe of the funeral ritual to the dead:

> Go, Go, by the ancient roads,
> there where our fathers went before, who preceded us!
> The two kings who revel in full liberty,
> you will see them, Yama and the god Varuṇa![10]

No one has sought to deduce, by a process of evolution, all of Jupiter's activity from his role in war, nor from his patronage of the festivals of the vineyard. Nor has anyone tried to explain the character of Varuṇa by starting from the hopes of the dying. This kind of operation is no more to be recommended for their parallel in Germanic religion. Let us add, as Jan de Vries has vigorously pointed out,[11] that even Odin's name, which is not obscure, obliges us to put at the center of his character a *spiritual* concept from which the most effective action issues. The Old Norse word from which it derives, *óðr,* and which Adam of Bremen translates excellently with *furor,* corresponds to German *Wut* "rage, fury" and to Gothic *wōds* "possessed." As a noun it denotes drunkenness, excitation, poetic genius

---

10 *Rig Veda,* X, 14, 7.

11 *Contributions to the Study of Othin, especially in his Relation to Agricultural Practices in Modern Popular Lore, Folklore Fellows Communications* 94 (1931), 45.

(cf. OE *wōð* "chant"), as well as the terrifying movement of the sea, of fire, and of the storm. As an adjective, it means sometimes "violent, furious," sometimes "rapid." Outside of Germanic, related Indo-European words refer to violent poetic and prophetic inspiration: Latin *vates*, Old Irish *faith*. It must thus have been a very important god, of the "first level," that such a name was destined to describe.

As for the consequences of the relative chronology that one deduces from the equation *Dyauḥ=Zeus=Jupiter=*Tiuz* (supposing that this equation is exact: there are reasons for deriving *Týr* and *Zio* rather from **deiwo-*, the generic Indo-European name for the gods), these consequences are founded on a simplistic and erroneous interpretation of this equation, and more generally on a false conception of the role and prerogatives of linguistics in such matters. In fact, in diverse areas of the Indo-European totality, the same divine function may be attributed, and myths illustrating this function may be applied, to gods with different names. Conversely, gods bearing similar or identical names, may, through particular evolutions that do not imply great changes in the structures of the religions, be endowed with different functions. The agreeable phonetic conformity of *Zeus, Jupiter*, and *Dyauḥ*, precious for the linguist, does not carry the mythologist very far. He quickly notices that the first two gods and the third do not in the least do the same things. The Vedic god, who is without great actuality, scarcely goes beyond the materiality of the luminous sky, which, taken as a noun, his name signifies. Jupiter and Zeus, on the contrary, are not the sky made divine (which Ouranos, the grandfather of Zeus, onomastically is), but the very real, very personal king of the gods and of men, and the lightning god. If one still wishes to compare them, functionally, to various figures from the Vedic pantheon, it is to the sovereigns Mitra and Varuṇa on the one hand and to the lightning god Indra on the other that one must address oneself. In other terms—speaking no more of Zeus, as Greek mythology escapes Indo-European categories—if one wishes to refer to the framework of the "three functions" defined in the preceding chapter, one sees that Jupiter, in this framework, occupies the first level, that of sovereignty, whereas in India Dyauḥ remains outside the framework, and the first level is occupied there by Varuṇa and Mitra. Under the same conditions, it is therefore possible that the old Indo-European name **Dyēu-*, in its supposed Germanic form **Tiuz*, does not apply to the god who is functionally analogous to Dyauḥ, nor even perhaps to Zeus and Jupiter. The functions of these last two may have been assumed, among the Germanic peoples, by a god bearing another name, a new name, properly

Germanic. It is possible, by the same reasoning that **Tiuz*, if indeed there was a **Tiuz*, might have coexisted with another god, **Wōðanaz*, Indo-European in function and in his position in the tripartite structure, but not in his name.

* * *

A solution to these pseudodifficulties was proposed in 1939, in the first edition of this book,[12] and further work has confirmed it. It was formed, albeit with a difference which defined a characteristic trait of the Germanic evolution, through consideration of the pair of Vedic gods that has twice been mentioned, Varuṇa and Mitra.

In the Mittanian document from the fourteenth century B.C. and in the mythology of the *Rig Veda,* as in the list of functional gods that Zoroastrianism transposed into archangels, the first level, the level of sovereignty, is not occupied by a single personage as is the second (Indra). Nor is it like the third, occupied by a pair of two hardly distinguishable twins (the Nāsatya), but by two clearly distinguishable gods with different characters, Varuṇa and Mitra. This doctrine is clearly expressed in many formulas in the Vedic ritual treatises. A certain number of passages in the hymns expressly presuppose it already. In most of these cases, the nature and object of the poems lead the poets to combine the two gods in a common praise, attributing indifferently the virtues of each of the two members to the pair which they form and sometimes even to the other member. To be complementary in their services, Varuṇa and Mitra are antithetical, each specification of one requiring a contrary specification of the other, to the point where a text can state: "That which is of Mitra is not of Varuṇa."[13] These multiple oppositions all have the same form, and it is easy, when one has familiarized oneself with a few, to predict with confidence which term, in such and such a formula, will be Varuṇa's and which will be Mitra's. Mitra "is this world" and Varuṇa "the other world." One Vedic hymn equates the first with the earth, the second with the sky. Others attribute to Mitra the visible and ordinary forms of fire or soma, to Varuṇa their invisible and mythical forms. Mitra is day and Varuṇa night (to which one of the hymns already makes an allusion). To Mitra belongs whatever breaks by itself, whatever is cooked by steam, whatever is properly sacrificed, milk, and so on. To Varuṇa belongs whatever is cut by an

---

12 Dumézil, *Mythes et dieux des Germains: essai d'interprétation comparative* (Paris: Presses Universitaires de France, 1939).

13 *Śatapatha Brāhmaṇa,* III, 2, 4, 18.

axe, whatever is "seized" by fire, whatever is improperly sacrificed, the intoxicating soma, and so on. Beyond these minute expressions produced by the accident of circumstance, the inner natures of the gods are clearly contrasted with one another, being defined by the very name (for Mitra), or (for Varuṇa) by their distinctive attributes and celebrated myths. The word *Mitra* is formed by adding the suffix of instrumental nouns to a root that means "to exchange regularly, peacefully, amicably" (from which also Latin *munus, communis,* as well as Old Slavic *mêna* "exchange" and *mirŭ* "peace, order"), and means simply "contract." This, according to a classic (1907) article by A. Meillet,[14] is not a natural phenomenon but a social phenomenon that has been deified. More precisely, it is a deified type of juridical act with its effects, the state of mind and reality which it establishes among men. The name of *Varuṇa* is of uncertain etymology, but his character is sufficiently defined by his usual attributes. On the one hand, he is par excellence the master of *māyā,* the illusionistic magic, creator of forms. On the other hand, materially and symbolically, from the *Rig Veda* up to the epic, he is armed with knots and strings, with which he seizes the sinner—even were it his son Bhṛgu—instantly and without possible resistance. There are demonic affinities in him, whether one compares or separates his name from that of Vṛtra. At the risk of being arbitrary or simplistic, I have proposed a summing up of the information about them in these formulas: Mitra "sovereign god of law," Varuṇa "sovereign god of magic."

Roman theology seems to have known a similar division of divine duties, with a *Dius Fidius* who bears the *fides* in his name, at first distinct from Jupiter, but later absorbed by the imperious figure of the Capitoline god. It is the epic, the legendary history of the origins of the city, however, which provides the best example of the opposition and the complementarity of the two equally necessary modes of sovereignty. It does so in the figures of the two founders. One is the demigod Romulus, accompanied by his retinue of "sheaf binders," the beneficiary of Jupiter's auspices and spectacular intervention. The other is the completely human Numa, founder of the laws and particular devotee of the goddess Fides. This parallelism of Indo-Iranian theology and the Roman epic, which can be followed in great detail, guarantees that the "bipartition of sovereignty" was part of the fund of ideas on which the Indo-Europeans lived.

There are reasons for thinking that the same structure of two

---

14 A. Meillet, "La religion indo-européenne," *Revue des idées* 4 (1907), 689–698; reprinted in Meillet, *Linguistique historique et linguistique générale* (Paris, 1921), pp. 323–334.

terms, warped in quite an interesting way, is the base of the duality of Odin-Tyr. From the Germanic point of view, neither one nor the other is "older"; both go back to Indo-European divinities.

The correspondence of Odin and Varuṇa is striking. Both are fundamentally magicians. To be sure, Nordic magic presents its own characteristics for which it would be vain to seek equivalents in India. But the gift of shape-changing so characteristic of the former coincides with the *māyā* that the latter employs so abundantly. The immediate and irresistible catch that Varuṇa makes, expressed by his lines and his knots, is also Odin's mode of action. On the battlefield he has the gift not only of blinding, deafening, and benumbing, but literally of binding his enemy with an invisible line. This process is the one Brynhild evokes in her dreamt malediction that she aims at Gunnar after the murder of Sigurd (*Brot af Sigurðarkviðu,* 16): "It seemed to me," she says,

enn þú, gramr, riðir, glaums andvani,	(that) you, king, rode cheerless,
fiǫtri fatlaðr í fiánda lið.	fettered into the enemy army.[15]

He is fettered by the *herfjǫtur* "army fetter," the enchantment that paralyzes the warrior. Now the poets personified this notion in the name of one of the Valkyries, that is, one of the minor goddesses who directly assist Odin: *Herfjǫtur* (*Grímnismál,* 36).

To the ambitious, disquieting, almost demonic aspects of Varuṇa correspond several traits of Odin, some of which have been mentioned above: his giant ancestors, his particular friendship with the demonic Loki, his blood brother. And Varuṇa, in celebrated legends, is no less fond of human sacrifice than are Odin and the Mercurius-*Wōðanaz of Tacitus.

As the *māyin* Varuṇa is a king, *rājan,* and even *samrāj,* the magician Odin is the king of gods and protector of royalty. Varuṇa, says the *Śatapatha Brāhmaṇa,* is the *kṣatra,* temporal power and principle of the warrior class (while Mitra is the *brahman*). In the language of the hymns, the *kṣatra* has an affinity for the elite, the nobles, the *ari* (while Mitra is closer to the *jana,* the masses).[16] Just so the famous lines from the *Hárbarðsljóð* let the god himself say (str. 24):

Óðinn á iarla, þá er í val falla,	Odin has the jarls, who fall in battle,
enn þórr á þræla kyn.	but Thor has the race of the thralls.[17]

The heroes killed in battle belong to Odin and continue in Valhalla a life of unending feasts and duels which are no more than

15 *Edda* (Kuhn), p. 200; cf. *Edda* (Bellows), p. 408.
16 L. Renou, *Études védiques et pāṇinéennes* 2 (1956), 110.
17 *Edda* (Kuhn), p. 82; cf. *Edda* (Bellows), p. 129.

sport, and this happy destiny is extended to anyone else who marks himself with the sign of Odin before death. Just so we have seen the Indian funeral ritual promise the Aryan dead—all the Aryan dead, it would seem—as the end of their journey the residence where they will see the two kings Varuṇa and Yama, while "tasting pleasure at their will."

Between the vast domains of one and the other there are of course numerous differences, the majority of which are minor and can easily be explained through the scenery, the neighborhood, and the conditions of life where the two religions were practiced. Varuṇa is not the poet or patron of poets which the *vates* Odin is. He has no animal auxiliaries reminiscent of the wolves and ravens surrounding Odin, nor the taste of the northern god for hangings (no doubt founded on shamanistic practices). These differences are of the magnitude that one might expect. But there is one of greater magnitude, which reveals one of the original traits of ancient Germanic civilization.

If it happens that Varuṇa is invoked for victory in war, that is not one of his ordinary functions, but a natural extension of his sovereign position. The warrior god is Indra, and several *Rig Veda* texts make an exact division of tasks. A group of hymns from Book VII which are addressed to them jointly (82–85) contains excellent differentiating definitions:

> One of you [Indra] kills the *Vṛtra* in battles,
> The other [Varuṇa] watches constantly over the laws. (83, 9)
> One [Varuṇa] keeps in order the frightened peoples,
> The other [Indra] fights the invincible *Vṛtra.* (85, 3)

And, with a slight twist:

> May the wrath of Varuṇa spare us!
> May Indra procure for us a vast domain! (84, 2)

One is struck immediately, however, by the number of ties between Odin and battles, or warriors, in this world and in the next. He is rarely a warrior himself, except in the historicization of the *Ynglingasaga* (quoted above), where he is called a *hermaðr mikill* "great warrior," and marches from one conquest to the next. He is present in battles, grants victory on the spot, expresses his decision with precise gestures, and aims at the enemy army—at it alone, it seems—the paralyzing "fetter" that he has in common with Varuṇa. From the frenetic type of the *berserkir* to the elegant type of a Sigurd, the distinguished combatants belong to him, participating according to their diverse natures. Finally it is only those who fall in battle or those others marked with a symbolic wound, whom he receives in Valhalla. In short, if he acts through all this in a manner conforming to his definition as sovereign, master of men's destiny, and often by purely magic or internal action, it remains no less true that war is one of the principal circumstances of that action. If, however, he leaves to Thor the care of Indra's thunder, he still enriches his "Varunic" aspect with many qualities that Vedic India reserves for the thunder and warrior god, the god of the second level. The Valkyries have reminded scholars, and justly so, of the Marut, companions of Indra, and the Odin-like heroes of the *Edda* and of the sagas recall Arjuna, son of Indra, to whom the epic has transposed the mythology of the father.

The explanation of this peculiarity of Odin is obvious. In the ideology and in the practices of the Germanic peoples, war invaded all, colored everything. When they are not fighting, those of whom Caesar gave the first sharp sketch think only of coming battles: *vita omnis in venationibus atque in studiis rei militaris consistit,* and that from a very young age, *a parvis labori ac duritiae student* (VI, 21, 3). If they are disdainful of agriculture, if they reject a permanent distribution of the soil, that is primarily *ne assidua consuetudine capti studium belli gerendi agricultura commutent* (22, 3). The sovereign god is deprived by the absence of a sacerdotal class and by the rudimentary state of cult, noted also by Caesar, of a part of the social base on which his Vedic analog rested. How should *Wōðanaz not have felt the effect on his internal equilibrium of this hypertrophy of warlike cares? From one end of our sources to the other, the picture varies only slightly. By the same token as to "Mars," it is to Mercurius, that is, *Wōðanaz, that the Hermunduri consecrate in advance the army they are about to confront, *quo voto equi viri cuncta victa occidioni dantur.*[18] In Uppsala in the eleventh century, says Adam of Bremen, Wodan *bella gerit hominique ministrat virtutem contra inimicos.*

* * *

This same character of Germanic societies explains the evolution, the deviation, otherwise considerable, of the Germanic equivalent to the second member of the pair Mitra-Varuṇa. It is certainly possible—the question is still debated—that the Indo-Iranian Mitra, although he is god of contracts, or rather because he is god of contracts, would have had more interest in war than his Vedic heir displays. Those who think so base their argument especially on the post-

[18] C. Tacitus, *Annales*, XIII, 57.

Gathic Avesta, where Mithra is "the" true warrior god, of whom Verethragna, spirit of Victory, is no more than an auxiliary. Personally, I see in his promotion rather an effect of the Zoroastrian reform. After having condemned the too autonomous type of warrior whom Indra patronized and having downgraded the great god to an archdemon, they assigned his formidable function to the god of law himself. The warrior should thereafter be nothing more than the submissive and disciplined auxiliary of Ahura Mazdā and his church. I shall maintain this opinion here; it is clear that if the other were adopted, the explanation I have proposed for the Germanic "Mars" would be even easier to defend.

The difficulty centers, in effect, in these few words: Tacitus and several inscriptions render with "Mars" the name of the god who among the continental Germanic peoples should balance Mercurius-*Wōðanaz and who is called either **Tīwaz* or **Tiuz*. The Scandinavian Tyr is first and foremost defined as a god of war: "There is a god called Tyr. He is the boldest and most courageous, and has power over victory in battle; it is good for brave men to invoke him."[19]

However, certain facts limit and orient this definition. First, it is not "Mars" to whom the warriors in Tacitus's *Germania* sing to prepare themselves for the heroic acts of war. It is to "Hercules," otherwise *þunraz, the equivalent of Thor: *fuisse apud eos et Herculem memorant primumque omnium virorum fortium ituri in praelia canunt.* Second, one could peruse all Scandinavian literature (except the eschatology, where as a rule all the gods must fight) without finding a scene where Tyr appears or does anything on a battlefield. The various special relationships that have been sought between Tyr and certain weapons are founded on false etymologies or wrongly interpreted facts.[20] The only example given by Snorri of the intrepidity of the god is anything but a battle scene. It is the deliberate sacrifice he makes of his right hand in the wolf Fenrir's mouth. Finally, epigraphy and place-names attest to an important link between "Mars"-Tyr and the *thing* (ON *þing*), the popular assembly where legal cases are tried and juridical difficulties heard. "Mars" is actually called *Thingsus* on an inscription carved by Frisians at the beginning of the third century in Great Britain. In Zealand in Denmark, *Tislund*

19 *Snorra Edda* (Jónsson), p. 32 (*Gylfaginning*, chap. 13); *Prose Edda* (Young), p. 53.

20 Dumézil, "Remarques sur les armes des dieux de 'troisième fonction' chez divers peuples indo-européens," *Studi e Materiali di Storia delle Religioni* 28 (1957), 7 n. 5.

was certainly a place of assembly. Furthermore, the translation of *Martis dies*, which is, for example *týsdagr* "Tyr's day" in Old Norse (cf. Eng. *Tuesday*), is *dingesdach* in Middle Low German, Middle Dutch *dinxendach* "Ding's day" (Dutch *dinsdag*). The first element, altered, is perhaps found in German *Dienstag*. These facts—except the last, which he does not accept—have inspired the thoughtful comments of Jan de Vries:

> In general, too much emphasis has been placed on the warlike aspects of Tyr, and his significance for Germanic law has not been sufficiently recognized. It should be noted that, from the Germanic point of view, there is no contradiction between the concepts "god of War" and "god of Law." War is in fact not only the bloody mingling of combat, but no less a decision obtained between the two combatants and secured by precise rules of law. That is why the day and place of battle are frequently fixed in advance; in provoking Marius, Boiorix offers him the choice of place and time (Plutarch, *Marius*, 25, 3). So is explained, also, how combat between two armies can be replaced by a legal duel, in which the gods grant victory to the party whose right they recognize. Words like *Schwertding* ["the meeting of swords," a kenning for battle], or Old Norse *vápndómr* ["judgment of arms"] are not poetic figures, but correspond exactly to ancient practice.[21]

Inverse reasons can be added to the above to make the gap even smaller. While war is a bloody *thing*, the *thing* of peacetime also evokes war: people deliberating have the appearance and ways of a battling army. Tacitus described these assemblies: *considunt armati ... nihil neque publicae neque privatae rei nisi armati agunt* ... and, for approval, they shake their spears, the most honorable sign of assent being *armis laudare*.[22] A few centuries later, Scandinavia offers the same sight: whatever may be the sanctity and the "peace" of the *thing*—as presented in the texts chosen by W. Baetke[23]—men gather there, armed, and in approval they brandish swords or hatchets or even strike their shields with their swords. And it is not only scene and protocol which recall war: the *thing* is a test of strength and prestige between families or groups, the more numerous or more menacing attempting to impose their will on the others. Despite the famous, noble, fearless jurists, the procedure itself is only an arsenal of forms on which one may draw, which one may divert from their destination, turning right to wrong. Properly used, law assures the equivalent of a victory, eliminating the poorly protected or weaker

---

21 De Vries, *AGR* 1 (1935), I, 173–174; *AGR* 2 (1957), II, 13–14.

22 Tacitus, *Germania*, 11–13.

23 W. Baetke, *Die Religion der Germanen in Quellenzeugnissen* (1937), p. 32.

adversary. The luckless Grettir, and a good many others, had this experience.

That is, furthermore, the lesson to be learned from the one mythic episode of which Tyr is the hero, that in which Snorri shows Tyr's bravery. It is linked to the very character of the god, because, says Snorri, after this adventure Tyr "is one-handed and he is not called a peace-maker."[24] This legend has stimulated more extensive reflections, which I can only briefly summarize here. We have seen above that Odin is voluntarily mutilated, that he obtained his knowledge of the invisible, the basis of his power, through the loss of one of his eyes. Tyr, too, is mutilated voluntarily, or at least with his tacit consent. At the beginning of time, Snorri recounts, when the wolf Fenrir was born, the gods, who knew that he was to devour them, decided to tie him up. Odin had a magic cord made, so thin that it was invisible, but strong enough to resist all tests. Then they proposed to the young Fenrir that he let himself be bound by this harmless fetter, in sport, to give him the pleasure of breaking it. More distrustful than youth usually is, the wolf accepted only on the condition that one of the gods put a hand in his mouth while this operation was going on, *at veði* "as a pledge," so that all should transpire without deceit. None of the gods was willing to pledge his hand, until Tyr stretched forth his right hand into the wolf's mouth. Naturally the wolf could not free himself: the harder he tried, the tighter the magic fetter became—and so he stays until the end of time, those gloomy days when all the forces of evil will be liberated to destroy the world and the gods with it. The gods, according to Snorri, "all laughed except Týr; he lost his hand."[25]

The function of the god of the *thing* and his mutilation thus agree closely with the function of clairvoyance and the mutilation of Odin. It is the loss of his right hand, in a fraudulent procedure of guarantee, as a pledge, which qualifies Tyr as the "god of law"—in a pessimistic view of the law, directed not toward reconciliation among the parties, but toward the crushing of some by the others. Tyr "is not called a peacemaker." This imagery has permitted an important observation that guarantees the antiquity of the symbolic mutilations of the two gods in Indo-European comparative mythology. In 1940 I pointed out a parallel Roman legend, as usual not in the nonexistent divine mythology, but in the epic.[26] During the first war of the Republic,

---

24 *Prose Edda* (Young), p. 53.

25 *Snorra Edda* (Jónsson), pp. 32, 35–37 (*Gylfaginning*, chaps. 13, 21); *Prose Edda* (Young), p. 58.

26 Dumézil, *Mitra-Varuṇa* (Paris: Presses Universitaires de France, 1940).

Rome, in the mortal peril it is thrown into by Porsenna and his Etruscans, is successively saved by two heroes, of whom one is one-eyed and the other becomes one-handed: Horatius the *Cyclops* and Mucius the *Left-handed.* While the Roman army retreats in disorder over the Tiber bridge, the former holds the attention of the enemy army by himself through a stance that disconcerts it, notably by casting terrifying looks at it: *circumferens truces minaciter oculos,* says Livy. The other hero, who has entered the enemy camp to stab Porsenna and has been captured after being tricked, burns his right hand in the king's brazier to lead him, by this proof of heroism, to believe that after him three hundred young warriors, equally resolved, will repeat the attempt—which is perhaps not true—and so convince him to consent to an honorable peace with Rome. Here are the comments I made about this Italo-Scandinavian correspondence in 1951:

> It is clear that the provinces of action of Cocles and Scævola are the same respectively as those of Odin and Tyr: paralyzing the enemy on the one hand and persuading through a pledge in a ceremony of oaths on the other. It is also clear that, in Rome as in Scandinavia, these actions are connected with the same two mutilations, and under the same conditions. Odin and Cocles have already become one-eyed through a previous mutilation when they paralyzed an enemy army. Tyr and Scævola lose their right hands before our eyes, right in the story, in pledge to a heroic false oath.
>
> However, the scope of these adventures is extremely unequal. In Rome they are only various illustrious feats, without stated symbolic value, with no other interest than that of patriotic propaganda. They have at first no other consequences for their heroes than honors once conferred and mutilations that have rendered them so completely incapable of all action and all legal service, that from now on they cannot even be considered. In Scandinavia, on the contrary, the two mutilations, clearly symbolic, first create and later manifest the lasting quality of each of the gods, the paralyzing visionary and the chief of legal procedure. They are the palpable expression of the theologeme that is the basis of the coexistence of the two highest gods, namely that the sovereign administration of the world is divided into two great provinces, that of inspiration and prestige, that of contract and chicanery, in other words, magic and law. This theologeme is, among the Germanic peoples, no more than a faithfully preserved inheritance from the time of the Indo-European unity, for it is found, with all the desirable extensions and commentary, in Vedic religion, where the binder magician Varuṇa, and Mitra, the contract personified, form a ruling pair at the head of the world of gods.
>
> Furthermore, the analogy between the Roman and Scandinavian stories is of the sort that at the same time excludes both the possibility that they may be independent and the possibility that one derives from the other. We are dealing here, in fact, with a complex and exceedingly rare theme. Since 1940, when the correspondence was first noted, a great many scholars have combed the mythologies of the ancient and modern

worlds in an attempt to find, with its double functional effect, this couple of One-eye and One-hand. Only the literature of another people related to the Germanic and Italic peoples, the Irish epic, presents something comparable although noticeably more distant. And yet the Roman and Scandinavian plots are too different to suppose a direct or indirect loan from one to the other. A loan would rather have conserved the outline of the scenes and some of the picturesque details and lost the sense, the ideological principle of the double intrigue. It is this principle—the link between the two mutilations and the two modes of action—which holds good between one part and another in scenes that have nothing else in common. The only natural explanation is therefore to suppose that the Germanic and Roman peoples retained this original pairing from their common past.

In addition, as this pair is richer in value when it is operating on the mythical plane, supported by the theology of sovereignty, it is probable that this was its primary form. Rome then transposed it from heaven to earth, from gods to men, its own men, in its own popular and national history. The dual rescue operation retains its decisive importance, but it is no longer at the beginning of the universe, nor in the society of immortals, nor even to found a bipartite conception of directing action. It is at the beginning of the Republic, in the society of Brutus, Valerius Publicola, the Horaces, and the Muciuses, and intended by a sampling of extraordinary self-sacrifice to give rise throughout the centuries to other patriotic acts of devotion.

The process of the transposition escapes us and will always escape us, but the transposition is certain. It is even perceptible in the embarrassment that Livy shows in telling the unlikely story of the one-eyed legionary, and in the cunning way in which he grants him, in a roundabout phrase, to signify "glances," a plural *oculos* that his surname and all of the tradition belie.[27]

"A pessimistic view of the law," I just said, in characterizing the Germanic evolution of the sovereign god of Law. And that is of great importance.

First for the equilibrium of the tripartite theology. By attenuating and blurring his originality and his raison d'être beside the "magician god," and excessively developing a military aspect, the "god of Law" has practically lost his place on the first level, and that very early. Chapter 9 of the *Germania* does not associate Mars with Mercury, but with Hercules: *Deorum maxime Mercurium colunt . . . ; Herculem ac Martem . . . placant.* Certainly, despite their theoretical equality, the Mitra of the *Rig Veda* had less relief than Varuṇa, and the Roman *Fides*, or the *Dius Fidius* were certainly pale in comparison with Jupiter. The reassuring gods occupy men less than the disquieting ones; at least the latter retained their sovereign rank. "Mars"-Tyr has in practice descended to the rank of "Hercules"-Thor.

---

[27] Dumézil, "Mythes romains," *Revue de Paris* (December, 1951), pp. 105–115.

But the evolution of the "god of Law" had a deeper effect on what might be termed the general tone of the religion. In vain do the Scandinavian gods punish sacrilege and perjury, avenge violated peace or scorned law.[28] No one incarnates any more in *pure*, exemplary fashion those absolute values that a society, even hypocritically, needs to shelter under high patronage. No divinity is any longer the refuge of the ideal, or even of hope. What divine society has gained in effectiveness, it has lost in moral and mystical power. It is now no more than the exact projection of the bands or the terrestrial states whose only concern it is to gain and overcome. To be sure, the life of all human groups is made up of violence and trickery. At the very least theology describes a divine Order where all is not perfect, either, but where a Mitra or a Fides keep watch as guarantors and shine as models of true law. Even if polytheistic gods cannot be impeccable, they should at least, to fulfill their role, have one of them speak for and respond to man's conscience, early awakened, surely already well awakened and mature, among the Indo-Europeans. But Tyr can do that no longer. The Germanic peoples and their ancestors were no worse than those Indo-European peoples who fell upon the Mediterranean, Iran, or the Indus. But their theology of sovereignty, and especially their god of Law, by conforming to the human example, was cut off from the role of protestation against custom which is one of the great services rendered by religion. This lowering of the sovereign "ceiling" condemned the world—the entire world of gods and men—to being no more than what they are, since mediocrity there no longer results from accidental imperfections, but from essential limits.

Irremediably? This is where Balder intervenes, son of Odin and regent of a world to come.

[28] Baetke, *Die Religion*, pp. 40–42.

CHAPTER 3

The Drama of the World: Balder, Hoder, Loki

Mitra and Varuṇa are not the only sovereign deities in the Vedic religion. They are the most distinguished of a group, the Āditya, who appear to have consisted initially, and already in the Indo-Iranian community, of not more than four members. These were unequally divided among the two levels of action which we have observed in the preceding chapter as defined by Mitra and Varuṇa. 1) *Mitra, Aryaman,* and *Bhaga* collaborate in the spirit of law and justice which manifests itself in Mitra's name; 2) *Varuṇa,* who is alone in his sternness, his magic, and his disturbing distance. There are reasons to think that it is this scheme, with its asymmetrical structure, which appears again, sublimated and clericalized, in that of the two first archangels of Zoroastrianism and the two beings closely associated with the first: 1) *Vohu Manah* ("The Good Thought"), *Sraoša* ("Obedience"), *Aši* ("Retribution"); 2) *Aša* ("Order").[1]

The presence of two auxiliary gods beside Mitra, the sovereign who "is this world," is easily explained. Aryaman, the one who carries the word *arya* in his name, is specially allotted the protection of the Aryan nation and assures it duration and cohesion: matrimonial alliance, hospitality, gifts, free circulation, and prosperity. The other, Bhaga, whose name means "allotment," presides over the just, calm, and peaceful distribution of goods among the Aryans. Zoroastrianism has simply, for Sraoša, replaced protection of the Aryan nation by

[1] For detailed analysis and comparison, I can only refer to chapter 2 in my little book, *Les dieux des indo-européens* (Paris: Presses Universitaires de France, 1952), especially as revised in the Spanish translation, *Los Dioses de los Indo-Europeos* (Barcelona, 1970), pp. 39–68.

that of Mazdean society, the church; and, for Aši, added to the distribution of worldly goods another distribution, or rather repayment, which is more important in their eyes: that of meritorious deeds by the faithful, before and after death.

It has often been noted that the Vedic Indians displayed relatively little concern about what follows death. Representations of the hereafter are contradictory and rarely flourish in the hymns, which are bursting with vitality and worldly ambition. By comparison with the state of Indo-Iranian things, this was, perhaps, an impoverishment. It is noteworthy that neither the hymns nor the rituals say anything of this which is the principal and nearly the only, business of Aryaman in the epic—which of course preserves at times pre-Vedic conceptions that the Vedas have not retained. In the epic Aryaman continues his mission into the other world where he is king of a badly defined category of ancestors, "the Fathers." The road that leads towards them is called "the road of Aryaman." It is reserved for men who during their lives have performed the rites exactly (in contrast to the ascetics to whom another road is open). But Zoroastrianism is preoccupied with the other world to the point of unbalancing the hopes of the faithful on its behalf. Yet it gives a similar role to the Being derived from Aryaman, an essential role among the "good" dead. It is Sraoša who accompanies and guards the soul on the perilous journey that leads it before the tribunal of judges, of which he is a member. This exact parallel confirms the idea that, in environments not properly Vedic, the Indians have preserved a pre-Vedic conception (waiting to manifest itself in the form of the epic), which made Aryaman the king and protector of the collectivity of Aryan dead as well as of the living Aryans.

I have pointed out a similar association in Rome, of two auxiliary gods to Jupiter. These divinities unfortunately are only known in the Capitoline cult, at a time in which Jupiter, as Optimus and Maximus, concentrated in himself the two aspects, "Mitrian" and "Varuṇian," of sovereignty. The great god lodges in his temple *Juventas* and *Terminus*. The former is patroness of the *juvenes*, the class most important to the Romans for the vitality of the city. The latter is protector of a just delimitation of the landowners' estates. Moreover, Juventas guaranteed eternity to Rome, while Terminus guaranteed spatial permanence for her site. Even less curious about the afterworld than their Vedic cousins, attached to the concrete and devoted to their city, the Quirites entrusted to a divinity only the "indefinite future" of Rome and of themselves, the Romans, that is, the Romans successively present on earth in waves of unceasingly regenerated life, like tidal waves in the mighty ocean.

The Vedic poets speak little of afterlife and do not engage their Aryaman with it, but neither do they allow what one could call a theory of destiny to appear, either apropos their Bhaga and the allotment of wealth, or apropos the other gods. Bhaga, in particular, is not charged in the accusation that reflection immediately stimulates on this matter: how to interpret the frequent injustice, the scandal even, of the "allotments," the caprice or the carelessness of the "distributor?" Bhaga is invoked by the poets of the hymns with visible trust, another evidence of the vitality and optimism that characterize their religion. Was it like this everywhere throughout the society, even among all the thinkers? Undoubtedly not, judging by an expression that appears to be a proverb, perhaps a popular one, which the ritual books have preserved and explained in their own way, but which can stand by itself: "Bhaga is blind." Bhaga makes up part of a little group of mutilated gods that can be readily compared in etiological stories. Their mutilation is as paradoxical as that of Odin, seeing because one-eyed, and Tyr, patron of quarrels at the Thing after having his right hand amputated in a procedure of guarantee. Bhaga, who distributes "lots" and who is blind, is associated with Savitṛ, the Impeller, who sets everything in motion and who has lost both his hands; with Pūšan too, protector of the "meat on the hoof" (the herds), who having lost his teeth can eat only gruel. It is probable that, in the case of Bhaga, this expression that the Brāhmaṇa quote as a proverb has no other meaning than that of the Occidental image that puts a bandage over the eyes of Tychè or Fortuna, distributors of fate.

There is a final group of problems that the reflections in the hymns do not consider: those of the eschatology, the end of the world, or at least of the present world. The poets speak constantly of demonic beings, under various names, but it is always in the past or in the present, to extol victories of the gods and to obtain new ones from them in the immediate future. The Brāhmaṇa often systematize this representation, opposing gods and demons like two rival peoples related by kinship, telling many episodes of their enduring conflict; but they never speak of "the end," nor does any ritual portray it or prepare for it. Furthermore, nowhere is any person presented as the "chief" of the demonic forces; they operate anarchically, in dispersed order. As is well known, Zoroastrianism, on the contrary, built its dogma, its ethics, and its cult on a sense of tragedy, obsessed with the struggle that the forces of Good maintain against those of Evil. In *The Avesta*, the two parties are organized hierarchically, each under a unique command. Their symmetry is even pushed to the extreme: each "good" being, Ahura Mazdā as well as the entities who attend him—and in whom the moralized figures of the gods of the three functions of ancient polytheism are reflected—has his own adversary, his "evil" counterpart. B. Geiger[2] has well demonstrated by his vocabulary studies that this grandiose conception is formed of elements that the *Rig Veda* is not ignorant of, and that, in particular, the two words Aša and Drudj ("Order" and "Falsehood"), which express the essentials of good and evil in Zoroastrian language, have the same function and the same articulation (*ṛta, druh*) in the Vedic language. Simply, in the hymns these words remain in a free state, clashing in formulas, but not sustaining on their confrontation an entire religious structure. Moreover, as it has been said, Zoroastrianism bases its concern and its efforts on the future, not on the past or the present. This is the case for the individual, who must unceasingly prepare for his salvation, as well as for the universe, which will liberate itself one day from the forces of evil which today are only too equal to those of good. At the moment of resurrection, says the *Grand Bundahišn*,

> Ohrmazd will seize the Evil Spirit, Vohuman will seize Akoman, Aša-Vahišt Indra, Štrivar Sauru, Spendarmat Taromat, that is to say Nānhaiθya, Xurdāt and Amurdat will seize Taurvi and Zairi, the true and the false word, and Srōš (that is to say Sraoša) Aēšma (demon of fury). Then two "drudj" will remain, Aharman and Az (demon of lust). Ohrmazd will come to this world, himself as a priest of *zōt* with Srōš as priest of *rāspī* and will hold the sacred belt in his hand. The Evil Spirit and Az will flee in the darkness, repassing the threshold of the sky through which they had entered . . . And the dragon Gōtchīhr will be burned in the molten metal, which will flow on the evil being, and the dirt and the stench of the earth will be consumed by this metal, which will make it pure. The hole by which the Evil Spirit had entered will be closed up by this metal. They will hunt thus in the distance the evil existence of the earth, and there will be renewal in the universe, the world will become immortal for eternity and everlasting progress.[3]

This eschatological vision, this definitive happiness succeeding the great crisis, is it a creation *ex nihilo* of mazdaism, or had the Indo-Iranians already dreamed of this great day when Good would take absolute and total revenge for the thousand trials that the

---

2 Bernhard Geiger, *Die Aməša Spəntas, Ihr Wesen und ihre ursprüngliche Bedeutung* (Vienna, 1916).

3 *Grand Bundahišn*, XXXIV, 27–32, ed. and trans. B. T. Anklesaria (1956), pp. 290–293.

forces of Evil inflicted on it? Until recently, the second hypothesis appeared excluded, but an article of twenty-two pages has reversed the probability.

* * *

In 1947 a Swedish scholar, S. Wikander, made a discovery that profoundly modified the perspective of the religious history of India.[4] It had been known for a long time that the great epic the *Mahābhārata* sometimes told, as a digression and in a new guise, legends that the Vedas do not mention, but of which the Iranians or other Indo-European peoples offer other versions. For example, the story of the fabrication and destruction of the giant Drunkenness, which has been analyzed in our first chapter. Now we know more: the central heroes of the poem, with their characters and their connections, also continue an Indo-Iranian ideological structure, in a form that in part is more archaic than are the hymns and the whole of Vedic literature. These heroes, five brothers, the Pāṇḍava or pseudosons of Pāṇḍu, are in reality the sons of five gods who, with and under Varuṇa, constitute the oldest canonical list of gods of the three functions: Dharma "Law" (obviously a new form of Mitra), Vāyu and Indra (two Indo-Iranian varieties of warriors), the two twins Nāsatya or Aśvin ("third function"). The order of their births conforms to the hierarchy of functions, while the characteristics and behavior of each son conforms to the functional definition of his father. Only Varuṇa has no representative in this list, but it has been easy to show that he is not absent from the poem. With some of his more specialized traits he has been transposed to the previous generation in the person of Pāṇḍu, supposed father of the Pāṇḍava.

The transposition is not limited to this father and his sons. The authors of the immense poem have explained it systematically at the beginning of the first book and recalled it many times later, that the heroes who oppose one another or cooperate are not men except in appearance. Whether they are sons or incarnations of either gods or demons, they represent in reality cosmic interests. It is the very drama of the mythical Great Times that they present, direct, or play. By a kind of projection, at a point of our space and in a moment of our times, they translate into past history what the myth distributes between the past, the present, and the future. Read in this perspective, translated with this key, which the authors themselves furnish and

[4] S. Wikander, "Pāṇḍava-sagan och Mahābhāratas mytiska förutsättningar." *Religion och Bibel* 6 (1947), 27–39.

which is confirmed by analyses that the Indians were no longer capable of making, the epic poem retraces from the beginning the trials, the injustices, and the depredations that the Evil Powers, at the command of a crafty leader, a "hero-demon," make the forces of Good, the "hero-gods," such as the Pāṇḍava, endure. Afterwards, it tells about the final battle, which in mythical language will be the eschatological battle, and in which the latter, taking their revenge, will annihilate their enemies. It depicts, finally, as a consequence of this terrible melee, the idyllic reign of the elder of the Pāṇḍava. I have analyzed the plot from this point of view elsewhere, and I am only summarizing the results here. Here is the succession of events, in their human form.

A certain generation of the dynasty of the Bharata gives birth successively to three brothers, each one marked by a deficiency, benign for the second but excluding the two others from royalty. Dhṛtarāṣṭra, the eldest, is blind; Pāṇḍu, who comes next, is sickly pale; Vidura, finally, is of mixed blood, his mother being a slave secretly substituted for the queen. Then Pāṇḍu becomes king. After a brief reign, marked by triumphs and unheard-of conquests, he is struck by a curse that forbids him the sexual act, and he has five sons begotten by the gods: the just and good Yudhiṣṭhira by Dharma; Bhīma, the giant with the club, by Vāyu; the chivalrous warrior Arjuna by Indra; finally, by the two Nāsatya or Aśvin, the humble twins Nakula and Sahadeva, servants of their brothers. When he dies, his brother Dhṛtarāṣṭra becomes the guardian of his sons, still young, while waiting until the eldest, Yudhiṣṭhira, can become king. But, Dhṛtarāṣṭra has sons of whom the oldest, Duryodhana, breathes a monstrous hatred and jealousy. Being unscrupulous with regard to his cousins the Pāṇḍava, he intends to deprive them of their heritage. During their common youth, he repeatedly tries to kill them. They escape only thanks to secret information given them by their uncle Vidura who is devoted to justice, moderation, and good familial concord. In revenge, Dhṛtarāṣṭra, although loving his nephews whose rights he acknowledges and declares, displays an extreme weakness in relation to his son, resists him only to yield a little later and sorrowfully permit his criminal attempts.

Not having succeeded in killing the Pāṇḍava, Duryodhana hatches another plan. The oldest of the five, the king-designate, Yudhiṣṭhira is an average, though passionate dice player. Duryodhana then asks his father's permission to challenge Yudhiṣṭhira to a match that he could normally win, but which he will lose, the adversary using treacherous, supernatural means. The blind man resists, hesitates for a long time between the wise advice and honest entreaties of Vidura and the violent entreaties of his son. Finally, he yields and gives the order to organize the fatal match, asking Yudhiṣṭhira to appear. Yudhiṣṭhira loses all his stakes one after the other: his property, his royalty, the freedom of his brothers and himself, even his wife who is just barely saved because of one of Duryodhana's excesses. Deprived of everything, the Pāṇḍava have to go into exile for a long period—twelve years in the forest and a thirteenth year in another country in disguise. At the end of this period they will be able to return and reclaim their heritage. But an irremediable hostility is henceforth established between the groups of cousins, and each one of the Pāṇḍava, before leaving the palace, chooses beforehand the enemy that he will demolish on the day of revenge.

The time having expired, Yudhiṣṭhira asserts his rights. Dhṛtarāṣṭra wishes to reestablish justice and at least arrive at a compromise between the rival claims. But his son overcomes him with recriminations and insolences and, dead in spirit, he responds negatively to his nephews' ambassadors. The result is war. All the kings of the earth take sides with one of the two camps, and an enormous and deadly battle follows which wavers back and forth for a long time, in the course of which the Pāṇḍava, keeping their word, kill the adversaries that they have selected in advance. Duryodhana falls under the blows of the herculean Bhīma. All the sons of Dhṛtarāṣṭra, all the "evil ones," perish, but the Pāṇḍava alone survive of the army of the "Good" along with a few sparse heroes.

On this ruin a new order is immediately founded. Yudhiṣṭhira reigns at last, virtuous, just, good. His two uncles are henceforth his advisers and his ministers: the blind Dhṛtarāṣṭra, whose only weakness was the cause of all their misfortune, and Vidura, the champion of peace, who constantly tried to avoid or limit misfortune. The wonders of the reign last until the successive deaths of the heroes: first of Dhṛtarāṣṭra who is consumed by the conflagration of his sacrificial fire; then of Vidura who, literally, is transfused into Yudhiṣṭhira; finally of Yudhiṣṭhira and his brothers who fall one after the other on their "Great Journey" towards solitude and who find again in the sky those whom they have loved or fought.

Such is the "historical" aspect of the narrative. Beneath this drama of men, another vast drama unfolds, that of the divine and demonic beings whom they incarnate or represent. The pseudosons of Pāṇḍu are sons (one passage says: "the partial incarnations") of the great gods of the three functions, the central axis of Indo-Iranian mythology. Pāṇḍu conforms to the type of Varuṇa (he too figured in certain rituals as sickly pale and was struck also, in one tradition, by sexual impotence). Just so, Duryodhana, the organizer of conspiracies, responsible for the evil plans that result at first in the misfortunes of the Pāṇḍava, and then in the extermination of nearly all the "Good" at the same time as all the "Wicked," is the demon Kali incarnated. Kali is the demon who carries the name of the age of the world, the fourth, in which we are living. When he was born, the most sinister signs and the most gloomy noises warned men, but his father, in spite of the advice of wise men, opened the series of his weaknesses by refusing to sacrifice him for the public good. So we have here in miniature a great cosmic conflict, which is presented with three "epochs": the crooked match by which Evil triumphs for a long time, removing from the scene the representatives of Good; the great battle where Good takes its revenge, decisively eliminating Evil; and government by the Good.

Two persons, in this perspective, are particularly important: the blind Dhṛtarāṣṭra and the mixed-blooded Vidura who, brothers of Pāṇḍu, dominate with very different attitudes the long conflict of cousins, only to become in the end collaborators, closely joined with Yudhiṣṭhira in his idyllic reign. It has been possible to show that, just as Pāṇḍu and Yudhiṣṭhira, the two successive kings, represent in the epic game the Vedic and pre-Vedic Varuṇa and Mitra (the latter rejuvenated in Dharma), just so the "half-kings" Dhṛtarāṣṭra and Vidura represent the two minor Vedic and pre-Vedic sovereigns, Bhaga and Aryaman. Vidura, says the poem, is an incarnation of this same Dharma of whom Yudhiṣṭhira is the son or a partial incarnation. When he dies, his being will return, throwing itself, dissolving itself into that of Yudhiṣṭhira. This is an excellent epic translation of the particularly intimate tie, confining sometimes to the point of identity, which exists in the hymns between Mitra and Aryaman. His character, his action are what one expects of Aryaman. He shows constant concern both for justice and for good understanding between members of the *kula*, the great family. He is only able to thwart for a time the fratricidal machinations of Duryodhana; although recognized as excellent, his advice is not followed and, during the battle, he says nothing more, and shows himself no more. He only reappears after the end of the conflict to collaborate closely with this Yudhiṣṭhira who is almost himself, and to apply finally the laws of justice and good understanding which he has always extolled. By a strange gap or a nearly unique exception, the poem does not make Dhṛtarāṣṭra into the son or incarnation of any god. But all through the drama, in words that he speaks and in the utterances of his interlocutors, his connection with fate *(daiva, kala,* etc.) is established and repeated a hundred times. This blind man is intelligent. He declares himself that his nephews are right; he knows (Vidura says so to him and he agrees) that the malice of Duryodhana can only lead to a catastrophe; but in the end, through lack of character, he makes decisions about the game and the war that this bad counselor suggests. He is, in all this, an image of fate. His hesitations, his capitulations, and his decisions laden with misfortune copy the behavior of fate, just as baffling as is he: "Bhaga is blind . . ." Vidura and Dhṛtarāṣṭra are never in opposition except in their speeches, on the subject of advice that the second asks of the first, which he approves of and does not apply. But there is no hostility between them and they will find their true vocation in the "aftermath of battle" when they will both collaborate, side by side, for the restored kingship of Yudhiṣṭhira.

It is interesting to note here, in the three brothers of the first generation, Dhṛtarāṣṭra, Pāṇḍu and Vidura, a new example of the curious representation, here pointed out several times, of mutilations or qualifying deficiencies. The first was born blind. He will have to make the most weighty decisions of the poem; for a brief moment he will have the choice in the gravest of circumstances of damming up evil or letting it loose. In short, he is the epic counterpart to Bhaga. The second, Pāṇḍu, who will have the most glorious descendants, "the Pāṇḍava," is struck by sexual impotence and, although king of the swarthy Aryas, born sickly pale. The third, dedicated with all his heart to the welfare and the internal cohesion of the noble race, is a bastard and of mixed blood. But it is above all the articulation of the great roles which I wish to point out here. In the first of the decisive "times" of the action, Duryodhana [= Demon] leads the blind Dhṛtarāṣṭra [=*Destiny] in spite of the warning of Vidura [=*Aryaman] to organize the match where normally Yudhiṣṭhira [=*Mitra] ought to be invincible. Nevertheless, by supernatural falsifying of the instruments of play, he will be beaten and, as a consequence, be obliged to disappear for a long time. In the second decisive "time," Duryodhana [= Demon] launches a formidable coalition against Yudhiṣṭhira [=*Mitra], his brothers and allies, and in the battle that follows, each of the Pāṇḍava [= functional gods] kills the adversary of his rank, including Duryodhana. Finally, in the revival that follows this crisis, the blind Dhṛtarāṣṭra [=* Destiny] and the just Vidura [=*Aryaman], entirely reconciled, maintain the work that is connected with the name and spirit of Yudhiṣṭḥira [=*Mitra]. Let us add that a deviant tradition, attested by a Buddhist Jātaka, manages without the person of Yudhiṣṭḥira and makes Vidura, here called "Vidhura," the stake of the crooked match.[5]

I have pointed out elsewhere the remarkable analogies between parts of this picture and "the end of the world" according to Zoroaster: in Mazdaism the long struggle between Good and Evil and the successes of Evil are followed, when ages have passed, by total liquidation of the forces of this Evil. In the course of this event, the Archangels (theological transposition of ancient Indo-Iranian gods of the three functions, as in India the Pāṇḍava are an epic transposition of them) "seize" and eliminate each one of the Archdemons who have opposed them. But the Scandinavian drama of Balder—the melancholy life and murder of Balder, the eschatological battle, the revival of the world under Balder—this is the myth that can most illuminatingly be compared with the Indian myth underlying the intrigue of the *Mahābhārata*.

* * *

The society of Scandinavian gods includes an extremely interesting person: Loki. Intelligent, astute to the highest degree, but amoral, loving to make mischief great or small, as much to amuse himself as to do harm, he represents among the Æsir a truly demonic element. Some of the assailants of the future Ragnarok, the wolf Fenrir and the great Serpent, are his sons, and his daughter is Hel, the mistress of the sinister abode where the dead will go that are not welcome at Odin's Valhalla.

On the other hand, among the sons of Odin the two diversely tragic figures of Balder (Baldr) and Hoder (Hǫðr) stand apart. Of the second, a single action is known, the involuntary murder of Balder, and a single trait: he is blind. He is not one-eyed and, as a paradoxical consequence, "better-seeing" like his father, but truly blind and incapable of managing by himself. The first unites in himself the ideal of true justice and goodness without subterfuge and the thirst for

[5] *The Jātaka*, ed. V. Fausbøll (London, 1896), VI, 355–379; *Jātakam, aus dem Pāli übersetzt*, Julius Dutoit (Leipzig, 1918), VI, 316–339.

"something else" that we remarked upon at the end of the preceding chapter. None of the great Æsir satisfies this thirst since Tyr has agreed to take part in trickery and in violence, and "is not at all a peacemaker among men." After this degenerate Scandinavian Mitra, it is Balder who takes up the function of maintaining peace. Snorri defines these two brothers in this manner:

> Höð is one of the gods. He is blind. He is immensely strong too, but the gods would rather there were no need to mention his name, since his handiwork will long be remembered amongst gods and men.
>
> Another son of Óðin's is called Baldr, and there is [nothing but] good to be told of him. He is the best of them and everyone sings his praises. He is so fair of face and bright that a splendour radiates from him, and there is one flower so white that it is likened to Baldr's brow; it is the whitest of all flowers. From that you can tell how beautiful his body is, and how bright his hair. He is the wisest of the gods, and the sweetest-spoken, and the most merciful, but it is a characteristic of his that [none of his judgments hold or come true]. He lives in the place in heaven called Breiðablik; nothing impure can be there.[6]

An interesting complement to Balder's nature can be deduced from what is said a little farther on about his son Forseti: "He owns the hall in heaven known as Glitnir. Without exception all who come to him with legal disputes go away reconciled; that is the best court known to gods and men."[7] Such are the principal actors of the drama, and here are its principal scenes:

> The beginning of this story is that Baldr the Good had some terrible dreams that threatened his life. When he told the Æsir these dreams, they took counsel together and it was decided to seek protection for Baldr from every kind of peril. Frigg exacted an oath from fire and water, iron and all kinds of metals, stones, earth, trees, ailments, beasts, birds, poison, and serpents, that they would not harm Baldr. And when this had been done and put to the test, Baldr and the Æsir used to amuse themselves by making him stand up at their assemblies for some of them to throw darts at, others to strike and the rest to throw stones at. No matter what was done he was never hurt, and everyone thought that a fine thing. When Loki, Laufey's son, saw that, however, he was annoyed that Baldr was not hurt and he went disguised as a woman to Fensalir to visit Frigg. Frigg asked this woman if she knew what the Æsir was doing at the assembly. She answered that they were all throwing things at Baldr, moreover that he was not being hurt. Frigg remarked: "Neither weapons nor trees will injure Baldr; I have taken an oath from them all." The woman asked: "Has everything sworn you an oath to spare Baldr?" Frigg

6 *Snorra Edda* (Jónsson), pp. 29–30 (*Gylfaginning*, chaps. 11 and 15); *Prose Edda* (Young), pp. 51, 55.

7 *Snorra Edda* (Jónsson), pp. 33–34; *Prose Edda* (Young), p. 55.

replied: "West of Valhalla grows a little bush called mistletoe, I did not exact an oath from it; I thought it too young." Thereupon the woman disappeared.

Loki took hold of the mistletoe, pulled it up and went to the assembly. Now Höð was standing on the outer edge of the circle of men because he was blind. Loki asked him: "Why aren't you throwing darts at Baldr?" He replied: "Because I can't see where Baldr is, and, another thing, I have no weapon." Then Loki said: "You go and do as the others are doing and show Baldr honour like other men. I will show you where he is standing: throw this twig at him." Höð took the mistletoe and aimed at Baldr as directed by Loki. The dart went right through him and he fell dead to the ground. This was the greatest misfortune ever to befall gods and men.

When Baldr had fallen, the Æsir were struck dumb and not one of them could move a finger to lift him up; each looked at the other, and all were of one mind about the perpetrator of that deed, but no one could take vengeance; the sanctuary there was so holy. When the Æsir did try to speak, weeping came first, so that no one could tell the other his grief in words. Óðin, however, was the most affected by this disaster, since he understood best what a loss and bereavement the death of Baldr was for the Æsir.[8]

This drama, as it appears also from the structure of the *Vǫluspá*, is the keystone of world history. Because of it, the mediocrity of the present age has become irremediable. To be sure, the goodness and gentleness of Balder were until then unavailing, since, by a sort of bad fate, "none of his judgments held, none came true." At least he existed and this existence was a protest and a consolation.

After his disappearance, Balder lived the life of the dead, not in the Valhalla of his father (he was not a warrior, he was not slain in battle), but in the domain of Hel—and without possible return as a result of an additional wickedness of Loki. To an envoy of Odin who asked him to free the god, Hel had responded:

that this test should be made as to whether Baldr was loved as much as people said. "If everything in the world, both dead or alive, weeps for him, then he shall go back to the Æsir, but he shall remain with Hel if anyone objects or will not weep."

Thereupon the Æsir sent messengers throughout the whole world to ask for Baldr to be wept out of Hel; and everything did that—men and beasts, and the earth, and the stones and trees and all metals—just as you will have seen these things weeping when they come out of frost and into the warmth. When the messengers were coming home, having made a good job of their errand, they met with a giantess sitting in a cave; she gave her name as Thökk. They asked her to weep Baldr out of Hel. She answered:

---

[8] *Snorra Edda* (Jónsson), pp. 65–68 (*Gylfaginning*, chaps. 33–35); *Prose Edda* (Young), pp. 80–82.

> Thökk will weep
> dry tears
> at Baldr's embarkation;
> the old fellow's son
> was no use to me
> alive or dead,
> let Hel hold what she has.
>
> It is thought that the giantess there was Loki, Laufey's son—who has done most harm amongst the Æsir. [9]

At least the gods succeed in seizing Loki and in chaining him, despite his tricks. He will stay there, tortured, until the end of time. Because time will end.[10] One day will come when all the forces of Evil, all the monsters, Loki himself, will escape their bonds and, from the four directions, will attack the gods. In terrible duels, each one of the "functional gods" will succumb, sometimes beating his adversary and sometimes avenged by another god. Odin will be devoured by the wolf Fenrir, which in turn will be torn apart by Vidar (Víðarr), son of Odin. The dog Garm and Tyr will kill each other. Thor will cleave asunder the World Serpent, but will fall immediately, poisoned by the venom that the beast spews forth. The demon Surt (Surtr) will kill Frey. Finally the primeval god Heimdall (Heimdallr) and Loki will confront and destroy each other. Then Surt will cast fire on the universe, the sun will be obscured, the stars will fall, and the earth will be engulfed by the sea.

But the disaster will be followed by a rebirth: the earth will emerge from the sea, green and beautiful, and, without sowing, grain will sprout. The sons of the dead gods will return to Asgard (Ásgarðr), the enclosure of the Æsir, those of Thor regain the hammer of their father. Balder and Hoder will leave Hel's domain together. All the gods will speak amicably of the past and of the future and tables of gold that had belonged to the Æsir will be found again in the grass . . .

The tragedy of Balder and the character of Loki on the one hand, and his "doom of the gods" (Ragnarǫk) on the other (or, by a mistake that Scandinavian pagans had already legitimized, this "twilight of the gods," *Götterdämmerung*) have been the subject of innumerable studies and hypotheses. As for the latter, several scholars have admitted an influence of Iranian and Zoroastrian eschatology. For "Balder the Beautiful," generally interpreted in the school of Mannhardt as a dying and reborn god of agricultural ritual, an in-

---

9 *Prose Edda* (Young), pp. 83–84.

10 *Snorra Edda* (Jónsson), pp. 70–73, 75 (*Gylfaginning*, chaps. 51–53); *Prose Edda*, pp. 86–92.

fluence has sometimes been supposed of some Attis or Adonis of the eastern Mediterranean. The presentation that was made at the beginning of this chapter of the Indo-Iranian material as a whole suggests an entirely different view. An important fact is immediately apparent: *more than the Iranian version of these cosmic events, it is the para- and pre-Vedic mythical ensemble, transparently preserved in the plot of the Indian epic, which reveals itself as parallel to the entirety of Scandinavian mythology*. As for the stories of Kvasir and Mada, studied in the first chapter, it is here again, paradoxically, Snorri and the *Mahābhārata* who present the most precise agreements. This geographic localization of the best analogy excludes borrowing. Thus, it is from common Indo-European material that the Germanic peoples and the Indo-Iranians have organized their stories of the great battle, and, among these last mentioned, it is not the Iranians who have been the most faithful. We know that after the Zoroastrian reform they must have rethought and sublimated these stories as they did all the others. Let us clarify this general impression.

Consider first the actors. Odin has two gods beside him, his two sons, one wise and merciful, father of the conciliatory god, but whose judgments remain without effect; the other blind, about whom nothing else is told and who does not participate in the whole of the mythology except on this unique occasion (as does his epic transposition "Hatherus" at the end of the saga of "Starcatherus"), for a murder, where he is visibly the incarnation of blind destiny. It is probable that we have here the Scandinavian end result of two minor sovereigns who have produced, among the Indo-Iranians, the gods Aryaman and Bhaga, then their Indian epic transpositions, the two brothers Vidura and Dhṛtarāṣṭra. In the Vedic hymns, Bhaga and Aryaman are the auxiliaries of Mitra rather than of Varuṇa. In the *Mahābhārata*, Vidura and Dhṛtarāṣṭra are indeed brothers of the person transposed from Varuṇa, Pāṇḍu, but it is as assistants to Yudhiṣṭhira, transposed from Mitra, that they fully realize their characters. In Scandinavian mythology, finally, where Tyr, homologous to Mitra, is not only degenerated in his definition, but fallen in importance, Odin remaining in fact the only "sovereign god," it is to Odin, as his sons, that Balder and Hoder are directly attached. As for Loki, with a coloration peculiar to Scandinavia, he is the homologue of the instigator of the great evils of the world, of the demonic spirit, whom certain Indo-Iranian stories doubtless knew although the Vedas do not. Zoroastrianism has magnified him in its Aṇra-Mainyu and the authors of the *Mahābhārata* have transposed him into Duryodhana, incarnation of the demon of our cosmic age.

The degradation of Tyr is the reason, moreover, that the latter does not play a role in the tragedy, except accessorily at the time of the final battle, and that it is Balder who concentrates in himself the essences of Mitra and Aryaman, the roles that the *Mahābhārata* distributes between Yudhiṣṭhira and Vidura. But we know how close Mitra and his principal collaborator were to Vedic and pre-Vedic times, and we have seen that the *Mahābhārata* goes so far as to make of Yudhiṣṭhira and of Vidura a kind of doubling of the same god, Dharma, a doubling that only the death of the second by "returning" into the first brings back into a unity.

Consider now the drama itself, in its three stages:

1) The demonic Loki uses the blind Hoder to eliminate the good Balder—here to send him, by death, into the long exile of Hel. He uses a game, which Balder, invulnerable in principle, has every right to believe harmless, but in which he is killed by the only weapon remaining which is dangerous to him, a weapon discovered by Loki and activated by the blind Hoder under Loki's direction. The method is parallel to that which results in the provisional elimination and long exile of Yudhiṣṭhira: the demonic Duryodhana wrings authorization from the blind Dhṛtarāṣṭra to stage the scenario that will destroy Yudhiṣṭhira. This scenario is a game that is apparently without any particular danger for Yudhiṣṭhira, who is an average player, but it is one in which his adversary, accomplice of Duryodhana, uses supernatural tricks that force him, beaten, into exile. The two principal differences are: (1) the differing specifications of the games (dice in India where dice are the typical game, and a more spectacular and romantic game in Scandinavia), and (2) the greater degree of blame on the part of the blind Indian who knows to what misfortune his action will lead and does it nevertheless through weakness, while the blind Scandinavian is entirely an involuntary instrument and is unconscious of the trick of the evil one. In Scandinavia, the responsibility is divided simply between Loki *ráðbani*, "killer by plan" and instigator, and Hoder, the blind *handbani*, "killer by hand" and purely a material agent. In India, responsibility is divided more complexly between a *ráðbani*, Duryodhana, and two *handbani* who participate consciously in his *ráð*, the blind Dhṛtarāṣṭra and the cheating partner of Yudhiṣṭhira. These differences allow the essential parallel to remain, but would be sufficient to set aside the hypothesis of a loan or even of literary influence by India on Scandinavia, if it were otherwise possible to form such a hypothesis.

2) The scene of the fatal game in the two stories opens a long, dark period: the whole course of the present world in Scandinavia, in

India only the time that Yudhiṣṭhira and his brothers are in exile. In India the time is reduced to a few years by the requirements of epic limits, but in the original myth it also must have been the final part of a cosmic age, since the one responsible, the demonic Duryodhana, is precisely the incarnation of the evil spirit of the present age. This period of waiting ends on both sides with the great battle where all the representatives of Evil and most of the representatives of Good are liquidated. The introductory circumstances of this battle are different, since, in Scandinavia it is initiated by the forces of Evil who were until then enchained, Loki being included among these as a result of Balder's murder, and are now abruptly loosed. In the *Mahābhārata*, however, it is initiated by the good heroes, reappearing after their temporary exile and claiming their rights. Another divergence is that in the *Mahābhārata* the survivors among the "good" are the Pāṇḍava, Yudhiṣṭhira and his brothers, each one of whom has killed his particular adversary without dying himself. In the Nordic myth, in contrast, the parallels of the Pāṇḍava, the functional gods, perish as well as their adversaries and the survivors or renascents are the sons of the gods, along with Balder and Hoder.

3) This difference is attenuated by the fact that the Indian parallels of Balder and Hoder, Vidura and Dhṛtarāṣṭra, who also have not taken part in the great battle, survive and receive new roles in the renewal that follows. Their ancient discord ended, they are, in complete and confident union, the two organs of Yudhiṣṭhira's perfect government. Thus, in the world that is reborn, purified, and delivered from Evil after the eschatological battle and the cataclysm, Balder and Hoder being reconciled, they take the place of the sovereigns—Balder holding simultaneously, as has been said, the roles of Yudhiṣṭhira and Vidura.

The fullness and the regularity of this harmony between the *Mahābhārata* and the *Edda* settles, I think, the problems of Balder, Hoder, Loki, and Ragnarok, which have been wrongly separated. And it brings order into this unique problem in an unforeseen manner, eliminating, except for a few accessory and late details, the solutions based on Iranian, Caucasian, or Christian borrowing. It brings to light a vast myth on the history and destiny of the world, on the relations of Evil and Good, which must already have been formed before the dispersal of at least part of the Indo-Europeans.

So the comparison is complete that I made in 1948 of the myth of Loki and Balder and of the Ossetic legend of Syrdon and Sozryko.[11]

---

[11] Dumézil, *Loki* (Paris, 1948), considerably revised in the German edition, *Loki*, trans. Inge Köck (Darmstadt, 1959).

The Ossetes, as is known, are the last descendants of Scythian peoples who, from before the time of Herodotus and until the Middle Ages, occupied vast territories in the south of what is now Russia. The Scythians were a branch of the Iranian stem, separated early, who did not undergo a profound influence from Zoroastrianism. It is all the more valuable to find among them, again in epic form, in a folklore noted down in the nineteenth and twentieth centuries, a near parallel, if not to the whole structure (the eschatology, the great battle are not represented), at least to the episode of the murder of Balder. The handsome hero Sozryko is also killed, at the instigation of the wicked Syrdon, a true Loki, and, according to a group of Tcherkessian variants, in a game that recalls very closely the one to which Balder succumbs. Sozryko is invulnerable except—it is a secret—in his knees. Syrdon discovers this secret. Then he engages the Nartes to organize a game of harmless appearance. They all place themselves on the summit of a mountain and Sozryko at the foot. From the height, they throw the cutting wheel on him and he returns it to them, making it rebound on the part of his body that they designate to him by their cries. What does he risk, since neither his forehead, nor his chest, nor his arms, nor almost any part of him could be cut? But soon, in the heat of the game, he forgets the only exception to his privilege and when they cry to him from above: "With your knees!", he opposes his knees to the wheel which is coming down and it cuts them off. It is probable that we read here the last remains of the Scythian version of the story whose Scandinavian, Indian, and—in the Zoroastrian remnant—Iranian versions we have considered.

CHAPTER 4

From Storm to Pleasure: Thor, Njord, Frey, Freya

The gods that form the second and third terms of the functional triad do not raise as many difficulties as the sovereign gods, Odin and his dramatic entourage. They are strongly characterized by the features that their rank demands. It is largely on the frontiers of their provinces, and through a few extensions that seem to transcend their definition, that they have given room for controversies.

The Germanic **þunraz* of whom Tacitus speaks was a "Hercules," and so the Thor of Scandinavian mythology remains: colossally strong, with a strength increased by the wearing of a belt and magic gloves, he spends most of his time on journeys, alone or in the company of his servant Thjalfi, on foot or in a chariot drawn by goats, in quest of giants to destroy. His weapon is the hammer Mjollnir, whose primary value is not in doubt. Like the *vajra* of Indra and the *vazra,* which the Iranian Mithra has stripped from Indra grown archdemon, it is the celestial weapon, the thunderbolt accompanying the "thunder" which has furnished its name to the god. There are other physical traits that make him resemble Indra: red beard and a fabulous appetite. He is the rampart of divine society, a position that no doubt earned him the place of honor which he occupied in the temple of Uppsala when Adam of Bremen described it. When he is absent from the divine enclosure, great perils threaten, but it is enough for the frightened Æsir to pronounce his name to make him rise up, menacingly, in an angry state, *mōðr,* which makes him resemble his monstrous adversaries. Nothing then restrains him, not even legal scruples: he does not recognize the promises and pledges that the other gods, even Odin, have imprudently made in his absence.

Examples are numerous. One day, says Snorri, a giant disguised as a master-craftsman came and offered to construct a castle for the Æsir. The bargain was made: the craftsman should complete his work in the course of a winter and with the aid of his only horse. If he succeeded, he would receive in payment the beautiful goddess Freya, the usual object coveted by the giants, and also the sun and the moon. The craftsman began to work and the dismayed gods quickly saw that he was going to succeed. Each night, untiringly, his horse brought him the huge stone slabs that he needed. Three days before summer, when only the small task of making the castle gate remained to be done, the gods, accusing Loki of having advised them badly, demanded that he cheat the craftsman of his salary. Thus, Loki turned himself into a mare and distracted the horse on which rested the chances of success.

> When the builder saw that the work would not be finished, he flew into a giant rage. When, however, the Æsir saw for certain that it was a giant who had come there, no reverence was shown for their oaths and they called on Thor. He came at once, and the next thing was that the hammer Mjollnir was raised aloft. Thor paid the builder his wages, and it was not the sun and moon; he would not even allow him to live in Giantland, but struck him such a single blow that his skull shivered into fragments and he sent him down under Niflhel.[1]

Thor's intervention is here grafted on a folklore theme that is well known in Scandinavia and elsewhere. Another adventure, where the god is involved not only in the final punishment, but in the initial risk, has produced up to the last centuries numerous popular ballads after having furnished the material for one of the most remarkable Eddic poems, the *þrymskviða*.[2] The giant Thrym has stolen Thor's hammer and has hidden it eight leagues under the earth. He will not return it, he informs Loki, who is sent as an envoy, unless the goddess Freya is handed over to him. Their champion thus stripped of the weapon of his victories, the gods are exposed to the greatest perils, and are ready to sacrifice the goddess. But she refuses with indignation. In the assembly Heimdall then proposes that Thor disguise himself as the betrothed and go to giantland under the name of Freya. Thor, in turn, is indignant, but Loki intervenes (str. 18):

---

1 *Snorra Edda* (Jónsson), pp. 45–47 (*Gylfaginning*, chap. 25); *Prose Edda* (Young), pp. 66–67.

2 *Edda* (Kuhn), pp. 111–115; *Edda* (Bellows), 174–182.

"þegi þú, þórr, þeira orða!
þegar muno iǫtnar ásgarð búa,
nema þú þinn hamar
þér um heimtir."

"Be silent, Thor,
and speak not thus;
Else will the giants in Asgard dwell
If thy hammer is brought not
home to thee."

Thor gives in: they dress him as a woman, with precious stones on his chest and keys clinking at his waist. Loki disguises himself as a servant and they both proceed in a wagon to giantland (Jotunheim) where Thrym, conceited, vain, and stupid, receives them. But Thor cannot overcome his nature: he eats an ox and eight salmon, and drinks three barrels of mead. The giant is anxious: he has never seen a bride so famished . . . Fortunately the crafty servant is there to find a response (str. 26):

"Át vætr Freyia átta nóttom,
svá var hon óðfús í iǫtunheima."

"From food has Freya
eight nights fasted,
So hot was her longing
for Jotunheim."

Deeply moved, Thrym leans forward to kiss her. The sharpness of the eyes under the veil makes him recoil. Loki explains (str. 28):

"Svaf vætr Freyia átta nóttom,
svá var hon óðfús í iǫtunheima."

"No sleep has Freya
for eight nights found,
So hot was her longing
for Jotunheim."

The giant's old sister comes to ask for the customary presents and Thrym, reassured, has the hammer brought in for benediction. Thor needs only make use of it. He gaily massacres the brother, the sister, and all who get in his way.

One of these stories contains strange traits, whose interest perhaps transcends mythology. Snorri[3] relates how, Thor being occupied far away in killing monsters, one day an undesirable guest enters the home of the Æsir, the giant Hrungnir in full "giant's rage." The Æsir can only invite him to their banquet. At the banquet he terrorizes them, threatening to carry Valhalla into his country, to kill all the gods, to leave with the goddesses Freya and Sif, and even as Freya fills his cup for him, to drink all the Æsir's beer. The Æsir then pronounce Thor's name and immediately Thor appears in the room, furious. Hrungnir, uneasy, remarks to Thor that he will receive little glory by killing an unarmed adversary and proposes an en-

---

[3] *Snorra Edda* (Jónsson), pp. 100–103 (*Skáldskaparmál*, chap. 25); *Prose Edda* (Young), pp. 103–105.

counter, man to man, in Grjóttúnagarðar on the "frontier." Thor shows the more alacrity in accepting this challenge since it is the first time that he has had an opportunity to proceed *til einvígis*, to a regular duel, with a place of rendezvous, the *holmr*.

Then is presented what appears to be an incoherence, but a significant one. Realizing the importance of the duel and not wanting Hrungnir to lose, the giants "make at Grjóttúnagarðar a clay man nine leagues high and three broad under his arms." They could not find a heart big enough to put in him, except the heart of a mare—again Thor arrived too soon. We would expect that this "dummy" was substituted for the real Hrungnir, and yet Hrungnir comes to the meeting place and takes up a position by the side of the dummy. It is true that he himself was a sort of statue: he had a heart made of hard rock, "with three corners, of the form that has become afterwards that of the runic sign that is called Hrungnir's Heart." He also had a stone head, a stone shield, and as an offensive weapon, a hone. He and the clay man wait at the meeting place, Hrungnir holding his shield before him and the stone man so frightened that, they say, he urinates when he sees Thor.

Thor is victorious, but partly thanks to a trick of his servant and companion, Thjalfi. The latter arrives first and, pretending to be a traitor, warns Hrungnir that Thor is apt to rise up from underground. It is, consequently, under his feet and not in front of his chest and face that he should place his shield. Scarcely has Hrungnir adopted this unusual posture, when Thor appears from the sky with thunder and lightning. His hammer shatters the hone (a piece of which lodges in the god's head) and shatters Hrungnir's skull. In his fall, Hrungnir catches Thor's neck under one of his feet. In the meanwhile, Thjalfi has attacked the clay man "who fell with little glory." Thjalfi tries to disengage Thor's neck, but Hrungnir's foot is too heavy. Learning that Thor has fallen, the Æsir try to save him: impossible. They are forced to appeal to Thor's son, Magni ("Force"), a child only three nights old, who easily lifts off the foot. As a reward, Thor gives him Hrungnir's horse, an act that earns him a lecture by Odin. Thor, according to Odin, ought to have given the prize not to his son, but to his father.

This story has recently become the subject of several highly improbable exegeses. In the first edition of this book,[4] I myself pointed out that one of the details, the dummy doubling for the real adversary, recalls the scene of the "initiation of a young warrior" described

[4] Dumézil, *Mythes et dieux des germains* (Paris, 1939), pp. 101–106.

in the saga of Hrolf Kraki, apropos of Hott (Hǫttr), a frightened young man. His "initiator," Bodvar (Bǫðvarr), having killed an enormous monster that was terrorizing his region, made him drink its blood and eat the heart. Hott immediately became strong and courageous. But the story continues. "Well done, comrade Hott!" says Bodvar, "let's go and set up the animal again and arrange it so that the others will believe it is alive!" The next day, the king's watchmen announce that the monster is still there near the castle. The king advances with his army and says: "I can't see any movement in the animal. Who wants to take it upon himself to fight him?" Bodvar suggests Hott who, to the surprise of the king, accepts. "You have changed a great deal in a short while!" says the king. Hott, who is weaponless, asks the king for his sword Gullinhjalti ("Golden Guard") with which he "kills" the monster's corpse without difficulty. The king is not a fool, and he says to Bodvar what he suspects to be true and adds: "This is nonetheless a good work by you to have made a hero where there was only Hott, who did not appear to be destined for great things." Finally, he changes the boy's name in order to mark the metamorphosis: after the sword which served in his semblance of an exploit, the new champion will be called Hjalti.

The use of a dummy in simulated exploits of valor is attested in the Indo-European world and elsewhere. In the story of Hrungnir and Thor, this detail appears with circumstances that render its interpretation difficult. Is it simple embellishment, taken from initiation rites, but stripped of its original value? Is it part of the story that then would be, as I thought in 1939, a true "initiation myth" either of Thjalfi (but this servant has nothing of the warrior in him either before or after the exploit) or of Thor himself–and, in this case, not "primary initiation, since Thor already is a redoubtable warrior, but of an initiation of a higher degree? Perhaps, since the text speaks of a beginning, of a sort of progress in the fighting experience of the god: "It was the first time" says Snorri, "that he had had a chance to take part in a regular duel." In the same sense would go the hone (*hein*) that henceforth will remain driven into Thor's skull as a distinguishing mark (the idols reproduce this trait by a nail driven in his head). It recalls one of the "shapes" manifested by the Irish hero Cu Chulainn after his first battle: "An emanation," says one text, "comes forth from the forehead of the hero, as long and as thick as the hone (*airnem*) of a warrior." Finally, it is possible that the three-cornered shape of Hrungnir's heart, a strange item of information, should be classified among the various triplicities of adversaries opposed to warring gods or heroes typical in a number of Indo-European legends (the three-headed adversary of the Indian Indra and of the Iranian Feridūn; Gēryon, adversary of Hercules; the three Curiaces overcome by the young Horatius; the three Meic Nechtain, adversaries of Cu Chulainn; the triple-hearted Meche killed by Mac Cecht, etc.). It would be vain to try to make these impressions more precise. At least they make one think that the mythology of Thor includes in certain of its episodes some rites, initiatory or otherwise, of young warriors.

The difference in the respective relations of Thor and Odin with warriors is brought out by several facts. First, the insulting phrase of Odin in the *Hárbarðsljóð* (str. 24) claiming for himself "the nobles (*jarlar*) who fall in battle" and for Thor "the race of thralls" (or slaves, *þrælar*). If this is only the caricature of an authentic belief and if J. de Vries is correct, as I believe he is, in thinking that the poet has here replaced a less ignominious notion (such as *karl*, "free peasant") with "thrall," there is surely a foundation of truth in this dual formula.

Outside the warrior domain, the essential distinction between Thor and Odin is expressed in the interesting Eddic poem, the *Hárbarðsljóð*, where the two gods exchange insults and boasts, many of which serve as definitions. Some have wished to see in this poem a document revealing a conflict of cults, a rivalry of religious groups marking the retreat of one god and the advance of another in the favor of the faithful. This is certainly wrong, as are the same type of conclusions that have been drawn sometimes from the parallel dialogue hymns of the *Rig Veda* where the sovereign Varuṇa and the warrior Indra address each other with sweet-sour words. In both cases the poets have only utilized the frame of the dialogue, the method of verbal fencing, in order to make more evident the natures of the two gods and the diverse services, sometimes contradictory, which they render in various parts of the same stable theological structure.

Other unwarranted deductions from well-established facts have tended to change the center of gravity of the character. The superstitions of modern Scandinavian folklore, survivals of old agrarian cults, and especially the fossil evidence that the Lapp loans have yielded in the skillful analysis by Axel Olrik of the ancient popular religion of the Norwegians—these have all tended to prove that in important layers of the population Thor had been something other than a warrior. Whereas the *Edda* presents him as a man in the prime of life, the Lapp tradition, in accord with several popular Norwegian expressions, makes him an old man with a red beard. The names that are given him by the Lapps reproduce or translate Scandinavian names of a uniform type as little Eddic as possible: *Hora Galles* (i.e. *Tor-Karl,* "the Good-man Thor," an appellation still known from popular songs of the end of the Middle Ages), *agja,* "the grandfather," *adschiegads,* "the little father" (name applied in the descriptions by Thomas von Westen), *Toraturos bodne* (a name noted by Skanke, the first word containing without doubt the name Thor and the second, "old man," taken from Scandinavian *bóndi* "peasant, head of the family"). In the south of Sweden Thor, the thunder, is moreover called by the peasants *go-bonden,* "the good peasant," *korn-* or *åker-bonden,* or *korngubben,* "the old man of grain, of the fields." These Swedish names recall the Lapp cult where Thor is a fertility god who gives rain or sun according to the needs of the soil and matures and protects the crops. We have seen, finally, that in the eleventh century, in order to define Thor, Adam of Bremen reported from his Swedish informants: *Præsidet in ære, qui tonitrus et fulmina, ventos imbresque, serena et fruges gubernat.* Curiously he does not leave the third god of the trinity, Fricco (Frey), anything but *pacem voluptatemque,* while concentrating on the first, the sovereign Wodan (Odin), all the properly warlike aspect of Thor (*Wodan, id est furor, bella gerit hominique ministrat virtutem contra inimicos*). A little farther on, speaking of the sacrifices at Uppsala, he limits the competence of the god in this way: *si pestis et fames imminet, Thor idolo libatur.* So it was Thor who gave Swedish peasants the atmospheric elements needed for their success. Summarizing Axel Olrik, Maurice Cahen[5] expressed it very well: the Lapp sacrifice unites the offering to the earth "in order that she shall nourish the herds, protect them from sickness and give them a vigorous mating"—with the offering to thunder "in order that he spare beasts and people and give the fecundating rain." All this is true, but does not permit one to relate "fecundity" to the essence of the divine concept: it is only through rain, the happy effect of his atmospheric battle and the exploits of his hammer, that he assists agriculture, and not by any power over germination. It is very natural that the poor Lapps, the pagan peasants of Uppland and modern

[5] M. Cahen, "L'étude du paganisme scandinave au XXe siècle," *Revue de l'histoire des religions* 92 (1925), 62.

folklore have retained only the fecundating result of this battle and of these exploits. Even in this function, Thor does not duplicate the great Vanir.

* * *

In the historicising perspective of the *Ynglingasaga,* Snorri makes Njord and Frey Odin's first and second successors after his death. Here is how he describes their reign.

> After him, Njorth of Nóatún took power among the Swedes and continued the sacrifices. Then the Swedes called him their king, and he received their tribute. In his days good peace prevailed and there were such good crops of all kinds that the Swedes believed that Njorth had power over the harvests and the prosperity of mankind . . .
>
> After Njorth, Frey succeeded to power. He was called king of the Swedes and received tribute from them. He was greatly beloved and blessed by good seasons like his father. Frey erected a great temple at Uppsala and made his chief residence there, directing to it all tribute due to him, both lands and chattels. This was the origin of the Uppsala crown goods, which have been kept up ever since. In his days there originated the so-called Peace of Fróthi. There were good harvests at that time in all countries. The Swedes attributed that to Frey. And he was worshipped more than other gods because in his days, owing to peace and good harvests, the farmers became better off than before.[6]

The *Gylfaginning* (chaps. 23–24: *Prose Edda,* pp. 52–54), more purely mythological, gives the three great Vanir the following description:

> The third *áss* is the one called Njord. He lives in heaven at a place called Nóatún ("enclosure of ships"). He controls the path of wind, stills sea and fire, and is to be invoked for seafaring and fishing. He is so wealthy and prosperous that he is able to bestow abundance of land and property on those who call on him for this.
>
> 13. Njord of Nóatún had two children after this, a son called Freyr and a daughter Freyja. They were beautiful to look at, and powerful. Freyr is an exceedingly famous god; he decides when the sun shall shine or the rain come down, and along with that the fruitfulness of the earth, and he is good to invoke for peace and plenty. He also brings about the prosperity of men.
>
> But Freyja is the most renowned of the ásynjor [*sic*]. She owns that homestead in heaven known as Fólkvangar ("Fields of the People"), and whenever she rides into battle she has half of the slain and Odin has

[6] *Heimskringla* (Hollander), pp. 13–14 (*Ynglingasaga,* chaps. 9 and 10).

half [cf. *Grímnismál*, str. 14] . . . She is most readily invoked, and from her name derives the polite custom of calling the wives of men of rank *Frú*. She enjoys love poetry (*mansǫngr*, lit. *Minnesang*), and it is good to call on her for help in love affairs.[7]

Stories, poetic periphrases (*kennings*), and some other information fill out and complete this picture, but everything important is here. Furthermore, with Freya as well as Frey—represented in the temple of Uppsala *cum ingenti priapo* and the object of such licentious ceremonies that Adam of Bremen did not wish to describe them—voluptuousness seems to have played a larger part than Snorri says. About Freya, even to Freya herself, the sorceress Hyndla can say (*Hyndluljóð*, strs. 46–47):

"hleypr þú, eðlvina,	You run about nights,
úti á náttom,	my good friend,
sem með hǫfrom	like a female goat
Heiðrún fari."	with the vagabond billy goats.[8]

And Loki's sarcasm (*Lokasenna*, str. 30) is of the same nature:

"þegi þú, Freyia!	"Be silent, Freya!
þic kann ec fullgerva,	for fully I know thee,
era þér vamma vant;	Sinless thou art not thyself;
ása oc álfa, er hér inni ero,	Of the gods and elves
	who are gathered here,
hverr hefir þinn hór verið."	Each one as thy lover has lain."[9]

In contrast, the tradition according to which Njord and his sister, or Frey and Freya, before their entrance to the home of the Æsir, had lived as husband and wife, as was usual among the Vanir, is not to be put down to shamelessness. It signifies only that the sexual mores of the Vanir, the "gods of the third function," in the free state, did not have the same framework or limitations as those of society after it became complete. Of Freya herself it must be said that the mythology hardly relates any specific adventures in support of the nasty remarks of Loki and Hyndla. Like Isis, however, she once traveled throughout the world in search of her lost husband, spreading tears of gold.[10]

The character of Njord (Proto-Scandinavian **Nerthu-*) is particularly famous in the history of Germanic religions because Tacitus

---

[7] *Snorra Edda* (Jónsson), pp. 30–31 (*Gylfaginning*, chaps. 11 and 13); *Prose Edda* (Young), pp. 52–54.

[8] *Edda* (Kuhn), p. 295; *Edda* (Bellows), p. 232.

[9] *Edda* (Kuhn), p. 102; *Edda* (Bellows), pp. 161–162.

[10] *Snorra Edda* (Jónsson), p. 38 (*Gylfaginning*, chap. 22); *Prose Edda* (Young), p. 59.

already identified him, but with female sex. This is the Nerthus of the *Germania*, honored by a sort of cultic union of little peoples somewhere in the south of Denmark (the Reudigni, Aviones, Anglii, Varini, etc.). Says Tacitus:

> These peoples, each one of which when isolated has nothing remarkable, worship Nerthus in common, that is to say Mother Earth. They believe that she intervenes in human affairs and passes from one to another of the tribes in a wagon. On an island in the ocean there is a sacred woods and, in this woods, a cart covered with cloth which is reserved to her and which only the priest has the right to touch. He divines the moment when the goddess is present in her sanctuary and he accompanies her, with all the marks of devotion, while she goes forward on her cart drawn by cows. These are days of rejoicing, and the places that she honors by her visit and from which she accepts hospitality are in celebration. They do not make wars, nor take up their arms; every iron object is locked up. It is the only period of time when peace and tranquility are known and enjoyed, and it lasts until the moment when the priest returns the goddess to her temple, satisfied with her contact with men. The cart with its cloth and, if one can believe them, the goddess herself, are then bathed in a secluded lake. The slaves who accomplish this ceremony are immediately swallowed up by the same lake. From there comes a mysterious terror, the sacred ignorance of the nature of a secret that is seen only by those who are going to perish.[11]

"Mother Earth," but lodged on an island in the ocean, distributor of joy and peace in spite of the final ritual of submersion, this old goddess of the northern Germans already has the principal traits of the Scandinavian Njord. People have often wished to derive one from the other, supposing that the cult spread toward the north from the spot where Tacitus located it. This is an improper use of the argument *ex silentio*. Even though the Roman historian established the presence of Nerthus on the continent, he did not say (nor could he say, knowing nothing about it) whether, male or female, she was at that time honored beyond the sea among the peoples in the southern part of the Scandinavian "island." He cites a few names from Scandinavia, including that of the Suiones, but he has noted no religious traits. The five place names, islands and fjords along the coast of Norway which are still called by names derived from Njord, **Njarð-ey*, "Island of Njord," and the four old **Njarð-vīk*, "Bay of Njord," can be as ancient as the *insula* of the continental coast that was all Tacitus knew. Just to the south of Bergen there is a little island formerly called **Njarðar-lög* (*-laug?*), the "District (Bath?) of Njord" where, in an exciting article (1905),

---

[11] Tacitus, *Germania*, chap. 40.

Magnus Olsen, using mythical elements in the place names and even the arrangement of the terrain, concluded there had been a cult very comparable to that of Nerthus.

As for the difference of sexes—Nerthus goddess, Njord god—it has been explained in many, rather unsatisfactory ways. Perhaps this is simply further testimony, and a very ancient one, of a common fact in Scandinavian marine mythology: most of the stories that tell of a sea spirit are known in variants where the spirit is masculine as well as in others where the spirit is feminine. In any case, the particular ties of Njord with the sea, not so much as a cosmic element, but as the locale of profitable navigation and nutritious fishing, have been thoroughly confirmed. His Lapp transposition, Bieka Galles, "the goodman Wind," is defined in these two terms: master of winds on earth and sea, and protector of fishing boats. I had the keen pleasure some years ago of coming across, in a collection of Norwegian folklore where it had remained unnoticed, an astonishing survival of Njord and his function in the popular beliefs of the eighteenth century. H. Opedal conveys precious information on the life of the inhabitants of Hardanger and especially on fishing, where he makes the following statement:

> The old folks always had good luck when they went fishing. One night the old woman Gunnhild Reinsnos (born in 1746) and Johannes Reinsnos were fishing in the Sjosavatn on Cape Finntopp. They had brought a torch and were busily fishing away. The fish were biting well on the fishhooks and little time passed before Gunnhild had enough fish to boil for the whole week. Then she wound the line around her pole saying, "Thank you, Njor, for this time."[12]

This essentially maritime character of Njord gave rise to a famous myth: his unhappy marriage with the eponymous earth goddess of Scandinavia, Skadi. This giants' daughter was wholly terrestrial. The couple made an arrangement, a compromise: nine nights in the mountains and nine nights on the coast. But in vain. Njord could not bear the Scandinavian Alps:

Leið eromc fiǫll, varca ec lengi á,	Mountains I loathed, no longer than nine
nætr einar nío;	nights did I stay there
úlfa þytr	the howling of wolves
mér þótti illr vera	seemed ugly to me
hiá sǫngvi svana.	compared with the hooping of swans.

[12] H. Opedal, *Makter og menneske, Norsk Folkeminnelag* 51 (Oslo, 1943), p. 49.

The sea of the North was no less trying for Skadi:

Sofa ec né máttac	I could not sleep
sævar beðiom á	by the shore of the sea
fugls iarmi fyrir;	for the noise of the mew
sá mic vecr, er af víði kemr,	that awakened me,
	the bird that flew
morgin hverian már.	each dawn from the deep.[13]

And she went back, alone, without returning, into her native mountains.

The attachment to the sea, to navigation, of at least one of the two gods who watch over the third function was doubtless not without Indo-European roots. One of the good deeds of the Vedic Nāsatya most often mentioned is her having saved a man from a shipwreck. As is well known, the Greek Dioscuri—who in spite of considerable differences retain several traits of the Indo-European twins—are the guardians of sailors. Before their dispersion the Indo-Europeans had a common word for "boat" (Sanskrit *nauh,* Latin *navis,* etc.), and it is exactly this word that is found again in the name of Njord's mythical dwelling, *Nóatún* "Enclosure (*tún*: German *Zaun,* English *town*; cf. Gallo-Roman *-dūnum*) of Boats." Aside from this specialty (it is said of Frey that he owns a magic boat that he can fold into his pocket and which goes faster than all others), Njord and Frey are closely united. They have the same function of fecundity, the same taste for peace, and the formulas associate them readily and without distinction.[14] One poet, Egill Skalla-Grimsson, was not even afraid to put in the singular a verb of which the two gods are the subject: "One is astonished by the generosity of Arinbjǫrn,"

en grjót-bjǫrn of gœddan her	but Frey-and-Njord
	has well endowed
Freyr ok Njǫrðr at féar afli.	this Arinbjǫrn
	with wealth abundant.[15]

It is worth noting that the Scandinavians had not transformed this quasi-identity of function, as did the other Indo-Europeans, by making the two twin gods. Njord is Frey's father. Various indications

[13] *Snorra Edda* (Jónsson), p. 30 (*Gylfaginning,* chap. 12); *Prose Edda* (Young), pp. 51–52.

[14] E. Wessén, *Studier till Sveriges hedna mytologi och fornhistoria, Uppsala Universitets Årbok* 6 (1924), 126–129.

[15] *Egils saga Skalla-Grímssonar,* ed. S. Nordal, *Íslenzk fornrit* 2 (Reykajavík, 1933), 264.

make one think, however, that other Germanic peoples, and even certain Scandinavians, had preserved the twin formula.[16]

Frey is the hero, or at least the beneficiary, of an enjoyable tragicomedy, the subject of a poetic dialogue in the Edda, the *Skírnismál*, in which some have wished to see the reflection of a ritual of sacred marriage. In love with the giantess Gerd to the point of wasting away, the god sends his servant Skírnir to her. The latter tries in vain to win her for his master by promising her gold and threatening her with his sword. She only yields when he threatens her violently with "spells," which she finds unsettling. One of the most interesting details of the poem is this: when leaving on this delicate mission, Skírnir asks Frey to give him his sword. Frey agrees, and he will never get it back. It follows that in the only duel one knows of him, against the enigmatic Beli, he will have only his hands or a stag's antler for a weapon, and, says Snorri, he will then regret his thoughtless gift. It follows, above all, that he will present himself condemned in advance, disastrously deprived, in the battle at the end of the world. This sword, as will be seen, is chiefly noteworthy in the god's career by its absence. It is obviously not sufficient, any more than the duel with Beli of whom we know only his name, to qualify Frey for the title of "warrior god," as those have sometimes done who try to obscure the fundamental difference between the Æsir and the Vanir. In India also, gods of the "third function" are sometimes armed, but they are so in a different, humbler way than the gods of the higher functions. This is the case of the twins, Nakula and Sahadeva, of the *Mahābhārata*[17] to whom the sword is assigned as "minimal" arms. This is surely less noble than the throwing of weapons in which Arjuna, the hero of the second function, excels, and more in the range of ordinary men than the enormous club of the colossal Bhīma. In the same way (because Tyr, in spite of what one reads currently, is not "god of the sword") the sword that Frey possesses and that he sacrifices to his passion contrasts with Odin's spear, the bow of the gods Vali and Ullr, and Thor's hammer. The arguments in favor of a warrior character for Njord and Frey which some have tried to extract from the *kenningar*, the periphrases so frequent in the works of the skalds, rest on a misunderstanding of the very precise rules of this poetic technique.[18]

---

16 See my *Saga de Hadingus*, chap. 8, in *Du mythe au roman* (Paris, 1971), pp. 107–120.

17 *Mahābhārata* I, 5270–5274; II, 2463–2465.

18 See Dumézil, "Remarques sur les armes des dieux de 'troisième fonction' chez divers peuples indo-européens," *Studi e Materiali di Storia delle Religioni* 28 (1957), 1–9.

Contemporary folklore has not preserved the memory of Njord nor—despite illusions dispersed today—that of Freya, but E. Brate[19] was doubtless right in thinking that mythical representations, in which Thor as well as Frey are engaged, abound in a tradition published in 1912 by T. Karsten.[20] In the archipelago off Nykarleby two ancient cult places are found, *Torsö* and *Frösö* "Thor's Island" and "Frey's Island." Near the second, one notices seven small islands whose name, "Islets of the Fiancée," is explained by a legend. One day three great holiday boats, three *kyrkbåtar*, took a wedding party to the old church of the "Island of Peter," Pedersö. The breeze was gentle and the most unrestrained gaiety reigned on board. Then the wind increased and the fiancée asked that they spend the night on the small islands. They agreed, but the young man proposed that they celebrate the feast without further delay and at the same place. This became a spectacle such as they had rarely seen: dancing, gorging, and drunkenness; general confusion. . . . Finally, men and women, lost in intoxication and debauchery, tumbled on all corners of the island. As at the last judgment, the sky was covered by clouds, a frightful storm burst out, and the bride and groom and all the wedding guests were swallowed up by the sea. Even though they are darkened by the Christian notion of sin of the flesh, has one not the impression of glimpsing here again some of the familiar themes of the ancient religion? Frey in marriage and in orgy; Nerthus swallowing up her servants after the feast; and, dominating everything, the furious rumbling of Thor?

---

19 E. Brate, *Vanerna, en mytologisk undersökning* (Stockholm, 1914), p. 21.

20 T. Karsten, "Einige Zeugnisse zur altnordischen Götterverehrung in Finnland," *Finnisch-ugrische Forschungen* 12 (1912), 307–316.

Bibliographical Notes

CHAPTER 1

Two extremely useful collections of documents pertaining to Germanic religion should be immediately mentioned: F. R. Schröder, *Quellenbuch zur germanischen Religionsgeschichte* (original texts, 1933), and W. Baetke, *Die Religion der Germanen in Quellenzeugnissen* (1937). (W. Baetke is the author of one of the masterpieces in our field, which all historians of religion ought to study: *Das Heilige im Germanischen* [1942]) .

The bibliography of the problem of the Æsir and the Vanir is given in the notes of Jan de Vries, *Altgermanische Religionsgeschichte,* 2d ed. (*AGR* 2), (1957), I, 208–214.

Bernhard Salin's article, 'Heimskringlas tradition om asarnas invandring" (*Studier . . . Montelius* [Stockholm, 1903], pp 133–141) was followed by his attempt to confirm his theory of the "migration of the Æsir" in his great book *Die altgermanische Thierornamentik* (Berlin, 1904). He undertook an extremely detailed examination of a category of fibulae along their supposed itinerary. The flimsiness of his historical deductions does not correspond to the precision or scrupulousness of proper archaeological study.

The most remarkable manual based on the thesis disputed here is that of Karl Helm, *Altgermanische Religionsgeschichte,* whose first volume is dated 1913 and the two parts of the second 1937 (*Die Ostgermanen*) and 1953 (*Die Westgermanen*); but the author decided to leave it unfinished. In a certain measure this lacuna is filled by E. A. Philippson, *Die Genealogie der Götter in germanischer Religion, Mythologie und Theologie* (1953). In the meanwhile, in 1925, in the *Festgabe G. Ehrismann,* pp. 1–20, K. Helm published an epoch-making methodological treatise, "Spaltung, Schichtung und Mischung im germanischen Heidentum." A useful discussion brought us into opposition in the *Beiträge zur Geschichte der deutschen Sprache und Literatur*: K. Helm, 77 (1955), 347–365; G. Dumézil, 78 (1956), 173–180. Of course, the discussion is rekindled and will be rekindled without ceasing, and probably without profit. The methods and the thesis of P. Buchholz, "Perspectives for Historical Research in Germanic Religion," *History of Religions* 18, 2 (1968), 111–138, are typical. Everything proceeds as if the author thought that a people who cannot write (not yet!) cannot have a theological system, and, correspondingly, that in reconstructing their history and chronology one can establish a prehistoric religion with the help of archaeological remains. Where would the study of Celtic religions be if one applied such findings to it? Their material vestiges are extremely scanty, and yet it is imperative to assume that their religious doctrines, the mythological and epic material, the legal system, and the like, must have been complex and sophisticated, since the training of future druids demanded so very many years. Only a comparison of the reports in the oldest written, discursive documents (Caesar, the Irish epics, the *Mabinogion*) with the oldest traditions of the other Indo-European peoples permits us to get a glimpse of what this religious and intellectual prehistory must have been.

Among other recent presentations made according to conceptions incompatible with my own, the principal is that of W. Baetke, *Die Götterlehre der Snorra Edda* (*Verhandlungen der sächsischen Akademie*, Ph.-Hist.-Kl., vol. 97, no. 3), 1950. Cf. also the fruitful article of A. Closs, "Die Religion des Semnonenstammes," *Wiener Beiträge zur Kulturgeschichte und Linguistik* 4 (1936), 549–674.

The thesis here maintained—that the Æsir and the Vanir are solidary parts of the same structure—was accepted by Otto Höfler, *Kultische Geheimbünde der Germanen* (1934), p. 295, and by Jan de Vries, in the first edition of his *Altgermanische Religionsgeschichte* [*AGR* 1] (1937), II, 278–279 (comparing the two divine groups to the phratries into which Australian clans are divided, for example). My precise interpretation of the war between the Æsir and the Vanir was formed progressively since 1940; see my *Archaic Roman Religion* (1970), I, 65–78. This interpretation was accepted and amplified in the two great works by J. de Vries and W. Betz; de Vries, *AGR* 2 (1957), I, 208–214 (on p. 212 a reconstitution of the scenario of the war is proposed which has the advantage of justifying the order of the strophes in the *Vǫluspá*; on a less satisfactory proposal of J. de Vries see my *Archaic Roman Religion* (1970), p. 72, line 15), and W. Betz, *Die altgermanische Religion* (1957), col. 2475 and *passim*. Cf. an attempt at conciliation with the theory of two races in E. Polomé, "La religion germanique primitive, reflet d'une structure sociale," *Le flambeau* 4 (1954), 437–463.

Finnur Jónsson (*Altnordische Sagabibliothek* 3 [1894], 180) construes verse 28 (chap. 56) of *Egil's Saga*, cited on page 4, differently and less naturally, but the theological structure remains the same (for the singular verb with a double subject, Njord and Frey, see the end of chap. 4). Bo Almqvists attempt (*Norrön Niddiktning* [1956], I, chap. 2) to establish a close tie between verses 28 (chap. 56) and 29 (chap. 57), and accordingly reduce *landáss* to some kind of sprite, is not convincing. Besides, it is a priori probable that the being named conjointly with Odin, Frey, and Njord is a god of the same rank as they. It may be objected that the expression *landáss* "God of the Land" (or "of the Earth, the occupied soil," in adopting the other sense of *land*, cf. line 2 of the verse) is not attested as a designation of Thor. But then one should recall the ritual behavior of the immigrants arriving in Iceland from Norway: in throwing into the sea the wooden posts consecrated to Thor, they entrusted to him the care of indicating to them the spot where they should debark and "occupy the land" (*landnám*). In this way the god became the responsible protector of their *land*.

On Gefjon see my *Mythe et épopée* II (1971), pp. 273–274.

CHAPTER 2

Fine analysis and bibliography appear in J. de Vries, *AGR* 2 (1957), II, 27–106 (Wodan-Odin), 10–26 (Tīwaz-Tyr), and in W. Betz, *Die altgermanische Religion* (1957), cols. 2485–2495 (Wodan), 2495–2499 (Ziu/Tyr). In these two authors, respectively pp. 25–26 and col. 2495, is a restatement (from O. Bremer, 1894, and W. Krause, 1940) of the etymology of Tyr (**Tīwaz* rather than **Tiuz*). De Vries, pp. 95–97 (based on R. Otto, *Gottheit und Gottheiten der Arier* [1932]) makes a very important comparison of Odin with the Vedic god Rudra, easily reconcilable, given the character of the latter, with the comparison of Odin and Varuṇa. See my *Mythe et épopée* II (1971), pp. 87–95 (and the whole first part, devoted to the hero Starkaðr).

On *Mars Thingsus*, see the study of S. Gutenbrunner, *Die germanischen Götternamen der antiken Inschriften* (1936), pp. 24–40; despite objections, it is still probable (W. Scherer, 1884) that the two feminine divinities with whom this god is associated are related to the names of the two kinds of *thing* known from Frisian legal texts, *bodthing* and *fimelthing* (*Deo Marti Thingso et duabus Alaesiagis Bede et Fimmilene*). On the location of the *thing*, see O. Lárusson, "Hov och ting," *Studier tillägnede V. Lundstedt* (1952), pp. 632–639 (numerous references to the sagas).

Germanic kingship and its relation to the sovereign gods has recently called forth three important studies: O. Höfler, *Germanisches Sakralkönigtum* I (1952); K. Hauck, "Herrschaftszeichen eines Wodanistischen Königtums," *Jb. f. fränkische Landesforschung* 14 (1954), 9–66; J. de Vries, "Das Königtum bei den Germanen," *Saeculum* 7 (1956), 289–310.

The bipartition of the function of sovereignty among the Indo-Europeans, outlined in the first edition of this book (*Mythes et dieux des germains* [Paris, 1939], pp. 35–43), was first developed in my *Mitra-Varuṇa* (1940; 2d ed., 1948; the Germanic data in chaps. 7, 8, and 9). I have subsequently treated it in several essays, notably *Les dieux des Indo-Européens* (1958), chap. 3, pars. 2–4. A book on the theology of sovereignty will appear later (University of Chicago Press); meanwhile, see my *Mythe et épopée* I (1968), pp. 147–157. For a consideration of differing opinions and objections (Thieme, Schlerath, Gershevich) see my articles referred to in *The Destiny of the Warrior* (University of Chicago Press, 1970), p. 53 n. 3. I shall shortly examine, in the *Revue de l'histoire des religions*, the astonishing arguments with which P. Thieme has attacked my thesis (1958). In the meanwhile, see *Journal asiatique* 246 (1958), 67–84, and *L'idéologie tripartite des Indo-Européens* (1958), pp. 108–118. I have not the space here to take up the parallel Ullr-Tyr, still valid (*Mythes et dieux des Germains*, pp. 37–41, and *Mitra-Varuṇa*, p. 145; cf. de Vries, *AGR* 2 [1957], II, 162).

The comparison of the mutilations of Cocles and Scaevola is in my *Mitra-Varuṇa*, chap. 9: "Le Borgne et le Manchot," summarized in *L'héritage indo-européen à Rome* (1949), pp. 159–169. Several points require revision. The present state of the problem was expounded at the Indo-European symposium at Santa Barbara, California, March 19–20, 1971.

CHAPTER 3

The bibliography of the myth of Balder and of Ragnarok is immense. One will find the essential and most modern items in the notes of J. de Vries. *AGR* 2 (1957), II, 214–238 (Balder), 239–405 (Das Weltende). Cf. W. Betz, *Die altgermanische Religion* (1957), cols. 2502–2508 and 2521–2523.

In the French edition of *Loki* (1948), pp. 227–254, I still entertained the interpretation of Balder as a spirit of fecundity in a seasonal cult. The German edition (1959) has rectified this view, in accord with the present chapter. The Mannhardtian theory is also maintained and renewed in F. R. Schröder, "Balder und der zweite Merseburger Spruch," *Germanisch-Romanische Monatsschrift* 34 (1953), 166–183. Cf. my "Balderiana minora," *Indo-Iranica* (Mélanges Georg Morgenstierne) (1964), pp. 67–72.

A definitive critique of this theory has been made by J. de Vries, "Der Mythos von Balders Tod," *Arkiv för nordisk filologi* 70 (1955), 41–60. I had myself rejected it in a course at the Collège de France, and largely with the same arguments, while J. de Vries was writing this article. But the new interpretation of my learned Dutch colleague—the death of Balder as a myth corresponding to a ritual of initiation of young warriors—seems to me to meet as many difficulties. Balder is no more a warrior than he is a god of fecundity, a Vanr. The blind Hoder, an invalid incapable of acting alone, can scarcely be a hypostasis of Odin, even if this illustrious one-eyed god is sometimes called "the blind god." The role and the attitude of Odin in this drama are too constantly in favor of Balder for one to suppose that, in a previous version, he had been responsible for his (Balder's) death. Balder does not "return to life," as he ought to do in an initiation myth, after a simulated death as well as after a real death in an agrarian ritual, and so on.

Balder, whose name signifies "Lord," is indeed Odinish, but he is not attached to the warrior aspect of Odin, but to his sovereign aspect of which he offers a purer conception, presently unrealizable, which is reserved for the future. As for Hoder-Hatherus, it is remarkable, and conforms well with the prehistoric evolution of Germanic ideology, that this incarnation of fate and blind death should be named wih a word that, as an appellative, signifies the "warrior." On other Germanic representations of Fate, see most recently the short but excellent commentaries by J. de Vries, *AGR* 2 (1957), I, 267–273, and of W. Betz, *Die altgermanische Religion,* cols. 2537–2541, and the documents assembled in W. Baetke, *Die Religion der Germanen in Quellenzeugnissen* (1937), 98–110. The distortion of these myths by Saxo was studied in my *Du mythe au roman* (1971), app. II, pp. 159–172 ("Balderus et Høtherus").

The classification of Aryaman among the sovereign gods which is made here, opposes that proposed by Paul Thieme (1938, 1958): v. *Journal asiatique,* 246 (1958), 67–84.

The interpretation of the Pāṇḍava (and of their collective family) has been presented by S. Wikander in his fundamental article, "Pāṇḍava-sagan och Mahābhāratas mytiska förutsättningar," *Religion och Bibel* 6 (1947), 27–39, which Wikander has completed, for the twins, in "Nakula and Sahadeva," *Orientalia Suecana* 6 (1957), 66–96. I have developed it and extended the mythic interpretation to other characters and even to the intrigue of the Indic epic in the first part (pp. 31–257) of *Mythe et épopée* I (see esp. chap. 8, "Anéantissement et renaissance"). I urge germanists who would wish to discuss my unitary interpretation of the murder of Balder and of Ragnarok to read this comprehensive exposé first. On Heimdall see below, chapter 7; on Víðarr see my "Le dieu scandinave Víðarr," *Revue de l'histoire des religions* 218 (1965), 1–13.

CHAPTER 4

On Thor, see the bibliography in the notes of the full account of J. de Vries, *AGR* 2 (1957), II, 107–153; cf. W. Betz, *Die altgermanische Religion*, cols. 2499–2502. The essay of Helge Ljungberg, *Tor, Undersökningar i indoeuropeisk och nordisk religionshistoria* I (1947)—the first since L. Uhland's remarkable book, *Der Mythus von Thor* (1936) —assembles a lot of material, but is based on conceptions of Indo-European religion incompatible with those developed here. One can only hope that, in spite of the burdens of the episcopal office in Stockholm, this distinguished scholar (author of an important book, *Den nordiska religionen och kristendomen* [1938]) will find time to bring the second volume to press. Cf. F. R. Schröder, "Indra, Thor, und Herakles," *Z. f. Deutsche Philologie* 76 (1957), 1 and following.

The myth of Hrungnir has been the subject of two divergent and improbable analyses in the *Festschrift Felix Genzmer* (1952): H. Schneider, "Die Geschichte vom Riesen Hrungnir," pp. 200–210; Kurt Wais, "Ullikummi, Hrungnir, Armilus und Verwandte," pp. 211–261 and 325–331.

On the Vanir, see the bibliography in the notes of J. de Vries, *AGR* 2 (1957), II, 163–208 and 307–313; cf. W. Betz. *Die altgermanische Religion* (1957), cols. 2508–2520.

Njord has also been the subject of several recent studies. The book of E. Elgqvist, *Studier rörande Njordkultens spridning bland de nordiska folken* (1952), developing in extensive detail the thesis of the immigration of Njord's cult into Scandinavia, has given J. de Vries the occasion for a very useful refutation, the scope of which transcends this problem: "La toponomie et l'histoire des religions," *Revue de l'histoire des religions* 145 (1954), 207–230. In *La Saga de Hadingus, du mythe au roman* (1953; rev. ed., 1970: *Du mythe au roman*), I have shown that this person and this saga, in the first book of *Gesta Danorum* of Saxo, are epic reductions of Njord and his myths. In the article "Njördhr, Nerthus et le Folklore scandinave des génies de la mer," reprinted as Appendix VI in *Du mythe au roman*, pp. 185–196, I have proposed an explanation of some difficult points in the record by the analogy of Danish, Norwegian, and Swedish mermen (or mermaids).

In refutation of the attempts to derive the "great gods" from the fertility of specialized "little spirits," see below, chap. 5.

H. Celander, "Fröja och fruktträden," *Arkiv för nordisk filologi* 59 (1944), 97–110, showed that, contrary to appearance, the goddess Freya has nothing to do with certain modern beliefs and practices concerning crops. N. E. Hammarstedt proposed the recognition of a "Ritual of Frey" in certain practices of Swedish weddings, "Kvarlevor av en Frös-ritual i en svensk bröllopslek" in the *Fests krift H. F. Feilberg* (1911), pp. 489–517 (French summary pp. 785–787). A possible but distant reminder of stories on the death and funerals of Frey-Frodhi has been pointed out in my note "La 'Gestatio' de Frotho III et le folklore du Frodebjerg," *Revue germanique* (1952), pp. 156–160, reprinted as Appendix V, pp. 178–184, in *Du mythe au roman.*

Part Two: Minor Scandinavian Gods

CHAPTER 5

Two Minor Scandinavian Gods: Byggvir and Beyla (1952)

No Scandinavian god could have a simpler dossier than Byggvir's: only a single, fairly explicit text. Furthermore, he is an obviously secondary god: as such, he formerly merited only a few lines or a brief remark in the handbooks. But celebrity and importance have come to him, since he presents one of the best observation posts for those who wish to comprehend the evolution and tendencies of mythological studies during a half century. If making this point today[1] requires us to abandon certain other recent views, the lesson to be gained from this is only the more valuable, and we must still express our admiration and respect for the masters who have devoted their care and craft to the scrutiny, appreciation and exploitation of this minuscule figure from the *Lokasenna*, the "Wranglings of Loki."[2]

I. BYGGVIR AND BEYLA

For some time now—we are at the forty-third strophe—Loki has been overwhelming the gods, one after another, with sarcasms that are the

[1] This discussion sums up several lectures that were held at the Collège de France in December of 1950.

[2] It seems that this Eddic poem is from the tenth century, perhaps the ninth, but certain critics place it in the first half of the eleventh. On the spirit of the *Lokasenna*, cf. my *Loki* (1948), pp. 155 ff.: I do not believe that it is the work of a Christian, nor of an "old pagan" who polemicizes against the pagan mythologizers of later times. In all polytheism, in all supernatural anthropomorphism, the gods have their weaknesses, of which the believers can make fun—as the listeners to the Homeric poems did—without impiety or bad intentions. The "Wranglings of Loki" does not have the tone of Lucretius. But the opposite opinion is still maintained by Jan de Vries, *Altnordische Literaturgeschichte* (1941), pp. 171 ff.

more cutting because there is some basis for their malevolence. The inhabitants of Asgarðr are, after all, men like us. Although more powerful than we, they still sin and make fools of themselves, just as we do. Bragi, the goddesses Idun and Gefjon, then Odin, then the goddesses Frigg and Freya, then Njord, and Tyr, and Frey have had certain memories recalled to them. These occasionally contain for us some valuable new facts, but to the gods they are disagreeable and laced with menace. When Loki has finished his sport with Frey, a small character takes the floor, Frey's servant, Byggvir.[3]

43. Byggvir qvað:
Veiztu, ef ec øðli ættac sem Ingunar-Freyr,
oc svá sællict setr,
mergi smæra mylða ec þá meinkráco
oc lemða alla í liðo.

44. Loki qvað:
Hvat er þat iþ litla, er ec þat lǫggra séc,
oc snapvíst snapir?
at eyrom Freys munðu æ vera
oc und qvernom klaca.

45. Byggvir qvað:
Byggvir ec heiti, enn mic bráðan qveða
goð ǫll oc gumar;
þvi em ec hér hróðugr, at drecca Hroptz megir
allir ǫl saman.

46. Loki qvað:
þegi þú, Byggvir! þú kunnir aldregi
deila með mǫnnom mat;
oc þic í fletz strá finna né mátto,
þá er vágo verar.

Byggvir spake:
Had I birth so famous as Ingunar-Freyr,
And sat in so lofty a seat,
I would crush to marrow this croaker of ill
And beat all his body to bits.

[3] Byggvir and Beyla are mentioned in the prose prologue that appears in the manuscripts at the head of the poem. They are named last among the guests of Ægir and qualified as "servants of Frey." There is no important variant for these strophes. The *Codex Regius* (ca. 1270) has *Beyggvir* in the prose prologue and in strophe 45, 1, but keeps *Byggvir* in the citation of the speaker before strophe 43 and in 45, 1, as well as the genitive in strophe 56, 1; cf. below note 25. The originals are from *Edda* (Kuhn), p. 105. The translations are from *Edda* (Bellows), pp. 165–169.

Loki spake:
What little creature goes crawling there,
Snuffling and snapping about?
At Freyr's ears ever wilt thou be found,
Or muttering hard at the mill.

Byggvir spake:
Byggvir my name, and nimble am I,
As gods and men do grant:
And here am I proud that the children of Hropt[4]
Together all drink ale.

Loki spake:
Be silent, Byggvir! thou never couldst set
Their shares of the meat for men;
Hid in straw on the floor, they found thee not
When heroes were fain to fight.

Loki's irony next turns against Heimdall, and then against the goddesses Skadi and Sif. Finally Beyla intervenes in order to announce the end of the jest; Hlorridi, that is Thor, is approaching, and will chastise the insolent one.

55. Beyla qvað:
Fiǫll ǫll sciálfa, hygg ec á for vera
heiman Hlórriða;
hann ræðr ró, þeim er rœgir hér
goð ǫll oc guma.

56. Loki qvað:
þegi þú, Beyla! þú ert Byggvis qvæn,
oc meini blandin miǫc;
ókynian meira koma með ása sonom,
ǫll ertu, deigia, dritin.

Beyla spake:
The mountains shake, and surely I think
From his home comes Hlorridi now;
He will silence the man who is slandering here
Together both gods and men.

Loki spake:
Be silent, Beyla! thou art Byggvir's wife,
And deep art thou steeped in sin;
A greater shame[5] to the gods came ne'er,
Befouled thou art with thy filth.[6]

---

[4] Surname of Odin still not definitely interpreted.
[5] *Ókynia*, literally "monstrosity of a race or of a family."
[6] *Dritin* is very precise: *dríta* is "cacare," *fugladrit* is "bird's dung"; it is the English *dirt* (OE *drit*). The Latin *fritillum* has been adduced, a dictionary word

The couple is well matched, if one is to believe Loki. In any case the husband is as devoted to his master as the servant of a fine home. He calls him by his grand title,[7] speaks of his lineage, his palace: "Ah, if I were the master," he almost says, "I would not fail to . . ."

The insults of Loki were difficult to comprehend at the time of Max Müller, when the two servants, as well as the master, had to be interpreted as part of some great spectacle of nature.

Even the admirable J. L. Uhland—I say admirable because nothing is more intelligent than his *Sagenforschungen*, and many of its pages have not been superseded[8]—and before him that Karl Müllenhoff to whom many good minds are returning today, fatigued with the Mannhardtian atomization of ritual and legend,[9] in short, the greatest names of the school found only poor explanations. Byggvir and Beyla would be the "Bieger" and the "Biegung," the curver and the curved, that is the summer winds that make foliage and flower clusters gently bend and sway. Or, since it was really an impossibility to derive Beyla from the same root as Byggvir, they would be the "Bieger" and the "Buckel," that is, more prosaically, the troughs and the crests of the undulations of waves on the sea in good weather.

---

of uncertain meaning, defined as "a leaking from the dung hill into the midden," as well as the Latin *forio*, "cacare," *foria*, "diarrhea, defecation" (Varro).

7 *Ingunar-Freyr*. This title (cf. again *Yngvifreyr*, mythic ancestor of the Swedish dynasty of the *Ynglingar*) evidently makes reference to a background concept of the *Inguaeones* of Tacitus (*Inguine* in *Beowulf, Ingunar* or *Yngunar* in the *Heimskringla* of Snorri), but has not yet been elucidated with reference to the ending *-ar* of its first term (cf. Jan de Vries, *AGR* 1 (1937), II, par. 221 and notes). Axel Kock, "Om Ynglingar," *Svensk Historisk Tidskrift* 15 (1895), 161, had suspected an erroneous division of **Inguna* (genitive plural) *ár-freyr*, "the Freyr [god] of harvest of the *Ingunar*." In one of his last articles, "Ingunar-Freyr," in *Fornvännen* 35 (1940), 289–296, Henrik Schück, following up an old idea of R. Much, saw in *Ingunar* a feminine genitive singular, "of the Inguioness," designating the inevitable Nerthus of chap. 40 of the *Germania* of Tacitus. In 1941, F. R. Schröder entitled one of his learned and original essays "Ingunar-Freyr" (*Untersuchungen zur germanischen und vergleichenden Religionsgeschichte*, I); p. 41 he also proposes: "*Ingwanaz* is the masculine partner, the son and the husband of *NerÞuz-Ingwanō*, the maternal goddess of the earth."

8 I am thinking of the courses that J. L. Uhland gave during his three years of professorship at the University of Tübingen (1830–1833), and which cause one to regret the remainder, political, of his career. The substance of these courses has been collected into several volumes of *Uhlands Schriften zur Geschichte und Sage* published after his death (1862), from 1865 to 1873, by the professors of Tübingen. The lines on Byggvir and Beyla are in Volume VI (1868), page 96, in an analysis of *Lokasenna*.

9 I am thinking of the preface that Karl Müllenhoff wrote in 1884 for the posthumous *Mythologische Forschungen* of W. Mannhardt and in which he admits, correctly, I believe, that, from the time of Tacitus, there existed in Germany systematized religions. The lines on Byggvir and Beyla are in an old article, "Der Mythus von Beovulf," *Zeitschrift für deutsches Alterthum* 7 (1849), 420.

Thus, either the German *Beule* or the Gothic *ufbauljan,* "to swell," was called on to justify the name of the maid servant of Frey.

None of all that was probable, but these explications of detail, given in passing, were carried along and maintained, without much attention from their authors, by the imposing torrent of naturalistic evidence. It is well known how this evidence has vanished.

II. BYGGVIR AND BARLEY

More positive in its principle, the school that disenchanted the myths, that of the *Wald-und-Feldkulte,*[10] took up the problem anew and recognized almost immediately a different piece of evidence, which was more limited but certain: Byggvir is a personification of barley. The Danish folklorist Svend Grundtvig, the editor of the *Folkeviser,* the imposing collection that was to be finished by his student Axel Olrik, stated this fact as early as 1874. In the second edition of his *Sæmundar Edda hins fróða* he attached this note, among very few others, to the forty-fourth and forty-fifth strophes of the Lokasenna:[11]

> Do we not have here a transparent allegory, which would link Byggvir, the nimble servant of Frey, to the Scotch Allan Mault and to the corresponding English Sir John Barleycorn? The peasants beat this figure to death, according to an old drinking song, and then bury him with a ploughshare. When the weather grows warm he comes to life, grasps the beard of his chin, and undergoes a new series of tests—cutting scythe, the heavy flailing, the hard millstone—and finishes nevertheless as a great lord, conqueror of the greatest heroes, winner of women's hearts. This lord is barley, *bygget,* from which the good old beer is made.

From the very start the explication was well founded, both in content and form, and it is astonishing that scholars continued to search elsewhere. In 1895, for example, Wolfgang Golther asked if Byggvir, servant of the god of fertility, was not simply "the peasant."[12] He saw a derivative of the verb *byggva,* an older form of *byggja,* "populate, colonize, inhabit," a derivative that occurs in poetry in several compounds: *jarð-byggvir,* "incola prædii, fundi,"[13] referring to a prince; *lopt-byggvir,* "incola tabulati, inhabitant of a stronghold (or of a ship), gubernator, dux"; *faðm-byggvir,* "incola sinus, inhabitant of

[10] The fundamental work of Wilhelm Mannhardt, a "summary" and the fruit of lengthy research, dates from 1875. In 1858, when he published his *Germanische Mythen,* he gave, understandably, more of the naturalism then fashionable.

[11] Svend Grundtvig, *Sæmundar Edda hins fróða,* 2d ed. (1874), p. 200.

[12] Wolfgang Golther, *Handbuch der germanischen Mythologie,* pp. 234–235. He interpreted *Lokasenna,* strophe 44 ("and under the millstone you will chatter"), as an allusion to the work of the peasant, the servant, at the mill.

[13] I give the translations of Sveinbjörn Egilsson, *Lexicon poeticum antiquae linguae septentrionalis* (1860), s. vv.

the bosom, husband . . ." But, besides the fact that this word *-byggvir* is not found outside of such compounds,[14] it is obvious that it means only "the inhabitant of," not "the peasant."

"Byggvir-barley," *Byggvir-bygg*, takes into account almost all the details and ironies of the text, or at least all those that an uncertainty of vocabulary does not obscure. Here is how I believe they can be interpreted.[15]

1. a) Byggvir, grain of barley, is truly a "little thing" (44, 1.).

b) The neuter *þat et litla*, whose contemptuous intention is moreover certain (M. Olsen, H. Gering, N. Lid), must have greatly amused the listeners because *bygg* is a *neuter* noun.

2. a) It is only fair to say about barley grain *und kvernom klaka*, "and under the millstone you will chatter."

b) Conversely, "Barley" covers himself with ridicule when he says: "If I were my master, I could *crush* that sinister crow finer than marrow." The verb he employs, *mølva*, corresponding to the Gothic *ga-malwjan*, "to crush," is a hapax in Old Norse literature, but exists in modern Icelandic in the sense of "to reduce to crumbs." Magnus Olsen has heard it used about a stream that has eroded its bed (*mölva og brióta*). The Icelanders could not help being aware of its synonym *mylja* (from **mulwjan*), but also words of more exact meaning, from the same root, which the little "Barley" would have done better not to evoke in his boasting: *mala*, "to grind," *mjǫl*, "flour."

3. The listeners must have been amused to hear "Barley" say: "If I were of as noble extraction as Frey is, if I had as he does a rich dwelling . . ." (43, 1–2). His own extraction is from an ear of grain; his dwelling is the mill or the vat for mashing and brewing.

4. a) In return, "Barley," raw material of beer, has good reason to be proud (45, 3–5) when he sees the gods drink the good brew that they owe to him.

b) He can be proud also that the gods and men call him "nimble, lively," *bráþr* (45, 1–2), not only because it corresponds to the spirit produced by beer (M. Olsen), but also because the listeners were perhaps aware that the root of the word is the same as that of the verb that denotes brewing, *brugga*, "to brew, brauen."[16]

5. Scandinavian drinking feasts, like those of the Celtic epic tra-

---

14 Cf. the plural *-byggjar* "inhabitants," also found at the end of compounds.

15 The interpretations 1b, 2b, 6, and 7b are presented here, I believe, for the first time.

16 That of the Latin *fervere*, "to boil," and the Celtic *Borvones* (Bourbonne-les-Bains, Bourbon-Lancy, etc.).

dition, are the scenes of struggles of precedence, of boasting, which can quickly turn into quarrels—the *Lokasenna* itself is such a contest—and Loki has a trump card when he responds to the little "Barley":

"You never knew how to divide (correctly, peacefully) the fare among (convivial) men." Loki has twice before used this formula *þú kunner aldrege*, "you never knew how to . . . " (22, 1; 38, 1), saying to Odin, the sovereign god who decides victory, "you never knew how to settle battles *(deila víg)* among men (combatants), and you have given the victory many times to the ones who should not have been granted it!" Loki then says to Tyr, the god of justice, "You never knew how to bring reconciliation between two (men in legal conflict)!" In both these cases, and consequently also in the case of Byggvir, Loki reproaches a *specialized* god for not having handled or directed men well *in his special domain*, be it battle, conflicts of *þing*, or drinking of beer.

6. Loki adds, "And when men do battle, you are never to be found among the straws of the *flet*." *Flet* refers to the bench attached to the wall on which straw is strewn (verb *stráa*).[17] Byggvir would appear to be reproached here for cowardice, but this is only the comic interpretation of a material fact, normal and inevitable, in the context of *bygg*, barley itself, not the character Byggvir: *there is no more barley grain in the straw that is spread out on the benches*; the barley grain is in the beer that creates the quarrels, not in the straw on the seats. And naturally the poet plays also on the sense of the preposition "í," the expression *í flets stráe* meaning "*on* the straw on the bench" when the guest is concerned, and "*in*" this same straw when grain is concerned.

7. In summary, only the second and third verses of the forty-fourth strophe do not immediately explain themselves by the civil status of the character.

a) The first contains the clash of the words *snapvíst snapa*. The verb *snapa* properly means "schmarotzen, to be a parasite," but Nils Lid states that it is used in a broader sense in modern Icelandic, for example when speaking of animals who graze on a rare herb in the frozen earth. No doubt the exact nuance of the word still escapes us.

b) As for the second, "At Frey's ear you will always be," it is probable that it can be clarified by a ritual or figurative usage. Through descriptions of Lapp practices gathered in the seventeenth

---

[17] Cf. in the Poetic *Edda* (Kuhn), *þrymskviða*, 22, 2: for the arrival of the false Freya, the stupid Thrym says to the giants who serve him: "Get up, giants, and put the straw on the benches *(stráeþ bekke)*!"

and eighteenth centuries, which continued in large part practices borrowed from Scandinavian paganism, we know that various more or less repugnant objects associated with fecundity were hung on Frey's idol, *Veralden Olmay*. Perhaps, although it is not declared in our sources, clusters of barley were also hung there? In fact, in the famous report of Johann Randulf[18] the missionary, known as the "manuscript of *Närö*," 1723,[19] the following is stated:

> They have a second idol, besides *Horagalles*, that is, Thor or Jupiter, whom they call *Weralden Olmay*,[20] that is the "man of the world," who is the same as Saturn. They decorate this idol with the magic drums that have, above the head, a curved line with several hooks, all of which are supposed to represent fecundity as much of the earth and sea as of animals. They pray to it that the barley may grow well in the country and that they may buy beer, alcohol, and all that which is made with barley. That is what they want to signify with the hoe he holds in his hand and with which he must dig the ground of Restmand (this is what they call Christ) when the seed is sown.

No doubt, the curved line garnished with hooks which one sees on the drums of the Lapp sorcerers is in fact a cluster of barley. Sometimes it dominates the character planted near it, leaning above his head,[21] sometimes he raises it in his right hand and, quite correctly, the height of the cluster, bent back, is "at his ear," *at eyrom Freys*.[22] It is thus probable that the allusion in the *Lokasenna* and the figures of the drums are explained by the same cult practice, a similar decoration of the idol.

---

18 This intelligent Pietist missionary has been reproached for mixing what he knew from his personal investigation with what he took from either his master Thomas von Westen or his colleague Jens Kildal, and for having confused nomadic and sedentary Lapps, exaggerating the Scandinavian characteristics of Lapp mythology. His report, the original of which is lost, but of which multiple copies still exist, is nonetheless extraordinarily important. On this alone are founded the articles of Axel Olrik, "Nordisk og lappisk gudsdyrkelse" (*Danske Studier* [1905], 39–63), and "Tordenguden og hans dreng i lappernes myteverden" (*Ibid.* [1906], 65–69), which clarified in such convincing manner traits of Scandinavian paganism through Lapp survivals.

19 The report of Johann Randulf was among the first published, when J. Qvigstad decided to make the observations of the old missionaries generally accessible. See J. Qvigstad, *Kildeskrifter til den lappiske Mythologi* (in the *Skrifter* of the Kgl. norske Videnskabernes Selskab of Trondhjem [1903], 1). The lines cited here are from page 101. They have been translated into German in K. Krohn, *Lappische Beiträge zur germanischen Mythologie* (*Finnisch-Ugrische Forschungen* [1906]), p. 169.

20 Adaptation and partial transcription of the title of Frey, *Veraldar goð* (*Ynglingasaga*, chap. 10, end), "the World God."

21 For example, J. A. Friis, *Lappiske Mythologi* (1871), no. 1, between pp. 30 and 31; the figures are quite realistic.

22 *Ibid.*, no. 10, between pp. 44 and 45; here the art is very abstract.

As the description of the *Lokasenna* agrees indeed with "Barley" personified, the derivation of the name is no less perfect. The Old Icelandic neuter *bygg* comes from a theme **biggwu-*, **beggwu-*[23] from common Germanic **bewwu-*, which produced elsewhere the Old Saxon *beo*, "harvest," the Anglo Saxon *béow*, "cereal grain." The masculine *Byggvir* is derived from it in the same way as a large number of names of characters in the two Eddas are, from appellatives in all three genders: *Eldir*, one of the servants of Ægir, who is the host when Loki makes his sarcastic accusations, is fire, *eldr*, personified. Ægir himself takes his name from that of running water, *á* (feminine), which is the Gothic *ahwa*, "stream," the Latin *aqua*. The giants *Ǫrnir* and *Brimir* are eagle, *ǫrn* (masculine), and the roaring sea, *brim* (neuter).[24] Moreover we find here, usually in a possessive sense, a quite common type of derivation: *hallr*, "large stone," gives *hellir*, "cavern"; *hjalmr*, "helmet," gives *hilmir*, "chief, prince," and so forth.[25]

Thus no doubt exists concerning the nature of Byggvir. But, once that is recognized, how should such a personification be interpreted? Several directions are possible and have been followed.

Certain scholars, such as Axel Olrik in 1905,[26] have thought that the name, which is found nowhere else, and consequently the character, must be only a pleasant conceit of the poet of the *Lokasenna*. Because the derivation from *bygg* is transparent, he did not risk seeing his allusions lost.[27] He would thus have exercised his ingenuity on the theme of "the career of the barley," as our school readers present the instructive adventures of a grain of wheat, as the Scotch and English ballads recalled by Svend Grundtvig develop the "passion" and glory of Allan O'Maut and of Sir John Barleycorn,[28] as the

23 The theme in *-u* appears only in the dative of *bygg*, *byggvi*.

24 Without forgetting one of the most interesting, *Kvasir* (personification of a fermented drink), from *kvas*: E. Mogk, *Novellistische Darstellung Mythologischer Stoffe Snorris und seiner Schule*, in the *Folklore Fellows Communications* 51 (1923), 24–25; cf. my *Loki* (1948), p. 98.

25 Magnus Olsen, in his *Hedenske kultminder i norske stedsnavne I* (Videnskabsselskabet i Christiania, II Hist.-fil. kl. 1914, 4), p. 107, says that, in a course, Sophus Bugge had legitimized the occasional variant of the *Codex Regius* (see above, note 3), *Beyggvir*. He thought it was an approximative notation of **Bøggvir*, which he explained by the Swedish dialect form, Dalecarlian *bägg* "barley" (although Swedish has *bjugg*). That is excessive precision, and *Beyggvir* doubtless does not need to be justified.

26 Axel Olrik, "Tordenguden og hans dreng," p. 139.

27 This against Chambers, *Beowulf* (see below, n. 63), p. 299 n. 2.

28 In the poem of Robert Burns (1759–1796):

A miller used him worst of all,
For he crushed him between two stones . . .

cf. Jamieson, *Popular Ballads and Songs* (1806), II, 239 ff.

edifying poets of the German Reformation illustrate the trials of the poor Christian by "the seventeen sufferings of linseed,"[29] as finally many unexpected and personal applications from our times have been made of the evangelical image, "except a corn of wheat die . . ." (John 12,24).

Other authors, and Axel Olrik himself five years later, preferred approaches that they judged to be more productive. The "Vegetations-geister," the "Spirits of the Corn," were in vogue. Through them it was hoped to find a means of exploring the oldest, but at the same time the most vital depth of European paganism. Byggvir offered a choice topic. But, before taking up these vast perspectives, we must assure ourselves that the wife given Byggvir by the poet, who proved so embarrassing to the disciples of Max Müller, fits in with the happy cereal restoration of her husband. Just who or what is Beyla? Let us state immediately that her case is more difficult and that she has not yet been explained in a satisfactory manner.

III. BEYLA

In the wake of his discovery, Svend Grundtvig proposed:[30] "The wife of Byggvir, who is qualified with *deigja*,[31] that is, properly, with 'one who kneads,'[32] must be either the foam or the yeast of beer." Both of these identifications are improbable. Next to Byggvir, one would expect a concept on the same level, and foam is definitely not on the same level as barley.[33] Further, one would expect an independent notion, one comparable to barley but not, however, one which has the same result, as yeast does. Furthermore, "to ferment" is not "to knead."

Twenty years later, E. Sievers recognized in *Beyla,* which he explained by **Baun-ilō,* a personification of the bean,[34] thus putting

---

29 Bibliography in J. Bolte, *Andreas Tharäus, Klage der Gerste und des Flachses,* in the *Schriften* of the Society of History of Berlin, 33, 3 (1897), 35–68; cf. C. M. Edsman, "Gammalt och nytt om sista kärven och årets äring," *Rig* (1949), I, 23–25. After the four days of steeping (retting), "Linen" (Lein) himself narrates in the poem of a Brandenburg pastor (in 1609; Bolte, p. 53):

> Wann dann im Leib die Knochen mein
> Gar weich und fast verfaulet sein,
> Als kommen bald her ungebettn
> Die Mägde wiederumb getrettn . . .

30 Grundtvig, *Sæmundar Edda,* p. 200 (see above n. 11).

31 Strophe 56, 4.

32 Svend Grundtvig says *bagerske* "Bäckerin."

33 The foam appears here as a curious cropping up of naturalism in vegetal mythology.

34 E. Sievers, *Grammatische Miscellen,* 8: "Altnord. Vali und Beyla," in the *Beiträge* of H. Paul and W. Braune, 18 (1894), 582 ff.

"Frau Bohne" beside "Herr Gerstenkorn." They are two good servants, homogeneous and yet autonomous, of the general god of fecundity. And such a personification is conceivable. Did not Walther von der Vogelweide amuse himself a few centuries later, by speaking of "Mrs. Bean?"[35]

> Waz êren hât frou Bône
> daz man sô von ir singen sol?
> si rehtiu vastenkiuwe!

In this perspective, the qualification *deigja*, "Teigmacherin," or "Bäckerin," can be explained: she evokes the thought of the "cake" of Epiphany, which closes the twelve days of winter. Is not the "bean" hidden there which well merits being called *dritin*, dirty, in a jesting and malevolent sense, when it later is found, sticky with dough?

This amusing interpretation meets with three major difficulties. As for the content: no matter what Sievers suggests, and although the name of the bean is indeed Common Germanic,[36] and although the plant has been cultivated in Scandinavia since the first centuries of our era, perhaps earlier,[37] it is impossible to put it on the same plane in life, religion, or ideology, as barley, which is a truly essential item of cultivation, without which there would be neither bread nor beer.

As for the content again: the custom of the "bean in the cake," the oracle of the bean, only penetrated into Germany, as Sijmons[38] has reminded us, under the influence of Greco-Latin practices. Thus it is unlikely that around the time when the *Lokasenna* was composed it could have been installed firmly enough in the Nordic countries—

---

[35] In the edition of *Walther von der Vogelweide* by Wilmanns (4th ed. by Michels; 1942), II, 102, and the important commentary.

[36] Old Icelandic *baun* (genitive *baunar*), Old English *béan*, Old Saxon and Old High German *bôna*; cf. the Frisian island of *Baunonia* in Pliny, IV, 94. The word is thus Common Germanic, although the plant is imported, and it does not overlap the name that is found in Latin (*faba*, cf. Basque *baba*) and in Balto-Slavic (Old Prussian *babo*, Old Slavic *bobŭ*), from which H. Petersson was right in separating it in "Etymologien," *Indogermanische Forschungen*, 23 (1908–1909), 390.

[37] Joh. Hoops, *Reallexikon der germanischen Altertumskunde* 1 (1911–1913), 301–302, s.v. *Bohne*, is very peremptory, because of the common Germanic word: "The absence of deposits of beans in the archaeology of Northern Europe before the great migrations is only due to chance."

[38] H. Gering and B. Sijmons, *Kommentar zu den Liedern der Edda* (1927), I, 304, which makes reference to Stemplinger, *Antiker Aberglaube in modernen Ausstrahlungen* (1922). Cf. the *Handwörterbuch des deutschen Aberglaubens* of H. Bächtold–Stäubli, I (1927), the articles *Bohne* (by Marzell) and *Bohnerkönig* (by Sartori) with the bibliographies.

and under paganism!—to support by itself *all* the malignant allusions Loki makes concerning the character of Beyla.

And finally with regard to form, the derivation of Beyla from *baun* with loss of the *n*, although it is clear to modern linguists, would risk remaining misunderstood by the listeners to the poems since it is far less clear than the transparent derivation of Byggvir. In this case the irony of *deigja* and *dritin* would be lost. Short of admitting that Beyla was a traditional and well-known personification of the bean, which would face the first basic objection just made, and vexingly recalls the "mysteries of the fig," invented at the beginning of the century by Salomon Reinach to explain *sycophante* in the light of *hiérophante*.[39]

Twenty years later still, Magnus Olsen proposed the derivation of *Beyla* from *baula*, "cow."[40] He saw in *Beyla* "milkmaid," a sort of living résumé of the tasks of cattle raising. Sophus Bugge furnished him with this solution in a still-unpublished lecture, as did a very recent work by the Icelandic scholar F. Jónsson.[41] This would clarify the word *dritin* immediately: the woman who works with cattle and doubtless also with the spreading of dung on the land is surely "dirty." As for *deigja*, if it is not explained here with its proper meaning "one who kneads," we must not forget that this word is extended to cover all varieties of servants in Old Norse and in rural dialects (*sæter-*, *rakster-*, *bakster-*, *reiddeigja*). It is particularly used in the compound *budeie*, "Milchmädchen, milkmaid," as also in the Swedish *deja*, *mjölkdeja*.[42] Perhaps the poet used it here already in its general sense. Magnus Olsen concluded:

> The two servants of Frey (*Freys þjónustumenn*, as the *Lokasenna* says in the prose introduction), the couple Byggvir-Beyla, represent the two principal aspects of Frey's activity. This god oversees the prosperity of all that lives and is simultaneously master of agriculture and of cattle raising. Thus it is fitting for him to have two servants whose names make reference, one to the cultivation of grain, the other to the care of cattle.

An eminent disciple of Magnus Olsen, Nils Lid,[43] has added that Byggvir and Beyla, understood as Barley and Cowmaid, evoke the

39 Salomon Reinach, *Cultes, Mythes et Religions* (1908), III, 92–118 reprinted from his article, "Sycophantes," *Revue des études greques* (1906), pp. 335–358.

40 Magnus Olsen, *Hedenske Kultminder*, p. 109.

41 F. Jónsson, *Goðafræði* (1913), p. 74.

42 Cf. also the English *day-woman* (Anglo-Saxon *dæge*).

43 Nils Lid, *Joleband og vegetasjonsguddom* (in the *Skrifter* of the Oslo Academy, Section on History and Philosophy [1928], 4), p. 147.

old rural division of labor between the sexes, which has long been attested in Scandinavia. Agriculture there is man's task, whereas women deal with cattle.

This explanation, too, meets with difficulties. Beyla, cowmaid, *woman* working with cows, is not homogeneous to Byggvir, *barley* personified. Rather more logical would be a couple "Milk (or Cow)-Barley," or a couple "Milkmaid-Brewer." The great disproportion of figure between these two beings makes their linking as husband and wife somewhat strange. To give the Eddic hapax *deigja* the broad meaning of "servant" which the word later acquired is also not satisfying. The Eddic language had other ordinary words to designate "servant," and, in a text like this one, in which all the interest is focused on the precision of the allusions, *deigja* must have been chosen for a nuance of meaning, for its clear relationship with *deig,* "dough (German "Teig").[44] The word *baula* itself,[45] the noun for "cow" on which the whole explication is based, is not usual enough for the poet to have been certain that the derived *Beyla* would be understood. Finally, a priori, the final *-la* has a good chance of being the suffix of a feminine diminutive (**-ilō*), as Sievers had thought, since these are frequent in Eddic proper names. There are, for example, the giantess Hyndla, "the little bitch," (**hund-ilō*); the giantess Bestla (daughter of *Bǫlþorn,* "thorn of evil"), who is without doubt **bast-ilō,* from *bast,* neuter. "interior part of the bark of the linden tree, or a cord made from this material"; Embla, the first woman, created from a certain tree (and married to Askr, "the ash tree"), which no doubt comes from **elmla, *alm-ilo,* "the little elm." The couple Byggvir-Beyla, with only the feminine noun being a diminutive, must be in some way comparable to the couple who were the first human beings, born of the ash and the elm, *Askr* and *Embla.* All these reasons make the interpretation of the learned Norwegian somewhat unlikely.

---

[44] From a root signifying "knead, shape"; that of the latin *fingere, fictile,* of the Greek *teikhos* "wall," and so on.

[45] See Ferd. Detter, "Zur Ynglingasaga, Freyr and Loki," in the *Beiträge* of H. Paul and W. Braune, 18 (1894), 88–89. *Baula* is a proper name for cow, but from words such as *baulufall,* "carcass," lit. "ruin of Baula," and *baulufótr,* "foot of Baula" (a nickname), Detter concluded that *baula* was also a generic term for "cow." A. Noreen, *Abriss der germanischen Lautlehre* (1894), p. 94, connects the feminine Baula with *boli,* "bull" (cf. *bylja,* "to bellow or low?" or cf. Greek *phallos*??), through which Detter also wants to explain the surname of Frey, *Belja dólgr* "the enemy of Beli." Beli would be a bull; one would thus compare the death of Frotho III killed by a sea cow (Saxo), with that of the King Egill killed by a bull (*Ynglingasaga*), and the like; there is no limit to such transformations.

IV. BEYLA AND THE BEE

I think that these inconveniences can be escaped through a simpler explanation, which has not yet been proposed.

Closest to beer, conceptually speaking, is the other fermented drink that the Scandinavians loved, mead. The sequence "barley-malt-beer" corresponds to the sequence "bee-honey-mead." The size of the two basic elements is of the same order, the use and effects of the two products are comparable and their being attributed to Frey's province (food, pleasure) equally natural.

Now, from the point of view of form, *Beyla* can be a diminutive of the Old Icelandic word for bee, *bý*, without the disfiguring loss of a consonant, and therefore transparent and immediately comprehensible.

This word *bý* is itself a strange form, a frozen neuter plural, which is usually interpreted as coming from **bíu*,[46] the normal plural of **bí*, which corresponds to the word presented by the other Germanic languages, directly or in derived forms: for example, the Old High German *bîni* (neuter), *bîna* (feminine), *bîe*; Old Saxon *bî-*, Dutch *bij*, Anglo Saxon *béo*, English *bee*. With other derivations the word is found outside of Germanic languages; definitely in Latin (*fucus*, "hornet"), surely in Irish (*bech*), in Baltic (Old Prussian *bitte*, Lithuanian *bitis*), in Slavic (Old Slavic *bičela*, a double diminutive from which the Russian *pčela* comes).[47]

The form *Beyla* seems to be a diminutive in *-la* (from **-ilō*) of this word for "bee."[48] The vocalism of the first syllable should not

---

[46] According to K. F. Johansson, "Indische Miszellen," *Indogermanische Forschungen*, 3 (1894), 225–226. Cleasby-Vigfusson, *An Icelandic-English Dictionary* (1874), thought that one has *bý* for **bí* "because perhaps an etymology from *bú* (household, farming) floated before the mind, from the social habits of bees"; this is quite unlikely. The usual form for "bee" is the compound *by-fluga* "bee-fly"; a poem from the Egilssaga calls air *byskip* "the vessel of bees," and arrows *unda bý* "the bees of wounds."

[47] The Vedic Nāsatya are the great "healers" (even in their name; cf. German *ge-nesen*), notably by the medicine from plants; but mead, *madhu* (same word as Old Icelandic *mjǫðr*), is variously associated with them.

[48] Despite Johansson, "Indische miszellen" (above, n. 46) it is doubtless not necessary to introduce here the Swedish (Dalecarlian) *billa, bylla, bylja, bölja, böla*, etc. (cf. Helsinglandish *bolla*) "wasps' nest," but, more generally, "little construction," or "heap." Sophus Bugge, *Svenska Landsmålen* IV, 2, 227–228 seems to be right in seeing in these the root of the Old Icelandic *búa*, "to set in order; to live in," and of the German *bauen* "to construct" (for the evolution of this meaning, cf. Latin *favus*). It is even less necessary to compare the Scandinavian name of the bee with the Norwegian (standard language and dialects) *bille* "insects in general," which corresponds rather to the English "beetle."

be pressed too much; the *-ey-* is perhaps as approximate (instead of *ý*) as the *-ey-* of the bad variant Beyggvir[49] of *Byggvir*. But it is also possible, since nothing can be definitely affirmed without exactly superposable examples, that an old **biu-ilō* could give not **Býla* but *Beyla*.[50]

As for the content of the matter, the diverse pejorative allusions that Loki makes concerning Beyla's nature are quite comprehensible if she is "Bee."

1. Just as beer and with it barley are responsible for quarrels (46, 1–2), so mead, no less intoxicating, and with it, the bee, justifies the expression *meini blandin mjǫk* (56, 2), "greatly mixed with evil." This expression is certainly vague;[51] indeed, in the same poem, Loki was able to apply it to Freya (32, 2) with regard to her sexual conduct. But it is noteworthy that by taking the verb *blanda* in its proper material sense, "to mix," it is particularly adapted to mead. In the beginning of the *Lokasenna*, as he forces his way into the banquet hall, Loki announces to the servant Eldir: "I am bringing to the sons of the Æsir uproar and quarrel, *ok blentk þeim svá meini mjǫþ*, and I am going to mix their mead with malice!" The adjective *meinblandinn*, "mixed with evil, poisoned," is an epithet of *mjǫþr* in the *Sigrdrífumál* (seventh and eighth strophes in the form in which it is cited in the *Vǫlsungasaga*).

2. *Deigja*, "one who kneads," is best applied to the insect capable of molding a beehive.

3. *Dritin*, "dirty," is only a derogatory expression for a definite trait[52] of the worker bee when it returns to the hive soiled with pollen and vegetal fragments.[53] Like the Greeks and Romans, the ancient Germans were ignorant of the true process behind the fabrication of honey and wax. In a famous page,[54] Pliny the Elder shows honey al-

---

49 See above, n. 3 and 25.

50 One could also think of the analogous action of strongly linked morphological pairs such as *drjúpa* "to drip," and its causative *dreypa* "to cause to drip," *bjúgr*, "curved," and its derivative *beygja* "to curve."

51 It could also be alleged that the bee stings and is venomous; cf. the sense of *meinblandinn* "poisoned," in the text I cite below (*Sigrdrífumál*).

52 Cf. Greek *konisis*, according to Aristotle, *Historia animalium*, X, 40, almost a synonym for *kêrôsis*, *melligo*; it comes from *konis*, "dust." See Olck, s.v. "Biene" in A. Pauly and G. Wissowa, *Real-Encyclopädie der classischen Altertumswissenschaft*, Vol. III (Stuttgart, 1897), cols. 440–441.

53 Folklore and children's books use this trait. I take a random example from recent reading. In a Georgian "first book," *Deda Ena*, I find this little fable, in prose: "The butterfly and the bee," which we know well in the Occident; the beautiful butterfly says to the bee who is returning fully loaded to the hive, "Watch out, soiled one (*thkhupnia*), do not dirty me!"

54 Pliny the Elder, *Naturalis historia*, XI, 12, end: sive ille est caeli sudor, sive

ready formed in the sky as part of sublime *excretions*, descending to the earth in stages, each of which dirties it, and of which the bee is only the last. This dirtied substance nevertheless provides one of the purest of pleasures. Scandinavian folklore,[55] and Germanic in general, still knows of the "honeydew" that is gathered up by laying out cloths during the night of the summer solstice and to which many precious qualities as remedies and also as yeast are attributed.[56] But with regard to the allusion of our text, there is something more precise. The *Edda* knows that the beautiful substance that is our honey contains in fact celestial filthiness. The *Vǫluspá*, right after describing the genesis of the first human couple from two trees, evokes through the seeress the "World Tree" (str. 19):

Asc veit ec standa, heitir Yggdrasill,
hár baðmr, ausinn hvítaauri;
þaðan koma dǫggvar, þærs í dala falla,
stendr æ yfir, grœnn, Urðar brunni.

An ash I know, Yggdrasil its name,
With water *(auri)* white is the great tree wet;
Thence come the dews that fall in the dales,
Green by Urth's well does it ever grow.[57]

Snorri comments on it in these terms:

It is said further that the Norns who live near the spring of Urð draw water from the spring every day, and along with it the *aurr* that is deposited around the spring, and they besprinkle the ash so that its branches shall not wither or decay. But that water is so holy that everything that comes into the spring becomes as white as the film (that is called *skjall* "skin") which lies within the eggshell . . . The dew which falls from it to the earth is called honeydew (*hunangfall*) by men, and the bees feed on it.[58]

---

quaedam siderum saliva, sive purgantis se aeris succus, utinamque esset et purus ac liquidus, et suae naturae, qualis defluit primo! Nunc vero e tanta cadens altitudine multumque, dum venit, sordescens, et obvio terrae halitu infectus, praetera a fronde ac pabulis potus et in utriculo congestus apium (ore enim eum vomunt), ad haec succo florum corruptus et alveis maceratus, totiesque mutatus, magnam tamen caelestis naturae voluptatem affert. Cf. Vergil, *Georgics*, IV, 1 (aerii mellis caelestia dona), Ovid, *Metamorphoses*, I, 112.

55 Swedish *honungsdagg*, Danish *honningdugg*, Old Icelandic *hunangsdǫgg*; cf. German *Honigtau*, English *honeydew*.

56 Evidence gathered in B. Pering, *Heimdall* (Lund, 1941), pp. 114 ff.

57 *Edda* (Kuhn), p. 5; *Edda* (Bellows), p. 9.

58 *Snorra Edda* (Jónsson), pp. 24–39 (*Gylfaginning*, chap. 6); *Prose Edda* (Young), pp. 45–46.

There has been much discussion concerning the meaning of this *aurr*, which is also found in the myth of Heimdall.[59] The word has, however, a constant sense. Despite the repugnance of many authors, it means only "mire, dirty water, diluted earth."[60] That is what is signified here. And if the honey that the bees bring from the sky comes from the Tree sprinkled with muddy water, the adjective *dritin*, which Loki applies, is unjust but plausible. And the listeners, in light of the mythological origin of honey, must have understood this almost as quickly as they understood *deigja*.

It would seem then that the *Lokasenna*, under the general alimentary power of Frey, associates or rather marries two beings, Barley and the Bee, who furnish men with two appreciated nourishments and above all with the two drinks with which they become intoxicated.

It is difficult to believe that the Bee thus personified in the world of the gods could be anything other than a fantasy of the poet. That, certainly, does not entail that Barley personified should be equally artificial, since the poet could have amused himself by marrying a small, authentic being with an entity of his own fabrication. But neither does that necessitate seeing in Byggvir an important figure of the mythology: the real Scandinavian gods do not have wives deriving from the caprice of authors. This present reflection should be kept in mind in the discussion of the interesting and ambitious hypotheses with which we are now going to deal in returning to Byggvir.

V. BYGGVIR AND PEKO

Since the last third of the nineteenth century, two propositions have tempted scholars concentrating on Byggvir: I have already mentioned the first, of taking him for a late representative of a form of religion more ancient than the one that the rest of the Edda presents, a religion according to the *Wald und Feldkulte*. The second is that of combining humble Byggvir with the hero of the Anglo-Saxon epic, Beowulf, who according to a reasonable but not certain

---

59 *Vǫluspá*, 19, 2, *Lokasenna*, 48, 3.

60 See the good discussion by B. Pering, *Heimdall*, pp. 113 ff., 125 f. (which is not destroyed by the amusing remark of Dag Strömbäck, *Folkminne och Folktankar* 29 [1942], 40). To the authorities whom he cites may be added the valuable dictionary of Björn Haldorsson, *Lexicon islandico-latino-danicum*, written in the eighteenth century and published by R. Rask (Copenhagen, 1814); he gives *aurr* "1) argilla lapidea, 2) lutum"; *aurgaðr* "lutulentus"; *aurmikill* (*vegr*) "via lutosa." The commentary of Gering and Sijmons on *Vǫluspá*, 19, 2 (*Kommentar*, pp. 23–24) is a good example of resistance to evidence adjudged inconvenient, which causes so many problems.

etymology,[61] has "barley" as the first element of his name, and who seems the double of a hero named simply Béow. These two temptations were combined, producing results that were sometimes exciting but obviously weak and on which one cannot insist. Axel Olrik, in the second volume of his inspiring and daring *Danmarks Heltedigtning* (1910), set an example for such flights of the imagination.[62] The *Beowulf* of R. W. Chambers presents the dossier with great moderation,[63] and the feeling he conveys is beyond doubt: short of being content with constant approximations it is impossible to conclude anything about Byggvir from Beowulf or the converse.

It was with greater rigor and clearer, more promising perspectives that Magnus Olsen in 1914 developed in his great book *Hedenske kultminder i norske stedsnavne*[64] an approach he had first proposed in 1909.[65] This work had considerable influence and was saluted as a brilliant stage in the revivification of our studies. The analysis was repeated several times and completed by new comparative methods, but Magnus Olsen had said all that was essential. In what follows, however, in order to avoid an unjustifiable fragmentation, I shall present the documentation not as it was in 1914, but as it has been developed up to today.

In the *Finnisch-Ugrische Forschungen* of 1906[66] a cultivated Estonian, M. J. Eisen, had published a picturesque article entitled "Ueber den Pekokultus bei den Setukesen." He certainly did not foresee the interest he was going to arouse. Thirteen years later, after

---

61 For example, in a completely different direction, the Old English proper name *Béow* has been associated with the Old Icelandic proper name *Bíar* (from **Biawr*, from **Bewar*). One will find the review of proposed etymologies in E. Wadstein, *Beowulf, Etymologie und Sinn des Namens*, in *Germanica, Miscellany in honor of Ed. Sievers* (1925), pp. 323–326, with an unsatisfying, personal solution (*Beowulf* would be "Wind-, Sturmwolf," hence a wind demon).

62 Axel Olrik, *Danmarks Heltedigtning* (1910), II, 256. Furthermore, in spite of the most certain phonetic laws, A. Olrik combines *Béow* with *Bóvi*, a straw figure used in certain Danish popular ceremonies concerned with birth, in the thirteenth century (cf. J. and A. Olrik, "Kvindegilde i middelalderen," *Danske Studier* [1907], pp. 175–176) and with the *Bous* of Saxo Grammaticus, the Danish name of the avenger of Balderus. Cf. Jan de Vries, *AGR* 1 (1937), II, par. 267.

63 R. W. Chambers, *Beowulf, an Introduction to the Study of the Poem with a Discussion of the Stories of Offa and Finn* (1921).

64 Magnus Olsen, *Hedenske kultminder*, pp. 110 ff.

65 In a note to his fine article on the runic inscription on the Fløksand (Nordhordland) knife, in which he convincingly clarified a verse of the *Vǫlsaþáttr* through the words *lina laukaR* of the inscription: see Magnus Olsen, *Bergens Museums Aarbog*, 1909 (Bergen, 1910), p. 30 n. 3.

66 M. J. Eisen, "Ueber den Pekokultus bei den Setukesen," *Finnisch-Ugrische Forschungen* 6 (1906), 104–111.

having gathered new information, he corrected and conscientiously completed his analysis.[67]

In 1551, in the preface to his translation of the Psalms, Bishop Michael Agricola, apostle of the Reformation and the founder of Finnish literature,[68] had reported among the false gods of the Karelians a certain *Pellonpecko,* who favored the growth of barley (*ohra*), next to a protector of rye (*ruis*) and oats (*kaura*), *Wirancannos.*[69] *Pellon* is the genitive of the Finnish word *pelto,* "field," itself a loanword from Germanic.[70] Whatever Pecko is, *Pellonpecko* is obviously "Pecko of the field."

Now the Setukesians are a small group of 16,000 Estonians in the former territory of Pskov, in the extreme southeast of the Estonian domain, who have always lived under Russian domination, escaping that of the Germans and Poles, and who have been able to preserve some striking usages. In this "ethnic reserve," thanks to two skillful collectors of folklore, Eisen had learned of the existence of a spirit of abundance, an idol-talisman called Peko ("with short *e* and geminate *k*").[71]

This talisman is made of wax and has in general the shape of a child—often it is specified, of a three-year-old child.[72] Such a volume of wax represents a certain value, about thirty rubles of that time, and ordinarily a village has only one, the inhabitants grouping themselves into circles for its sustenance, circles "comparable to our reading circles." Each year under conditions that will be specified, the *Peko* changes hands. The man, who is called its "priest," keeps it locked up, protected from the indiscreet, in a chest in his barn.

The *Peko* is the object of five celebrations during the year, the

---

[67] M. J. Eisen, *In Eesti mütoloogia* (1919), translated into German by E. Erkes, *Estnische Mythologie* (1925), where the passage on *Peko* is pp. 115 ff.

[68] Mikael Agricola (1508–1557), student of Luther and of Melanchton in Wittenberg (1536–1539), coadjutant, then bishop of Åbo, first Finnish bishop. On this list of "gods" see K. Krohn, *Das Götterverzeichnis bei Agricola, Folklore Fellows Communications* 104 (1932).

[69] It would perhaps be a bit hasty to explain these names by elements taken from Scandinavian. This interpretation seems to have been rejected today.

[70] Pelto could be the Common Germanic **felþa-* or the Proto-Germanic **felþo-* (see the bibliography in E. N. Setälä, *Finnisch-Ugrische Forschungen* 13 [1913], 424). This would be, in the latter case, one of those rare substantives where the Indo-European *-o* of the stems in *-o* would appear pure, and not already changed into *-a* as in Common Germanic; cf. *jukko-* (*jukka-*) "yoke."

[71] It would therefore be better to write *Pekko,* as in Finnish. But I naturally respect Eisen's orthography.

[72] Eisen reports, however, with an Estonian reference, an aberrant form where Peko must be "furnished with a veal's head and multi-colored."

principal two taking place around the time of planting in the spring and in the autumn after the harvest. Each year, during this last celebration, lots decide the next lodging for the talisman. It is celebrated on a night with clear moonlight; both men and women participate in it. They assemble at the priest's home for worship and they eat and drink from night until morning provisions such as eggs, butter, brandy brought by the members of the "circle." This festival takes place around the *Peko*, which the priest and the two acolytes have solemnly fetched from its coffer, wrapped up like an infant, and which they have placed in the middle of the chamber. At first they eat with their backs to the *Peko*, then they march around it nine times in a circle singing:

> *Peko* our god (*Peko mie jumala*), protect our flocks, protect our horses, protect our crops . . .

Then everyone goes out into the courtyard and a veritable debauchery of violent actions ensues, whose object is to make blood appear, by chance, the accident of a scratch or wound. It would naturally be a sacrilege that no one would commit to feign or to provoke this bloodshed, which must be natural, for it is just this that designates the future guardian of the talisman. As soon as the precious sign has appeared, everyone congratulates the wounded one. They reenter the house to continue the celebration, that is, to drink and to eat. Finally the new priest joyously takes the *Peko* home wrapped in a piece of cloth.

Peko gives benediction and abundance to all who worship him, but chiefly to the household he stays with. Also, he is carefully kept from the deprecating pleasantries of the nonbelievers, who do not hesitate to mutilate him; there has been preserved, in one village, the memory of a veritable "affair of Hermes."

In the spring festival, near the time of planting, only the men participate and they are not allowed to drink brandy, which on this occasion, they say, is made with the "grain of God" (or "of the god?"), *jumala vili*. Discreetly, the *Peko* is taken from the barn and installed in the field to preside over the work from a spot that will later be infused with power: in such "places of Peko" (*Pekokoht*) people used to make offerings, in passing, of salt, grain, flax, and pieces of money. The presence of the talisman assures a rich crop.

Besides this, at Candlemas, *Peko*, well hidden in a rug and placed on a sledge, was supposed to give victory to his guardian in a race. The first Sunday after Easter a communal festival of beer took place, for which the worshippers of *Peko* had already brought their share of the malt to the priest in advance. The drinking took place in front of *Peko,* who was invited to participate and who was asked to protect the cattle and the fields. Finally, during a fifth celebration, the eve of Saint John, men and women in conjunction carry *Peko* to a pasture, offer him butter, milk, and wool, and ask his favor for their cattle raising.

Eisen and Magnus Olsen thought, evidently correctly, that this Setukesian Peko was none other than the Karelian Pellonpecko of Agricola. They thought also that the very general value as protector of rural richness which the first presented is a secondary extension from the protection of barley, specified by Agricola. That too is probable: the great Finnish folklorist E. N. Setälä brought together in 1927 several observations made since 1551 which confirm that particular value of *Pellon Pekko*—with an important variant *Pekka*—but which also show the allurement of generalizations.[73]

It was under these conditions, knowing as yet only the forms in *-o,* that Magnus Olsen proposed to recognize in *Pekko, Peko,* a very old loan from Proto-Scandinavian **beggwu-*, from which comes *bygg,* or else from a closely related form **beggwa-*.

It is known, since Vilhelm Thomsen,[74] that the Finnish dialects are full of words taken at various times from North or East Germanic, from Scandinavian or from a Gothic dialect, the oldest of which are preserved in astonishingly archaic forms: only the initial consonant groups, which are repugnant to Finnish, suffered. Maurice Cahen used to enjoy savoring with his students the Finnish word for ring, *rengas,* where the final *-az* and the radical vocalism *-e-* of the Ger-

---

73 E. N. Setälä, *Sanastaja* (1927), p. 47; a résumé in Norwegian by Nils Lid, *Joleband* (see above, n. 43), p. 148. Following are the four pieces of evidence:

1) In the eighteenth century, C. Ganander, in a manuscript dictionary, names *Pellon Pekka* as the god of barley and grains and attributes him to Tavastland (Tavastehus, today Häämenlinna, northeast of Åbo-Turku). In his *Mythologia Fennica* (1789), Ganander adds that *Pellon Pekka* (or *Pekko*) aids the spring sowing and that he is sometimes called *Pellon maito* "the milk of the field."

2) G. Renvall, *Lexicon Linguae fennicae* (1826) gives *pelto-pekka* (or *-pekko*), which he glosses "spirit of the field," (*peltoin haltia*); he adds that *pekka, pekko* also signifies "animal of the forest," and designates notably the bear and the hare.

3) In modern Tavastland folklore, there are reports of the custom of placing a knife on the slope that separates two fields "so that *Pellonpecko* will not eat the flower clusters"; when barley sprouts unequally, it is said that *Pellonpecko* has eaten the young shoots.

4) In the Finnish *runot* on the planting of barley, one finds *Pekka, Pikko, Pikki* named as clearer of the land. See several facts cited in K. Krohn, *Das Götterverzeichnis* (see above, n. 68), pp. 56–57.

74 Vilhelm Thomsen, *Ueber den Einfluss der germanischen Sprachen auf die finnisch-lappischen, eine sprachgeschichtliche Untersuchung* (1870), in which all the essential evidence has been gathered.

manic **hrengaz* (German *Ring*) are still heard, although they have already been altered in the oldest attested forms (in Scandinavian to *-aR* and *-i-*). In 1936, near Lake Saima, in a "sauna," I personally was amazed to hear the old, warmly wrapped-up woman (who, in the steaming vapor of the reddened stones, was flogging with a birch branch the torso of a young friend who was traveling with me), express her admiration—except for the initial *s*, but with the final **-iz* and the original diphthong—by the very form that would have been used by a consort of Ariovistus before a companion of Caesar's: *Kaunis! Kaunis!*; that is, the Germanic **skauniz* "beautiful" (German *schön*).

As Finnish does not possess voiced consonants except in alternations,[75] a Scandinavian **beggwu* had to result in **Pekku, Pekko.* A related form, not attested to but conceivable, **beggwa,* could give *Pekko,* as the Germanic **felþa* (German *Feld,* etc.) has given *pelto* "field" (Karelian *peldo,* Lapp *bälddo,* etc.). Thus formed from two Germanic words, *Pellonpecko* signifies "the barley of the field," and presents a personification of **beggwu* comparable to *Byggvir* of the *Lokasenna.* The determiner *Pellon* further recalls, as Magnus Olsen noted, the god **Fillinn,* which is revealed by the Norwegian toponomy studied in his book of 1914. This is **Felþinaz,* that is, properly, "(the chief) of the field," as the old Scandinavian *dróttinn* (**druxtinaz*) "king" and the Latin *dominus* are the chiefs of the *drótt* (people) and of the *domus.* This guarantees the authenticity and age of Byggvir.

In detailing his facts, Magnus Olsen pointed out correspondences between the strophes of the *Lokasenna* and the discussion of Eisen, some general, deriving from the name (relationships with barley and beer); others, or rather one other, more specific: the size of Byggvir (*þat et lítla* "this little thing," str. 44, 1) calls to mind that of Peko (dimensions of a three-year-old child). He pointed out that, in the generalized conceptions of the Setukesians, Peko, protecting all the aspects of a rural economy, had been given the scope of the Scandinavian Frey, "is" Frey rather than Byggvir. Now, in the poems of the *Edda,* Frey is the only god whose childhood is alluded to,[76] which is in accord with his nature as patron of fecundity. One might then consider that Frey, **Fillinn, Byggvir* are basically one and the same personage, and that the last more particularly is only an aspect, a surname of the first, more or less precociously detached.

---

[75] "Alexander Street" in Helsinki is *Aleksanterin katu* (Germanic **gatwō*).

[76] *Grímnismál,* 5, 3–4: "In former times, the gods gave Frey Alfheim (house of the elves) as a gift of toothing."

This demonstration was received with—the word is not too strong—enthusiasm: after the light that Axel Olrik had just thrown on Scandinavian cults and myths from Lapp borrowings surviving in the eighteenth century, it proved that Finnish and Estonian folklore made it possible to affirm and measure the importance of Byggvir. I remember the emotion with which my master, Maurice Cahen, in his course at the École des Hautes Études, less than two years before his death, spoke of this triumph. He even went further than the Oslo scholar, whose discovery he interpreted in accord with the systematic views on the development of religions which he held from Durkheim.[77]

VI. PEKKA, PEKKO, AND SAINT PETER

Since then the critics have been at work. Besides his colleague and emulator, the rigorous toponomast of Uppsala, J. Sahlgren, Magnus Olsen found opposed to him linguists, such as B. Collinder,[78] who do not think that, phonetically, *Peko, Pekko* can be derived from the Proto-Scandinavian word from which *bygg* is derived. In point of fact, the final *-u* of **beggwu* (which is the only form to consider, **beggwa* being only an arbitrary construction), would probably not have given a final *-o* in Finnish; *u* is retained. For example, it is the Finnish *sielu,* "soul," which corresponds to the Old Swedish *siæl, sial,* Old Icelandic *sál,* in composition *sálu-,*[79] and *-u* would be re-

[77] Cf. the memoir in which Cahen summed up his 1924 course, "L'étude des paganisme scandinave au XXe siecle," in the *Revue de l'histoire des religions* (1925), pp. 73–75: "the god Frey, who in his majesty assumes the care of all vegetation, succeeded specialized demons of the type of *Byggvir-Pekko,* whose functions were more modest; but he has retained them in his service. . . . Magnus Olsen has well underlined (*Hedenske kultminder,* pp. 112 ff.) the interest that the Finnish documents present. They are the evidence of a religious state already past even when the Eddic tradition began. Pekko shows us the inferior stage of vegetation spirits from whose ranks Frey rose to become a major god. We see here in illuminating fashion how the Finnish tradition clarifies not only an isolated detail, but all the development of vegetation divinities." In the assurance of his Mannhardtian and Durkheimian faith, Maurice Cahen here attributes to his master deductions that, happily, cannot be read in *Hedenske Kultminder.* It is furthermore a fruitful subject of reflection to see how the admirable philologist, rigorous and scrupulous, that Maurice Cahen was, becomes dogmatic, and begins to extrapolate and invent, when he comes to the plane of religious data. Like Salomon Reinach, he arranges them into abstract, simplistic schemes, which permit one to "see" before analyzing and affirm without demonstrating.

[78] B. Collinder, *Die urgermanischen Lehnwörter im Finnischen,* in the *Skrifter* of the Humanistiska Vetenskapssamfundet of Uppsala 28, 1 (1932), 191.

[79] Finnish *paljo,* Estonian *palju* "a lot, multitude" probably have nothing to do with Gothic *filu,* Old Icelandic *fiǫl* (from **felu*). Finnish *pallo* "ball" is not necessarily the Germanic **ballu* (Old Icelandic *bǫllr*): many languages designate round objects with such consonant sounds.

tained here even more firmly because it was confirmed in its timbre by the preceding *-w-*. Besides, Finnish *-o-* alternating with *-a-* (as is known to be the case today in *Pekko, Pekka*) comes in general from Germanic stems in *-a* (Indo-European *-o*):[80] for example in *jukko, jukka* "yoke." Finally, if the name for barley had been borrowed by the Finns from the Scandinavians, it is what would have been used for barley, just as rye is usually designated *ruis*, genitive *rukiin*, borrowed either from Scandinavian (Old Icelandic *rugr*), or Baltic (Lithuanian *rúgys*); but the Finnish word for barley is *ohra*.

For their part, Finnish folklorists have little by little related what is known about *Pekko, Pekka* to a group of indigenous practices and names which separate him from the "little thing" of the *Lokasenna*.

Even in Estonia, talismans comparable to Peko had long been reported.[81] These are wood or wax figurines, kept in the homes, guarantors of the fecundity of fields, as well as that of cattle and men. Their name ordinarily is *Tonnis*, that is "Antonius," because offerings to him are made on Saint Antony's day. But, in certain localities, the offerings take place on Saint Catherine's, or Saint George's, or on other days, too. In these cases the talisman is no longer called *Tonnis* but *Katri* or *Juri*.[82] The first observer of *Peko* himself reported the analogy of the autumnal festival of this talisman with the ritual of Saint Catherine by the other Estonians.[83] Could not Peko be simply the diminutive of the name of a saint?

In 1924, in a note to his work on "double fruits in folk beliefs,"[84] the historian of religion Uno Holmberg reported, among the White Russians of the neighboring territory of Mogilev to the east of Minsk, practices that were analogous, only more Christianized. The wax talisman receives here the form of a taper that every year is lodged at a different farm. While he is being transported to his new location, a song is sung in which the "saint" (who is not specified) is supposed to be thanking the previous host for his hospitality.[85] The Russian

---

80 Cf. above, n. 70.

81 Edwin Jurgens, "Ein weiterer Beitrag zum Tonniscultus der Esten," *Journal de la Société Finno-Ougrienne* 18 (1900), 1–9; in a foreword (p. 2) Max Buch writes: "Grain is sacrificed to it at harvest time, an article of clothing at the birth of each child, and a tidbit of every animal bought or slaughtered; and one prays to it to permit the birth of calves to take place successfully and unhindered."

82 *Ibid.*, pp. 2–3.

83 M. J. Eisen, "Ueber den Pekokultus," p. 106 (above, n. 66).

84 Uno Holmberg, *Doppelfrucht im Volksglauben*, in the *Mémoires de la Société Finno-Ougrienne* 52 (1924) (*Miscellanea E. N. Setälä*), 48–66. As is well known, the late Uno Holmberg had finnicized his name and signed himself Harva.

85 *Ibid.*, pp. 58–59, from A. S. Dembovetzkij, *Opyt opisanija mogilevskoj gubernii*, I (1882), 494.

folklorist Zelenin has also reported, again in White Russia, that the peasants around the time of planting take up as a talisman a wax taper that has been blessed three times: at Candlemas, on Maundy Thursday, and at Easter; they stand it in the grain to be sown, light it, and address their prayers to it; they bring it also into the field, where it is to protect the barley.[86]

The blow that can be foreseen through these facts was given to *Byggvir-Pekko* in 1924 through the efforts of the Helsinki folklorist Kaarle Krohn, in an article[87] where, taking up certain traits reported by Holmberg, he elucidated another Karelian "god" mentioned in 1551 by the Bishop Agricola in the same text in which he spoke of *Pellonpecko*. He cited *Egres*, the one who "creates peas, beans, and turnips, and produces cabbage, flax, and hemp." At the beginning of the twentieth century, in the two Karelias, it was still possible to recover traces of this rather active spirit, under the name *Ägräs, Ägröi*, generally preceded by *pyhä*, "saint," and serving to designate those mystically valuable things, double turnips. Holmberg had suggested that the etymology of this Ägräs be searched for among the saints of Roman Catholicism, without finding it, merely pointing out as an analogy, that the Russian population of the territory of Arkhangelsk makes Saint Onuphre the patron of turnips, because they are sown around the day of his festival. The wished-for saint was discovered by Kaarle Krohn: it was Saint Gregory, whom Agricola himself called *Pyhe Greus* in a prayer published in 1544, and who, by a false division had become *Pyh' Ägrä(u)s*, only to be restored as *Pyhä Ägräs*, or a form of special interest to us, *Pellon Ägräs*, "the Gregory of the field." The latter is invoked, with a very general value as protector, around the planting and mowing times, in the parish of Paltame, which is in eastern Österbotten.[88]

Pellon Ägräs, Pellon Pekko (or *Pekka*) are two expressions that seem parallel. They are, in fact, and completely. In a brief note to his article,[89] after having recalled the talisman of Mohilev reported by Holmberg, and underlining how this White Russian doublet makes the authenticity of Pekko as a *pagan* demon suspect, K. Krohn

86 D. Zelenin, *Russische Volkskunde* (Berlin-Leipzig, 1927), p. 28, cited by Nils Lid in the dossier of Byggvir-Pekko, *Joleband* (see above, n. 43), p. 152.

87 Kaarle Krohn, "Ägräs Gregorius," *Finnisch-Ugrische Forschungen* 16 (1923–1924), 180–185.

88 K. Krohn recalls that other names of "gods" from Agricola's list have also been more or less certainly interpreted as deformed names of saints; *Nyrckes*, who is concerned with squirrels, would be *Jyrki*, Saint George; *Hittauanin* (that is *Huittavainen*), who drives out devils, would be Saint Hubert.

89 K. Krohn, "*Ägräs*," p. 183 n. 1. Reprinted as "Pellon Pekko," in *Folklore Fellows Communications* 104 (1932), 56–57.

gave the long-awaited explanation: *Pekka,* which alternates in folklore with *Pekko,* is in Finnish an ordinary diminutive of *Pietari,* "Peter." *Pellon Pekko/a* is the "Peter of the field," the modifier *Pellon* being perhaps intended to distinguish the farmer's Peter from the fisherman Peter. We are dealing here, he says, with a "paganization" of a character taken from the orthodox calendar, as is also the case with *Iilia,* with whom the chants of the festival of Ingermanland associate him in prayers for prosperity.

In order to make the demonstration complete, it would be necessary to show that in Finnish folklore barley is indeed linked or has been linked with the festival of Saint Peter—for it is incontestable that the initial and proper specialty of *Pekko, Pekka* is barley. To my knowledge, our colleagues in Helsinki have not provided this last link. I cannot substitute myself for them, but I will add to the dossier one fact that by analogy makes the connection quite probable.

It is known that Siberia, peopled in the eighteenth century by colonists from various districts, had preserved for folklorists at the beginning of the century a harvest of valuable survivals that were no longer observed in Europe. Now, in the district of Yenisei,[90] that is, in a climate not too far removed from that of certain provinces of Finland, the two days June 29 and 30, called "Peter's days" or "the Peter and Paul" are not only the festival days of fishermen[91] and the end of the "fast of Peter." They also assume particular significance for the cultivation of barley:

> From this day on (it is said), "the cuckoo strangles on barley";[92] that means that he must stop singing "cuckoo" when the barley has grown into flower clusters, which takes place between Saint John's Day and Saint Peter's Day. If the cuckoo continues to sing, that means that the barley will have unsubstantial grain. Then it is said "the cuckoo has covered it with his cuckoos."[93]

---

[90] Al. Makarenko, *Sibirskij narodnyj kalendarj v etnografičeskom otnošenii* (*Vostočnaja Sibirj, Enijsevskaja gubernija*), forming volume 36 (1913) of the *Zapiski* of the Imperial Russian Geographical Society, Section on Ethnography, pp. 87–92: "Petrov denj" or "Petry-Pavly." On page 88 the author reports that facts similar to those that he records do not appear in the folk calendar of Russia: here as in other cases, Siberia was more conservative.

[91] On the Angara river one must consume at this festival freshly caught fish, notably the red fish from which the soup is made which the Russians call *uxa* and the Siberians *šerba;* at the table, one of the elders of the family addresses both saints with the invitation: "Peter and Paul, sit down, eat bread and salt. To you the wheat flour (*kaša*), to us the glass (*caša*): to you the fish (*rybka*), to us the fish soup (*šerba*)." A missal from 1776 gives, for this day, a formula for blessing the new nets and for the assurance of good fishing.

[92] *Kukuška davitca jačmenem.*

[93] *Kukuška obkukuvala.*

An analogous observation will probably be found some day concerning the origin of the Finnish and Karelian "Peter of the field" and of the patronage he exerts over barley.

VII. BYGGVIR IS NOT PEKO

Upon calm reflection, furthermore, the identification of Byggvir and Peko can only be seductive if it is necessary to admit, as was done a little too easily by the Mannhardt school,[94] that all agrarian spirits and "figures" are more or less equivalent and omnivalent; that, as soon as one has recognized in a mythic or folkloristic figure some limited and precise relationship to a feature or practice of rural economy, one has the right to attribute to this being all sorts of other relationships that are not directly attested.

If one takes the precaution of establishing a systematic parallel between Byggvir and Peko, by tables of what is present and what is not, one will discover that, outside the given initial fact of a relationship to barley (different, furthermore, since Byggvir *is* barley and Peko, a wax puppet, only *protects*, through barley, rural prosperity), and with the beer of the festivals issuing from barley, *the two descriptions have nothing in common.*

The *Lokasenna* only retains about Byggvir, as an "economic act," his passage under the millstone: it is one of the factors in the life of grain which Peko (and Pellon Pekko) does not know. He presides on the contrary over the planting and harvesting of grain, of which neither Loki nor Byggvir himself speaks. For Byggvir there is no allusion to a cultic act or activity (unless, if I am right, his presence by the ears of [the idol of] Frey). It is, on the contrary, the cult that dominates the reports about Peko, with precise rites such as nocturnal celebrations, seasonal festivities (with or without the participation of women), cult associations with contributions, a priest, and the like . . . Nothing about Byggvir makes one think of what Peko essentially is, a talisman that periodically changes its lodging and which must be carefully hidden and occasionally removed from its hiding place. Finally, the small size of Byggvir, which surely makes reference to the dimensions of barley grain, cannot legitimately be equated, as Magnus Olsen proposed, with the size of a three-year-old child, which Peko is said to resemble.

---

94 A good example of these hasty generalizations is the interpretation of the mythical Swedish king *Fjǫlnir* as **FelðuniR*, that is, "spirit of the field," although his legend has no connection with fields or rural life: being drunk, he drowns in a vat of mead. See Wolf Von Unwerth, "Fjǫlnir," in the *Arkiv för nordisk Filologi* 29 (1917), 320–335.

In brief, everything is different. Now, as elsewhere in our studies, even and especially in comparative problems, probability is achieved only through complete and precise measures, through the appreciation of differences as much as similarities.

It does not seem possible, therefore, to maintain the handsome identification of 1914.[95] Magnus Olsen brought enough other riches of scholarship, opened up enough fertile prospects for us to be able to renounce philosophically and without regret a hypothesis that well merited testing and which for thirty years excited the best minds of Norse mythography.

This great effort having come to an end, must we admit that Byggvir, in the *Lokasenna*, is only an amusing and artificial personification, without mythological reality? As for me, this is the interpretation that seems most likely. We have seen artifice issue forth in Beyla, "Bee," his wife. All that he himself says, and all that Loki says, amounts to a description of the behavior of barley grain, or of the temper inspired in men by beer, without religious resonance and without even the shadow of an allusion to a myth, however poor. Now, if one observes the *Lokasenna* in this regard, one will see that all the strophes, except those that concern Byggvir and Beyla, presuppose knowledge of mythological traits—which we either know or do not know—and go beyond the simple definition, or denomination of the character; so that Byggvir, servant of Frey, seems no more of a barley god than Eldir, his colleague and servant of Ægir, seems a "fire god."[96]

Nevertheless, in the light of minute and exciting researches by Nils Lid, one may prefer to believe that the ancient Scandinavians effectively animated the grain of barley into a minor figure under specific circumstances, at the mill, for example. The folklore examples he has gathered[97] are in any case all that has been reported as analo-

---

95 It is useless to attempt a reconciliation, like the one that Nils Lid seems to sketch, *Joleband* (see above, note 43), p. 148 n. 2; *Pekko* would indeed issue from the Germanic **beggwu*, and the variant *Pekka* would be "redone" by false interpretation, on the diminutive *Pekka* from *Pietari*. No: the analogous series *Tonnis, Katri, Jüri, Ägräs*, etc. proves certainly that *Pekko, Pekka* is primarily the name of a saint.

96 On the contrary the mythology attaches to Frey an authentic servant, Skírnir, "the sparkling." He is known from myths, and there is no doubt that he is the one always depicted at his master's side on the drums of Lapp magicians. Similarly Thor the thunder god has an authentic "servant," which gave much pleasure to Axel Olrik.

97 Nils Lid, *Joleband* (see above, n. 43), chap. 6, "Vetle-Gudmund, Kornvette og Kornguddom" ("Little Gudmund, grain spirit and divinity of grain"). The "Vetle Gudmund" (*vetle* "small," dialect variant of *vesle*) makes one think of *þdt et litla* of *Lokasenna* 44, 1. Nils Lid justly remarks that in what the *Lokasenna*

gous to Byggvir, whether they be about personified grain in riddles under the name of "Gudmund" (whose head is cracked by the millstone),[98] or about the *kvernknarren*, spirit of the millstone, to whom the peasant must make an offering or see his wheat mysteriously disappear, and who displays at the same time some traits of a "grain spirit."[99] But this mythology does not go very far: it is always concerned with evanescent figures, linked to an action or a place, whose names are neither ancient nor stable, by-products of that "mythopoeic faculty" that man will never forsake.

And so Byggvir takes up his little place again, the one the poem assigns him. He is not evidence of an older "form" of religion, does not explain or double for his master, has neither produced him nor issued from him by evolution. Barley and the Bee accompany the god of rural economy and the delights that he produces, as elsewhere Love and the Graces escorted Aphrodite, as Pavor and Pallor, perhaps furnished by Greek literature, second the Roman Mars. And with no more importance. If one wishes to understand, in the north, the mythology of fecundity, it is to Freya, Frey, Njord, in brief, to the great gods, today as before the Mannhardtian revolution, that one must address oneself.

"Deux petits dieux scandinaves: Byggvir et Beyla,"
La nouvelle Clio 3 (1952), 1–31.

---

says of Byggvir, aside from allusions to beer, it is the association between this little creature and the mill that comes into play: *und kvernom klaka* (44, 4) recalls the modern onomatopoeic name of the mill spirit *Kvern-knarren*. But this scholar goes beyond the facts when (p. 147) he translates the preceding verse (44, 3) "you *sing* always at Frey's ears" and adds that, in this "umsyngjingi" there may be an allusion to the sound of a mill; the verse itself contains nothing which could justify talking of songs or noise: it simply says "to be (*vesa*) at the ears of Frey."

98 Nils Lid, *Joleband* (see above, n. 43), p. 140, first variant "kløvde hòve pao han Vetle Gudmund."

99 *Ibid.*, pp. 147–148.

CHAPTER 6

The Rígsþula and Indo-European Social Structure (1958)[1]

Since the beginning of research into the three Indo-European functions (magic and juridical sovereignty, physical force, fecundity) and their expressions, a characteristic fact has emerged concerning the Germanic domain which doubly opposes it to the Celtic domain.[2] The Celts, as well the Gauls as the Irish, present in their social organization a formula almost superposable on the Indo-Iranian structure (druids, *flaith* or warlike nobility, *bó airig* or breeders-farmers). But in their theology one observes a complex picture in which it is not easy to find the equivalent Vedic and pre-Vedic lists of patron gods of the same three functions ("Mitra-Varuṇa, Indra, Nāsatya"). On the contrary, the Germanic peoples profess a clear trifunctional theology (presented in Scandinavia as "Odin, Thor, Frey"), but do not divide their societies according to these three functions. Caesar, who knew the Gauls well, was struck by this difference.[3] The Germans, he remarked, have no class comparable to that of the Druids and show little interest in ritual. As they no longer apply themselves to agriculture, only one type of man exists among them, the warrior: *vita omnis in venationibus atque in studiis rei militaris consistit.*[4]

This statement, assuredly too simple and too radical, nevertheless

---

1 These remarks were made in a course at the Collège de France, March 1, 1958. For the text of *Rígsþula* see *Edda* (Kuhn), pp. 280–287; *Edda* (Bellows), pp. 201–216.

2 Georges Dumézil, *Mythes et dieux des Germains* (1939), pp. 6–13.

3 Caesar, *De bello gallico*, VI, 21, 1; 22, 1.

4 *Ibid.*, VI, 21, 3.

brings together the essentials of Germanic originality, at least on the Continent and near the Rhine, for, as far back as one goes, Scandinavia has nourished a peasant mass, conscious of its function, under the sign of the gods Njord and Frey. But even in the north the absence of a sacerdotal class keeps the social structure from being superposable on the Indo-Iranian or Celtic model. In looking more clearly at *Rígsþula,* the famous Eddic poem in which this structure is exposed, or rather formed under our eyes, I should like to show that it can nevertheless be explained on the basis of the Indo-European functional tripartition.

Traveling incognito throughout the world under the name of Rig (ON Rígr)[5] the god Heimdall presents himself in a first house, a very poor one, in which he is met by the couple Great Grandfather and Great Grandmother. He spends three nights there in the conjugal bed and leaves after begetting a son. At his birth this son is named *þræll* "slave (thrall)." His descendants, boys and girls, bear only pejorative names. Rig then presents himself in a second house, more wealthy, where he receives the hospitality of the couple Grandfather and Grandmother. After three nights, he again goes off, leaving Grandmother with child, a son who at his birth receives the name *Karl,* "freeholder." The children fathered by Karl bear names the majority of which make allusion to peasant life and one of which, *Smiðr,* is even the word meaning "artisan (smith)."[6] The names of his daughters, less characteristic, are flattering. Finally Rig appears in a third house, this one luxurious, where Father and Mother receive him sumptuously. Here the product of his passage receives the name *Jarl,* "noble (earl)." In an action contrasting with the way he treated his other children, Rig does not abandon this one, but assists in his education and adopts him as a son. To this "Rig-Jarl" only male descendants are attributed, who all have names signifying "boy, son, heir," and who live like their father. Only the last, the young Konr, "Konr ungr," detaches himself from the mass and becomes the first king (*kon-ungr*).

---

[5] On the god Heimdall in his Indo-European perspective, see Dumézil, *Les dieux des Indo-Européens* (1952), pp. 104–105; J. de Vries has written on "Heimdallr, dieu énigmatique" in *Études germaniques* 10 (1955), 257–268, and in *Altgermanische Religionsgeschichte,* 2d ed. (1957), II, 238–244. Also see my article below, chapter 8, where one will find a justification of the use of *Rígr,* a foreign (Irish) name for king, which does not imply, contrary to what is often said, that the poem is of Celtic inspiration. In particular, the social division presented in the *Rígsþula* is certainly Germanic.

[6] See my article "Métiers et classes fonctionelles chez divers peuples indo-européens," *Annales, Économies, Sociétés, Civilizations* 13 (1958), 716–724.

This social structure has long been confirmed by juridical documents from the most diverse parts of the medieval Germanic world:[7] *adalingus, liber, servus* (Angles); *edhilingi, frilingi, lazzi*; or, *nobiles, ingenui, serviles* (Saxons); *satrapa* (or *nobilis*), *ingenuus, servus* (Danish: Saxo Grammaticus). We are certainly concerned here with a tradition, almost a Germanic theory. But it must be noted right away that in the *Rígsþula*, þræll and his descendants remain heterogeneous with the superior classes. The derisory or even defamatory names they bear are proof of it. They are not only found secluded at the bottom, but are even outside of the "good" social division, just like the śūdra of classical India in relation to the three superior varṇa; such that the following equivalence can be established, with a gap in the first term only:

—	brāhmaṇa
Jarl	kṣatriya
Karl	vaiśya
——————	——————
þræll	śūdra

In fact, the description that the poem contains (strs. 22–23) of the life Karl leads corresponds, *mutatis mutandis*, to the definition of the Indian breeder-farmers, the vaiśya:

Hann nam at vaxa oc vel dafna;
øxn nam at temia, arðr at gørva,
hús at timbra oc hlǫðor smiða,
karta at gørva oc keyra plóg.

Heim óco þá hanginluclo,
geitakyrtlo, gipto Karli;
Snør heitir sú; settiz undir ripti;
biuggu hión, bauga deildo,
breiddo blæior oc bú gørðo.

He began to grow, and to gain in strength,
Oxen he ruled, and plows made ready,
Houses he built, and barns he fashioned,
Carts he made, and the plow he managed.

Home did they bring the bride for Karl,
In goatskins clad, and keys she bore;
Snör was her name, 'neath the veil she sat;
A home they made ready, and rings exchanged,
The bed they decked, and a dwelling made.

---

[7] J. Grimm, *Deutsche Rechtsalterthümer*, A. Heusler and R. Hübner, eds., 4th ed. (1899), pp. 312–314. N. Wittich, "Die Frage der Freibauern, Untersuchungen über die soziale Gliederung des deutschen Volkes in altgermanischer und frühkarolingischer Zeit," in *Z. d. Savigny-Stiftung, Germ. Abt.* 22 (1901), 262–263.

Similarly, the occupations of Jarl—and also of Father, in whose house he is born—are those of the Indian kṣatriya; it is said about the Father (str. 28):

Sat húsgumi oc sneri streng,
álm of bendi, ǫrvar scepti.

There sat the house-lord, wound strings for the bow,
Shafts he fashioned, and bows he shaped.

Then about Jarl (str. 35):

Upp óx þar Iarl á fletiom;
lind nam at scelfa, leggia strengi,
álm at beygia, ǫrvar scepta,
flein at fleygia, frǫccor dýia,
hestom ríða, hundom verpa,
sverðom bregða, sund at fremia.

To grow in the house did Jarl begin,
Shields he brandished, and bowstrings wound,
Bows he shot, and shafts he fashioned,
Arrows he loosened, and lances wielded,
Horses he rode, and hounds unleashed,
Swords he handled, and sounds he swam.

As for the first term of the Scandinavian and Indian table, consideration of the precise kind of royalty represented by "Konr ungr" reduces considerably the difference, at first glance irreducible, produced by the absence in one group and presence in another of a sacerdotal caste. "Konr ungr" in effect is and can only be defined as a *magician*, with the notable exclusion of the warrior traits that still characterize his father and his brothers. He owes his promotion and success solely to his magic knowledge (strs. 43–46):

Upp óxo þar Iarli bornir;
hesta tǫmðo, hlífar bendo,
sceyti scófo, scelfðo asca.

Enn Konr ungr kunni rúnar,
ævinrúnar oc aldrrúnar;
meirr kunni hann mǫnnom biarga,
eggiar deyfa, ægi lægia.

Klǫc nam fugla, kyrra elda,
sæva of svefia, sorgir lægia,

. . . .
afl ok eliun átti manna.

Hann við Ríg iarl rúnar deildi,
brǫgðom beitti oc betr kunni;
þá ǫðlaðiz oc þá eiga gat
Rígr at heita, rúnar kunna.

Soon grew up the sons of Jarl,
Beasts they tamed, and bucklers rounded,
Shafts they fashioned, and spears they shook.

But Kon the Young learned runes to use,
Runes everlasting, the runes of life;
Soon could he well the warriors shield,
Dull the swordblade, and still the seas.

Bird-chatter learned he, flames could he lessen,
Minds could quiet, and sorrows calm;
. . . .
The might and strength of twice four men.

With Rig-Jarl soon the runes he shared,
More crafty he was, and greater his wisdom:[8]
The right he sought, and soon he won it,
Rig to be called, and runes to know.

Thus the first function, magic sovereignty, if it does not have for support a whole class of men opposed to the class of warriors and to that of breeder-farmers, does at least appear, and in the expected hierarchical place. It is concentrated, however, in the person of the king, whom the function has colored even to the point where there remains in him only "the" magician par excellence.[9] The *konungr* is thus clearly distinguished from the Indian *rājan*, coming in general, like "Konr ungr," from the warrior class, but who, pre- or juxtaposed to the class of priests, is characterized by temporal power more than by talent or knowledge, and must double, for the purpose of religious acts, with the priest par excellence who is his chaplain, the *purohita*.

The picture the *Rígsþula* gives in "Konr ungr" of royalty is in any case schematic and insufficient.[10] If one turns to the mythology, which is doubtless closer to social reality, one sees that the god of the first function, Odin, is to be sure a king-magician similar to "Konr ungr," but that he is also (and how could it be otherwise in the Germanic world?) a warrior god, even the great ruler of combats and fighters, the patron of the *jarlar* as well as of the *konungar*, and in

[8] It has been stated above that Rig (Heimdall) taught Jarl, beside the art of war, "the runes." But with Jarl this magic science did not prosper; it was retained as a seed that only flowered with Konr ungr.

[9] This seemed so astonishing that it was supposed that the poem was broken off, and that the last strophes, lost, told of the exploits of war of "Konr ungr." In fact, nothing supports this hypothesis.

[10] J. de Vries, "Das Königtum bei den Germanen," *Saeculum* 7 (1956), 289–309, brings a solution to the difficult problem proposed by Tacitus, *Germania*, 7, *reges ex nobilitate, duces ex uirtute summunt.*

the other world, of the *einherjar,* dead heroes skilled in combat whom the Valkyries bring to him. I have shown on several occasions how certain Scandinavian peoples or groups, while maintaining the Indo-European structure of the three functions in the triad Odin-Thor-Frey, modified the distribution of conceptual material among the three levels.[11] This is true first for Odin, with whom the accent is often placed on the warrior aspects at the expense of the magical aspects of his province. But this is also true for the one who strikes, the thundering and lightening Thor. He, in return, often lost his contact with the warriors, and interested society instead, and especially the peasants, with the fecund result of the atmospheric battle that he produces through rain. This confusion has either brought Thor closer to the proper, terrestrial gods of fecundity, Frey and Njord, or it has pushed these two, in turn, into the parts of their province where Thor does not compete, such as human fecundity and voluptuousness. The following were, for example, according to Adam of Bremen, the values of the three gods associated with the temple at Uppsala: *Wodan, id est furor, bella gerit,* says this keen observer, *hominique ministrat virtutem contra inimicos; Thor praesidet in aera, qui tonitrus et fulmina, ventos imbresque, serena et fruges gubernat*; and Fricco—the god *ingenti priapo*—has no more to himself than *pacem voluptatemque.* Consequently, one addresses oneself to Wodan *si bellum imminet,* to Thor *si pestis et fames,* and to Fricco *si nuptiae celebrandae sunt.*

Even in Norway, where the former dominion of Frey has been largely preserved, and where Thor, in the literature, has certainly remained the "one who strikes," modern folklore and Lapp borrowings attest nevertheless to a clear and ancient evolution of this god, through the benefits of storms, toward fecundity and the service of peasants. This can easily be seen in the verses of the *Hárbarðsljóð* (str. 24) in which Odin hurls into Thor's face the celebrated insult:

> Odin has the *jarlar* who fall in battle,
> And Thor has the race of the *þrælar.*

Jan de Vries has plausibly surmised[12]—for Thor has nothing to do elsewhere with the *þrælar*—a caricature, a parody of a more exact

---

[11] In the latest place, see my *Les dieux des Indo-Européens,* pp. 25–26; also my *L'idéologie tripartite des Indo-Européens* (collection "Latomus," vol. 31) (1958), chap. 2, pars. 19–22.

[12] Jan de Vries, "Über das Wort Jarl und seine Verwandten," *La nouvelle Clio* 6 (1954), 468–469: "Hier möchte ich an eine bekannte Verszeile des Harbardliedes erinnern:

saying, where, corresponding to Odin, patron of *jarlar*, one should find Thor the patron of the *karlar*: is not *karl* the stereotyped surname that Thor bears in Lapp mythology (*Hora Galles*<**Kar*(*i*)*laz*)? And, in folklore from the South of Sweden, is the god not designated by a quasi-synonym of *karl, go-bonden, korn-, åker-bonden*?

These breaks and overlappings in divine functions permit a justification of the parallel displacement which is observed in the attribution of symbolic colors that the *Rígsþula* makes to the social classes.

We know that this usage is very old, even Indo-European; it is well known among the Indo-Iranians (with whom the notion of "class, caste," is expressed by the words, *varṇa, pištra*, which are connected with color). This has recently been reported among the Hittites, and has also left clear traces in Rome.[13] In these various domains the colors retained were white (first function: priests, the sacred), red (second function: warriors, force), and dark blue or green (third function: breeder-farmers, fecundity). Only post-Rigvedic India, which placed a fourth class, that of the servant śūdra, below the three *ārya* classes, adjusted this system at the same time, attributing yellow to the vaiśya and reserving for the śūdra the dark color in its extreme form, black.[14] The *Rígsþula*, too, associates colors with the eponyms of the Germanic social classes.[15] It presents the baby Thrall, at his birth (str. 7), as *svartan*, black. Then it describes the baby Karl (str. 21) as *rauþan ok rjóðan*, red of hair and face; and finally the baby Jarl (str. 34) is *bleikr*, a bright white. And apparently "Konr ungr," for whom color is not indicated, is himself also *bleikr*, in his quality as the son of Jarl. We see that, if the black attributed to Thrall and his slave descendants is no more surprising than the

---

Óðinn á Jarla þá er i val falla
en þórr á þræla kyn.

Damit beschimpft der göttliche Fährmann den Weitgewanderten Thor. Dass Odin der Gott der Jarle, der Fürsten im allgemeinen war, wissen wir schon längst, aber ebensosehr war Thor der Gott der Karle, hiess er ja selber *þorrkarl*, wie uns die lappische Entlehnung *Horagalles* bezeugt. Der Spotter des Harbardliedes hat sich nicht gescheut, den biedern Bauerngott als den Schutzherrn der Sklaven zu verunglimpfen; aber das war nun eben die Bösartigkeit seines Witzes. Ich vermute, dass er eine alte Verszeile, die ursprünglich *þórr á karla kyn* lauten mochte, umgebildet hat. Dann wurde der Gegensatz *jarl*: *karl* auch hier zutage treten und sogar seine Entsprechung im Götterpaar Odin: Thor finden."

[13] See Dumézil, *Les rituels indo-européens à Rome* (1954), III, "Abati russati virides," IV: "Vexillum caeruleum," pp. 45–72; also my *L'idéologie tripartite des Indo-Européens*, chap. 1, pars. 20–21.

[14] There are ritual traces of the ancient system (white-brahmaṇa, red-kṣatriya, black-vaiśya): *Gobhila G. S.*, IV, 7, 7; *Khādira G. S.*, IV, 2, 12.

[15] On the precise value of these adjectives of color, see the notes of H. Gering and B. Sijmons, *Kommentar zu den Liedern der Edda* (1927), 349, 354, 360.

black of the Indian śūdra, in return the white and red, attributed respectively to the noble warriors and freeholders, are lowered by one level in comparison with Indic and also with the Indo-European prototype. The table below will show how the overflowing of Odin into the warrior function and that of Thor into the function of fecundity can explain this "descent" of white and red:

Indo-European State	Scandinavian Theology	Rígsþula
White∼Magic→Odin	Magic	Konr∼ungr
	War	Jarl∼white
Red∼Force, War→Thor	Atmospheric Combat	
	Fecund Rain	Karl∼red[16]
Blue∼Fecundity→Frey	Terrestrial Fecundity	
		Thrall∼black

In other words, the aspect of Odin (war) incorporated with Jarl and the aspect of Thor (fecund rain) incorporated with Karl caused the transfer to Jarl and Karl, respectively, of symbolic colors that, originally, were associated with aspects of Odin (magic) and Thor (atmospheric combat) which were not incorporated in Jarl and Karl. The transfer could only have been facilitated by the fact that the magic function, being no longer assured to a class of men but only to an individual "Konr ungr," was no longer felt to be homogeneous with the functions assured to Jarl and the *jarlar*, Karl and the *karlar*, and could, without opposing an already broken symmetry, remain outside the play of colors.[17]

These reflections permit the *Rígsþula* to be put into the dossier of our study and afford a glimpse of the simple and coherent evolution that transformed the Indo-European prototype into an original structure among the Germanic peoples.

"*La Rigsþula* et la structure sociale indo-européenne,"
Revue de l'histoire des religions 154 (1958), 1–9.

16 Among the continental Germanic peoples in the Middle Ages, the colors of the peasant are brown (or grey), blue on holidays. O. Lauffer, *Farbensymbolik im deutschen Volksbrauch* (1948), pp. 20–22; G. Widengren, "Harlekintracht und Mönchskutte, Clownhut und Derwischmütze," *Orientalia Suecana* 2 (1953), 53 n. 3 (in all of this work, several valuable indications and corrections on the symbolism of blue and brown will be found).

17 It was rather as a fighter, and as the Scandinavian equivalent of Indra, that Thor had a red beard—which passes, with the hammer, to Saint Olaf; cf. also the red shields of the Vikings, and, on the continent, the red-tinted hair of certain Germanic warriors (Tacitus, *Histories*, IV, 61). But red has several other values: J. T. Storaker, *Rummet i den norske folketro, Norsk Folkeminnelag* 8 (1923), 51–54, par. 14 (significance of the color red). Along with red, blue too was a color of Thor: J. T. Storaker, *Elementerne i den norske folketro, Norsk Folkeminnelag* 10 (1924), 113 n. 1.

CHAPTER 7

Comparative Remarks on the Scandinavian God Heimdall (1959)[1]

The god Heimdall poses one of the most difficult problems in Scandinavian mythography. As all who have dealt with him have emphasized, this is primarily because of a very fragmentary documentation; but even more because the few traits that have been saved from oblivion diverge in too many directions to be easily "thought of together," or to be grouped as members of a unitary structure.

The two latest studies on Heimdall, since the publication of the book by the Swede, Birger Pering,[2] are: (1) the two pages (104–105) where I summarized, in the appendix to *Dieux des Indo-Européens* (1952), a course given at the École des Hautes Études in 1947–1948; (2) the article that J. de Vries has published in our *Études germaniques* 10 (1955), 257–268, under the title, which is still justified, of "Heimdallr, enigmatic god."[3]

In 1947–1948 I noted that a large part of the information given us by the Eddic poems and Snorri's prose can be harmonized if we place in the center of the divine concept the notion of beginning: Heimdall would be a "first god; initial." This is a type of divinity that not only Rome, with Janus, but the religions of the Indo-Iranians know well. Their theologies and their rituals in many circumstances

---

1 Lecture delivered at the University of Oslo, September 26, 1956. The homology of Heimdall and Bhīṣma-Dyauḥ was explored in several lectures at the Collège de France, in February and March 1958.

2 Birger Pering, *Heimdall, Religionsgeschichtliche Untersuchungen zum Verständnis der altnordischen Götterwelt* (Lund, 1941).

3 See also de Vries, *AGR* 2 (1957), II, 238–244, pars. 491–493.

present or make use of a god who is not the greatest, the *summus*, but who passes as the first, *primus*, with the risks and privileges connected with this advanced position.[4] Heimdall also, without being the principal god nor chief of the gods, is "first" in different respects and according to the same specifications as Janus; in time, he is born in the beginning, *í árdaga* (*Hyndluljóð*, 35); he is the ancestor of humanity (*Vǫluspá*, 1),[5] the procreator of the classes and the founder of all social order (*Rígsþula*); in space he is posted at the threshold of the divine world, "at the limits of the earth" (*Hyndluljóð*, 35), "at the edge of the sky," at the lower end of the bridge that leads to the sky (*Snorra Edda*, ed. F. Jónsson [1931], pp. 25, 32–33), and so, like Janus, he is the watchman, the sentry, *vorþr goþa* (*Grimnismál*, 13; *Lokasenna*, 48) with the qualities that can be desired of such a sentry. He does not sleep, he can see at night as well as he can during the day, he has prodigious auditory acuity; finally, in the few mythical contexts where he not only appears but also acts, he starts the action. At the gods' meeting, he is the first to speak (*Þrymskviða*, 14–15); in the eschatology, as watchman he announces the tragedy that will destroy the world, by the sound of his horn (*Vǫluspá*, 46; *Snorra Edda*, p. 72).

Jan de Vries did not consider this unitary balance sheet to be false, but he found it insufficient, and several more years of reflexion lead me to the same opinion. To my mind, this conception, which dates ten years back, has two principal weaknesses.

First, the notion of "first god" does not seem to me to be so simple. It is simple in Rome, where Janus is entirely explained by the definition given him by the ancient scholars: god of the *initia*, of the *prima*. But a closer examination of the Indian and Iranian facts shows that this too-convenient term covers different though connected concepts: in the *Rig Veda* and in the Vedic rituals, Aditi the Non-attached,[6] Daksa the Energy,[7] Uṣas the Dawn,[8] Savitṛ the Impeller,[9]

[4] Dumézil, *Tarpeia* (1947), pp. 97–100; Dumézil, *Les dieux des Indo-Européens* (1952), pp. 79–105; cf. also Dumézil, "La triade Jupiter Mars Janus? *Revue de l'histoire des religions* 132 (1946), 115–123 (contrary to V. Basanoff) and Dumézil, "Jupiter Mars Quirinus et Janus," *ibid.*, 139 (1951), 208–215 (contrary to J. Paoli).

[5] And of the gods? But it is not certain that the second line of *Vǫluspá*, 1, must be understood in that sense. In other contexts, Heimdall is in any case subject to the norm and is declared a son of Odin, like all the gods, which does not really agree with *Hyndlul jóð*, 37–40 (see below, n. 25).

[6] Dumézil, *Déesses latines et mythes védiques* (1956), p. 98.

[7] *Ibid.*, pp. 93–96.

[8] *Ibid.*, pp. 9–43.

[9] *Ibid.*, p. 36 n. 6 and p. 98 n. 6.

Vāyu the Wind,[10] Tvaṣṭar the craftsman,[11] Dyu (nomin. Dyauḥ) the Sky, are, for different reasons, gods who "begin" and they coexist without being redundant. This is not the place to elaborate on this point, to define differentially the categories of the Indo-Iranian "first gods." It will suffice to say that there exists, among these gods—and, in epic transpositions, among the "first heroes"—one variety that I propose to call "frame gods (or heroes)." These characters are the first in time and in action but they are also the last; they open, but they also close; and because of that, when heroes are concerned, they do not live according to the same temporal rhythm as the others, whom they "enframe." The *Shah Nameh* notably presents some of these characters who age more slowly, who live several generations and who in this way watch over a long history that they first set in motion.[12] Today it seems to me that Heimdall belonged to this kind of primordial figure. In a work, already old and written in Dutch, Jan de Vries anticipated this explanation, comparing Heimdall to some Greek concepts like ακαμας χρόνος, πανεπὶδκοπος δαίμφν.[13] The comparison is fruitful and will have to be taken up again, but the mythical being who, because of his characteristics, seems to me to be the closest to Heimdall, is the Indian, the pre-Indian god, Dyauḥ.

Up until very recent times we have been able to say very little about this sky god, ancestor of many gods and sometimes even of all the gods. The discovery that Stig Wikander, in 1947, published on the "mythical groundwork of the *Mahābhārata*"[14] permits us to know this god better, no longer solely by the direct studying of mythological texts that speak too vaguely of him, but through the magnifying refraction of his epic transposition. Wikander indeed points out that the "good" heroes who are in the center of the *Mahābhārata*, the five Pāṇḍava and their common wife, are the transposition, on the human level, of the central divinities of the Vedic and even the pre-Vedic religions. The poets have, in any case, made this process

---

10 Dumézil, *Tarpeia*, pp. 66–76, 80–94.

11 W. Norman Brown, "The Creation Myths of the Rig Veda," *Journal of the American Oriental Society* 62 (1942), 86–87; Dumézil, *Tarpeia*, p. 69.

12 S. Wikander, "Sur le fonds commun indo-iranien des épopées de la Perse et de l'Inde," *La Nouvelle Clio* 7 (1950), 324–326.

13 J. de Vries, "Studiën over Germaansche mythologie, 9: De Oudnoorsche god Heimdallr," *Tijdschrift van Nederlandse Taal- en Letterkunde* 54 (1935), 53–76, notably p. 61; de Vries, *AGR* 2 (1957), II, 240.

14 Stig Wikander, "Pāṇḍavasagan och Mahābhāratas mytiska förutsättningar," *Religion och Bibel* 6 (1947), 27–39; for further references see Bibliographical Notes to chap. 3.

perfectly clear,[15] since their book introduces these heroes either as sons, or as incarnations of the gods whose characters, modes of behavior, and affinities they reproduce. They are grouped as the prototype gods were grouped in the theology. This remark of 1947 has great significance, which extends beyond the Pāṇḍava[16] group, and the listing of its applications has yet to be finished. Here is the application that we are interested in. The action of the *Mahābhārata* is completely embraced by a "frame hero," Bhīṣma, who is none other than the Sky, Dyauḥ, incarnated. As punishment for a fault, the god has been condemned to be born in a human form, and, in this incarnation, receives a life cycle much longer than that of ordinary humanity, enduring and aging without weakening. He sees things come and go, he raises the successive generations of princes, his nephews, his essential role being precisely to raise and protect them, without himself ever marrying. The firstborn of his family, he dies only at the end; wounded, he defers his death until after the great battle of the Pāṇḍava against the Kaurava which constitutes the main subject of the poem and which Wikander, in a bold and sound view, compared to the eschatological battle of Mazdaism. Without a doubt, we can see, in the story of Bhīṣma, an epic transposition of the behavior of the pre-Vedic *Dyaus, sky god and frame god, not sovereign (the sovereigns were Varuṇa and Mitra) but procreator and vigilant observer of active gods, though not himself active.

Heimdall is of this type. Born at the beginning of time, *í árdaga*, it is also he who survives the longest in the Ragnarǫk battle. When all the gods who must perish in battle have perished, it is he who fights the last duel, against the pernicious Loki, and who is the last to die, along with his adversary.[17] In contrast, his transcendence with respect to the generations is well marked in the Eddic *Rígsþula*, where we see him beget the social classes of humanity by successively going to three couples and begetting three children to the women of these couples. The couples are curiously named "Great Grandfather and Great Grandmother," next "Grandfather and Grandmother," next "Father and Mother."[18] One of his functions is therefore to provide

15 That is the too absolute theory presented in a section of the prologue of the poem, I, 2636–2797.

16 See the developments in the first part of Dumézil, *Mythe et épopée* I (1968), pp. 31–257.

17 *Snorra Edda* (Jónsson), pp. 71–73 (*Gylfaginning*, chaps. 37–38); *Prose Edda* (Young), pp. 87–88.

18 See above, chap. 6.

for successive births by procreating each time unofficially under the name of another, just as one of the functions of Dyauḥ incarnated in Bhīṣma is, from generation to generation, to ensure the births necessary for the continuation of the race, notably, at the most important time (for the births of Pāṇḍu and his two brothers) by having a brother of a dead man procreate under the name of this dead man. Furthermore, Heimdall is not the sovereign of the world that he could be thanks to his very ancient birth. He is no more king than is Dyauḥ incarnated in Bhīṣma who formally renounced this royal right that he held by primogeniture, and, as with Dyauḥ incarnated in Bhīṣma, his whole work in the *Rígsþula* tends, all things considered, to give men a king,[19] who is not himself. It is only the more remarkable that Heimdall's second name, the one under which he procreated the social classes of humanity, is *Rígr*, that is to say the Irish name—a *foreign* name, and therefore *inefficacious* in a Germanic country—of the "king." Note finally that, in this perspective and by comparison with the Indian Dyauḥ, the celestial traits of Heimdall are fully justified, for, if he is not strictly speaking the sky, he is the most celestial of the Scandinavian gods. He is more celestial than Tyr who, even if he corresponds phonetically with Dyauḥ, has acquired a completely different significance.[20] As Jan de Vries[21] said, Heimdall "lives at the edge of the world, at the foot of the rainbow, but his palace is above the skies, in the Himinbjǫrg . . . The rainbow is the path that joins the limit of the horizon to the center of the sky; it is from above the sky at the top of the central axis, that the watch-god watches the whole circumference of the world."[22]

The second insufficiency of the 1947–1948 explanation is this: even if it takes account of most of the god's deeds, it fails to account for several traits that are symptomatic rather than dramatic, and

---

19 See especially the discussion of *konungr*, above, chap. 6.

20 Cf. my *Mitra-Varuṇa*, 2d ed. (1948), chaps. 7 and 9; also my *L'idéologie tripartite des Indo-Européens* (Coll. Latomus, 31, 1958), chap. 3, sect. 4.

21 Jan de Vries, "Heimdallr, dieu énigmatique," *Études germaniques* 10 (1955), 253.

22 The Romans—I do not say the Latins—who have no eschatology—have no "frame divinity" either: Janus embodies the diverse nuances of the notion of a "first divinity," but not the latter; nevertheless his connection (which has been greatly exaggerated) with the *rex* and certain celestial traits, recall Dyauḥ-Bhīṣma and Heimdall. Heimdall also embodies whatever remains, in Scandinavia, of the theology of the *prima* (aside from the giants, the other *primi*), but he himself is, above all, the "frame god." His role in the "beginnings of actions" is primarily limited to two mythical interventions, and it does not seem that he was invoked to open religious or lay undertakings, as is the case with Janus, Savitṛ (and, in sacrifice, Vāyu). We know almost nothing about Germanic rituals.

which are surely important. For example, Jan de Vries is right[23] in considering as artificial the way in which I applied an epithet characteristic of Heimdall: "the white god," "the whitest of the Æsir," to the type of "first god"—therefore white, with white hair. More important than this whiteness, there are relations between Heimdall and the ram in one instance, with the waters and especially the sea in the other. These two kinds of relations are expressed in a series of precise traits of which I had to declare at the end of a brief sketch in 1952 that they remained unexplained by the concept of "first god." Before testing to see if they agree more with the one of "frame god," I would like first to attack a smaller problem, leaving aside the overall perspective and remaining close to the given data. These aberrant traits, indeed, have not only remained rebellious to my explanation as to all others that had preceded it, but moreover it is not easy to see how they harmonize simply with each other: they seem if not incompatible at least to be incoherent. Is this impression irremediable? I do not believe so.

But first there is one manner of treating such problems against which we must vigorously protest, the one that consists in causing them to vanish. Readers who have followed my work, especially *Loki* (1948) will not be surprised to see the statements of Heimdall which we read in Snorri accepted here as honest and authentic facts. I have put forth many reasons for confidence in the learning and the conscientiousness of the great Icelander, while refuting Eugen Mogk and his hypercritical school on the very points they had chosen to discredit him.[24] Birger Pering's book on Heimdall, so useful in other ways, shows the arbitrariness we fall into when, without objective criteria, we try to separate what is valid in Snorri's assertions from what is not.

This is why, in agreement with Jan de Vries, I do not think that we have the right to ascribe the multiple connections between Heimdall and the ram to misunderstandings or word play on Snorri's part. In the first place, *Hallinskíði* "bent stick" is a nickname of the god, but primarily of the ram, referring, according to the most natural inter-

---

23 De Vries, "Heimdallr" (see above, n. 21), p. 259.

24 Dumézil, *Tarpeia*, pp. 253–274 (war between the Æsir and the Vanir: contrary to E. Mogk, *Zur Gigantomachie der Vǫluspá* = *Folklore Fellows Communications* 58 [1925]); Dumézil, *Loki* (1948), pp. 97–106 (birth and death of Kvasir: contrary to E. Mogk, *Novellistische Darstellung mythologischer Stoffe Snorris und seiner Schule* = *Folklore Fellows Communications* 51 [1923]); Dumézil, *Loki*, pp. 133–148 (Loki et le meurtre de Baldr: contrary to E. Mogk, *Lokis Anteil am Baldrs Tode* = *Folklore Fellows Communications* 57 [1925]). (See above, chaps. 1 and 3.)

pretation, to the bent horns on both sides of his head. *Gullintanni,* "the golden-toothed," another of the god's strange nicknames, has long been explained by the fact that the teeth of old rams take on a color that recalls gilding. In the second place, Snorri also presents a pair of complementary periphrases, one of which designates the sword as Heimdall's head, *Heimdallar hǫfuð,* while the other designates the head as the sword of the same god, *hjǫrr Heimdallar.* Many modern authors have pointed out that these two images are well explained by the affinity between the god and an animal whose offensive and deadly weapon is precisely the head. Finally, with J. de Vries and contrary to B. Pering, I remain aware of the near identity of the proper noun, *Heimdallr,* and the ram's poetic name, *heimdali,* whatever the much-debated etymologies of one or the other may be. These allusions to a "ram's nature" or at least to a mode of acting comparable to that of a ram, surprises us, but the strangeness does not give us the right to eliminate them by subjective criticisms. On this point as on so many others, Snorri knew what he was saying better than we do.

The ties between Heimdall and water, especially the sea, have fortunately been less contested. They too are multiple. Firstly, through his sarcasm, in stanza 48 of the *Lokasenna,* Loki pities him in an ironic way for having to exercise his occupation with his back muddy (or wet?), *aurgo baki.* Secondly, as for his first duel with Loki, which the two fighters wage in the form of seals, *í selalíkjum*: given the fact that Loki, as we know from other sources, can assume any shape, it must be that this precise shape was imposed upon him by the nature of his opponent Heimdall, of whom we have no reason to believe that he was gifted with the same general talent of metamorphosis. Finally and above all, there is the god's birth, a veritable enigma, on which we also have no right to pronounce an arbitrary judgment. Let us recall the texts. In the *Húsdrápa,* a skaldic poem of the end of the tenth century which mentions the duel between Heimdall and Loki, Loki's opponent is said to be *mǫgr mœðra einnar ok átta,* "child of one mother and eight." In the *Heimdallargaldr,* it is Heimdall who presents himself in these terms: "I am the child of nine mothers, I am the son of nine sisters." The "Little Vǫluspá" inserted in the *Hyndluljóð* (str. 35) makes the setting even more precise:

Varð einn borinn í árdaga,
rammaukinn miǫc, rǫgna kindar;
nío báro þann, naðgǫfgan mann,
iǫtna meyiar við iarðar þrǫm.

One there was born in the bygone days,
of the race of the gods, and great was his might;
nine giant women, at the world's edge,
once bore the man so mighty in arms.[25]

We see what the "world's edge" is, two stanzas further, when the poem says of this primeval being:

Sá var aukinn iarðar megni,
svalkǫldom sæ oc sonardreyra.

Strong was he made with the strength of earth,
with the ice-cold sea, and the blood of swine.

As early as 1844,[26] W. Müller explained Heimdall's nine mothers, who begat him at the nutritious meeting point of earth and sea, by the *níó brúðir* of a poem of Snæbjǫrn's (beginning of the eleventh century) who are clearly the waves of the sea; and also by the "nine daughters of Ægir," god of the sea, of whom Snorri speaks, quoting another skaldic poem, and who are still certainly the waves; and generally by the *meyjar* who represent the waves in several texts (*Baldrs draumar*, 12; the riddles that Heiðrek was asked). This strange statement of facts must be accepted even though, as B. Pering says, "der Mythos von dem Gott, der durch neun (Meeres)jungfrauen geboren wurde, hat im nordischen Sagenschatz wohl keine Spur hinterlassen."[27]

These are the facts that must be reconciled. What can their principle of unity be? How can we harmonize this filiation starting with nine sisters who are the waves with the appellations and attitudes which evoke the ram? How can we understand that this ram-god, who, without doubt as an old ram has "golden teeth," is also said to be "the whitest of the Æsir?" A lucky accident recently led me to

---

25 This text (*Edda* [Kuhn], p. 294; *Edda* [Bellows], pp. 229–230) contains a striking opposition between Heimdall as *primi-genius* (stanza 37: *varð einn borinn í árdaga*) and Odin as *maximus* (verse 40: *varð einn borinn ǫllum meiri*); it is the formula of the relation of Janus and Jupiter, Saint Augustine, *City of God*, VII, 9: *penes Janum sunt prima, penes Jovem summa.* Analogous Iranian formula in *Yasna*, 45, first verses of stanzas 3, 4 and 6, see Dumézil, *Tarpeia*, pp. 86–88.

26 See the good article by Pering, *Heimdall*, pp. 166–170; cf. R. Meissner, *Die Kenningar der Skalden* (1921), p. 98 ("Welle").

27 To these mythical connections with the sea, J. de Vries has added an onomastic connection by noticing an exact parallelism in the formation of the god's name *Heim-dall* and the name of the barely known goddess, *Mar-dǫll*, the first element of which means "sea," *AGR* 2 (1957), II, 244, 328: "sie [=Mardǫll] steht also wohl in einem ähnlichen Verhältnis zum Meer wie dieser Gott zur ganzen Welt."

discover a parallel where these different traits are also brought together but in a clearer manner and with an immediately perceptible meaning. It is the Celtic countries that provide me with a means of explanation, in a different way than for Jean I. Young.[28]

Medieval and modern Welsh folklore naturally has spirits who live in the sea or at the edge of the sea.[29] The great anthology published in 1901 by John Rhŷs, *Celtic Folklore, Welsh and Manx,* cites numerous examples. The one that will be useful to us is to be found elsewhere, in the little book which a local author, J. Jones, under the ambitious pseudonym of Myrddin Fardd, in 1909 consecrated to the Caernarvonshire folklore: *Llên gwerin sir Gaernarvon.* On page 106 there are interesting bits of information relative to *y Forforwyn,* to the Mermaid, which we see from time to time, he says, on the rocks, above the sea, combing or arranging her hair: "Morforwyn is described as being of a dark brown color with a face similar to a human face, a wide mouth, a large nose, a high forehead, small eyes, with neither a chin nor ears, small arms without elbows, and the hands similar to human hands, except that the fingers are linked by some kind of thin skin; below the waist, it is a fish . . ." Although this curious species whose faces and upper limbs so oddly recall a seal, includes theoretically both males and females, Myrrddin Fardd notes that the folklore deals only with females, *morforwynion,* and he adds: "In old Welsh stories, we read that there was one which was called Gwenhidwy, whose frothing waves were the ewes and the ninth wave, the ram."

---

28 Jean I. Young, "Does Rígsþula betray Irish influence?" *Arkiv för nordisk filologi* 49 (1933), 97–107. The comparison made in this article is interesting, but seems to me rather to belong in the category of influences of Scandinavian literature on Irish literature. The two general reasons that the author gives in support of Irish influence on the *Rigsþula* have no validity: it has been noted, above, that recourse to the foreign word *Rigr* is explained by a deep-seated reason (Heimdall is only a potential king, the real king, created by him, having to be "Konr ungr" at the end of the poem, that is to say, in good Scandinavian, *konungr* "king"). In contrast, the procreative behavior of Heimdall-*Rigr* in the beds of his hosts has nothing in common with the "droit de cuissage" of Conchobor and other Irish kings. It must be added (see chapter 6 above) that the type of social division illustrated by the *Rigsþula* is specifically Germanic and distinguished from the Irish type by essential traits.

29 Besides J. Rhŷs, see W. Sikes, *British Goblins* (1880), pp. 47–48 (Mermaids); J. Ceredig Davies, *Folk Lore of Welsh and Mid Wales* (1911), pp. 143–147 (Mermaids). Cornish folklore contains the same concept and the same word, H. Jenner, "The Cornish Drama, II," *The Celtic Review* 4 (1907–1908), 48, in a fifteenth-century *Passio Domini*:

Myreugh worth an morvoron
hanter pysk ha hanter den.

"Look at the Mermaid, half-fish, half-man."

This belief fits into a known structure. Many folklores compare waves which, under a strong wind, are topped with a white foam (this is how Myrddin Fardd expresses himself: *tonau brigwynion*) to different animals, especially to horses or mares, to cows or bulls, to dogs or sheep.[30] We say in France, "moutons, moutonner, moutonnant" (white sheep, to break into white sheep, breaking into white sheep) and the English "white horses." The modern Welsh, like the Irish, speak of "white mares (*cesyg*)" but the old tradition linked to the name of Gwenhidwy, as in French, Basque, and other folklores, turned these waves into sheep. Conversely, in many countries the sailors or the coast dwellers attribute to certain wave sequences particular qualities or forces, sometimes, even, says Sebillot, a supernatural power: it happens that the third, or the ninth, or the tenth wave is the biggest, or the most dangerous, or the noisiest or the most powerful.[31] But what I have found nowhere else but in the Welsh tradition concerning Gwenhidwy is a combination of these two beliefs, the final result of which is *to make the ninth wave the ram of the simple ewes that are the eight preceding waves.*

This concept furnishes a satisfactory explanation of that section of Heimdall's dossier which we are considering: it allows us to combine his birth—nine mothers who are waves, at the confines of the earth—and his attributes of a ram. We understand that whatever his mythical value and functions were, *the scene of his birth made him, in the sea's white frothing, the ram produced by the ninth wave.*[32] If this is the case, then it is correct to say that he has nine mothers, since one alone does not suffice, nor two, nor three. An exact succession of nine is necessary to produce him, and the ninth one, if she is the only one to beget him, begets him only because there are eight well-counted ones before her. In this way is best explained the singularly analytic expression of the *Húsdrápa*, which calls Heimdall "son of one and eight waves." This decomposition of the number nine is excellent, emphasizing the one decisive wave in the group. In this

30 For example, P. Sebillot, *Légendes, croyances et superstitions de la mer*, I (1886), 153–157 (the waves interpreted as horses, sheep, cows or bulls, dogs, and even lions), 170–178 (the waves and the numbers), 176–177 (the ninth wave).

31 On the "nine waves" in pagan and Christian legends, see H. d'Arbois de Jubainville, *Le cycle mythologique irlandais et la mythologie celtique* (1884), pp. 256–257.

32 Neither in the Folklore Archives of Oslo, nor in the large collection of monographs that they have already published, have I found anything concerning the frothing of the sea. Other accounts survived until the eighteenth century, linked to the name of the god Njord; see my "Njǫrðr, Nerthus et le folklore scandinave des génies de la mer," *Revue de l'histoire des religions* 147 (1955), 210–226, esp. p. 215).

way we can also most easily explain one of the god's nicknames, *Vindhlér*, which has given rise to many hypotheses and which it will suffice to take in its literal meaning. *Hlér* is a common poetic name for the sea: *vind-hlér* can therefore be the sea, *hlér*, agitated because of the wind, *vindr*, and it appropriately indicates the god born at the place most noted for this vast frothing. It is finally understandable that Heimdall is characterized as "the whitest of the Æsir," *hvítastr ása*: in the epic transfiguration of frothing, the white of the foam is often put forth ("white horses," "white mares," etc.) and the Welsh *morforwyn*, owner of these white herds who run on the waves, is herself called *Gwenhudwy*,[33] in which the first term, the only clear one, means White.

Myrddin Fardd's text came to my attention in 1954, at Bangor, and, having been struck immediately by the analogy with Heimdall, I endeavored to learn a bit more about Gwenhidwy—for this good folklorist shows himself here to be irritably negligent: *yn yr hen Chwedlau cymreig ceir fod un* . . . How we would wish for a precise reference to these "old stories"! [34] I looked into the most recent book on Welsh folklore, by T. Gwyn Jones, professor of literature at Aberystwyth, *Welsh Folklore and Folkcustom*. In the section "Fairies," page 75, he quotes Myrddin Fardd and he also deplores the imprecision of Fardd's language. He further reproduces two verses of a sixteenth-century poem, taken from a manuscript at Oxford which Myrddin Fardd surely did not know. In this poem Rhys Llwyd ap Rhys ap Rhicert describes a boat trip to the small island of Bardsey,

---

33 The attested forms are *Gwenhudwy, Gwenhidwy, Gwenhidw*. As for the suffix *-wy* (*-w*), see K. Jackson, *Language and History in Early Britain* (1953), p. 376. As for the second member of the composite, only the reading *-hud-* makes sense. Old Welsh *hud* "witchcraft, charm," *hud-aw* "to enchant," Old Cornish *hud-ol* "magus" is related to Old Icelandic *seiðr*, name of a kind of magic, see D. Strömbäck, *Sejd, Textstudier i nordisk religionshistoria* (1935), and my *Saga de Hadingus* (1953), pp. 70–82.

34 Since this lecture was given, I have perhaps found Myrddin Fardd's source; it would be—as it often happens, alas, in anthologies of folklore in Welsh—an English book: Fletcher S. Bassett, *Legends and Superstitions of the Sea and of Sailors in all Lands and at all Times* (1885), cited on p. 26: "Welsh fishermen called the ninth wave the ram of *Gwenhidwy*, the other waves her sheep." He only gives as reference: "Brewer, *Reader's Hand Book*." The book in question is E. Cobham Brewer, *The Reader's Handbook of Allusions, References, Plots and Stories*, 2d ed. (1880), where we read, p. 416: "*Gwenhidwy*, a mermaid. The white foamy waves are called her sheep, and the ninth wave her ram," with, as its only justification: "Take shelter when you see Gwenhidwy driving her flock ashore. Welsh Proverb." There is disagreement in the lack of precision of the Welsh sources: the "hen chwedlau Cymreig" of Myrddin Fardd does not coincide with Brewer's "Welsh proverb" nor Bassett's "Welsh fishermen."

Ynys Enlli, the island of twenty thousand saints, a place of pilgrimage famous throughout the Middle Ages, at the southwestern tip of the Lleyn peninsula; this is how he describes the waves that break in this tumultuous strait:

haid o ddefaid Gwenhudwy	a flock of ewes of Gwenhudwy
a naw hwrdd yn un â hwy.	and nine rams with them.[35]

Soon after, my colleague and friend Brinley Rees, the folklorist from the University of Bangor, informed me that in a recently published book (1954) by Francis Jones, *The Holy Wells of Wales,* on pages 134–136 one could fortunately find collected all the passages from the old literature and collections of folklore concerning Gwenhudwy. The oldest document, two verses by Lewis Glyn Cothi, dates back to the end of the fifteenth century but obviously presupposes an ancient tradition.[36] He leads us to believe that Gwenhudwy, moustached, was no more desirable than the *morforwyn*-type that we saw described by Myrddin Fardd. In a folklore text of 1824, the flood that destroys a city is called "Gwenhudwy's oppression." A manuscript by Iolo Morganwy cities, among three poetic names for the sea, Maes Gwenhidwy, "the plain of Gwenhidwy." W. Y. E. Wentz, in a book published in 1911, *Fairy Faith in Celtic Country,* page 152, says that he heard his mother call the small fluffy clouds that appear in good weather, "Gwenhidwy's sheep," In *Y Cymmrodor* 23 (1921), page 367, G. Hartwell Jones says that in Cardiganshire and in Powys, the term *gwenhidwy,* pronounced *cnidw* in Powys, was formerly used to designate an insignificant or decrepit creature and especially a sickly lamb. All this suffices to prove that there has existed an authentic and complex mythology about Gwenhudwy, of which not much remains. The essential thing for us is her flock, the waves that go by groups of nine, of "eight plus one," producing, at each ninth one, a ram.

---

35 That is to say doubtless "9 x 9," an infinite number of waves.

36 In a poem to ask for a razor, *Gwaith Lewis Glyn Cothi,* ed. E. D. Jones (1953), p. 135, line 64.

Ni adaf mal Gwenhidwy
ar vy min dyfu barf mwy.

"Like Gwenhidwy, I no longer grow a beard on my lip."

In a satire against Thomas Hanmer and Rhys Cain, Thomas Prys, an Elizabethan poet, writes (*The Cefn Coch MSS,* ed. J. Fisher, [Liverpool, 1899], p. 147):

Ail yw Rhys yn ael y rhiw
wan hydol i Wenhidw.

"Similar is Rhys, at the edge of the hill, feeble magician, to Gwenhidw." Is it an allusion to magic, *hud,* that Gwenhudwy seems to have in her name, or merely an assonance?

I do not at all pretend to suggest here that Gwenhudwy, or rather her waves and her ram, were of old, in the mythology, the homologues of Heimdall's mothers and of Heimdall himself; on the contrary it seems to me that, aside from this point, the two areas of mythology have nothing in common. But Gwenhudwy's strange flock nonetheless permits an interpretation without artificialities of the most picturesque section of Heimdall's dossier. We now see how a being born at the confines of the world, from nine sisters who are the waves, can not only have aquatic characteristics but can also be characteristically white, and behave like a ram. In our studies, to explain is most often only to bring together, to understand as a whole what seemed to be incoherent.

Can we push this unification further? This birth that has just explained in an unexpected way why Heimdall is also a ram—can it be made to agree with the character that earlier enabled us to organize the rest—the main part—of his description and which we summarized in the expression "frame god"? Here again, we are offered a precise correspondence.

We return to the celestial, Vedic and pre-Vedic god, Dyauḥ and his mythology as it appears in epic transposition in the story of Bhīṣma, "frame hero" of the *Mahābhārata*. I have recalled that it was for committing a fault that Dyauḥ had to be incarnated.[37] How was this punishment administered? As it often happens in the poem, the compiler has juxtaposed two versions, which occidental criticism would be in the wrong to "choose" between.[38] Moreover, they are very similar, though Dyauḥ's name is pronounced in only one of them. Here, in three points, are the characteristics:

1. Dyauḥ is not alone. There are eight delinquents and eight defaulters, he and his seven brothers,[39] he being the principal delinquent and the others accomplices, but all condemned to the same penalty of temporary incarnation.

2. Out of pity, to spare them the stains of a human womb, the great

---

37 *Mahābhārata*, I, 3843–3963.

38 I remain sceptical of the formal, stylistic criteria used with regard to these two versions by Ronald M. Smith, "The Story of Ambā in the Mahābhārata," *Brahmavidyā, the Adyar Library Bulletin* 19, 1–2 (1955), 91–96.

39 These eight brothers are the group of the Vasu gods. According to the *Brāhmaṇa*, it occurs that Dyauḥ is also counted among the Vasu: for example, *Śatapatha Brāhmaṇa* XI, 6, 3, 6. Elsewhere (for example *ibid.*, IV, 5, 7, 2), Dyauḥ and Pṛthivī, Sky and Earth, form the two complementary terms that bring the number of gods to thirty-three, after the twelve Āditya, the eleven Rudra and the eight Vasu. These affectations are surely artificial.

aquatic goddess, the Gaṅgā (personification of the Ganges, as much a celestial as an earthly river that, in the Indian Weltanschauung, is more important than the Ocean and which, moreover, serves as mythical wife to the Ocean) then decides to be their mother; she transforms herself into a woman and gets herself pregnant by a king.

3. She gives birth to all eight of them, successively, with quite different destinies. As for the first seven, complying with the prayers that they addressed to her before their incarnation, she throws them scarcely born into her own waters saying: "I love you!" and drowns them, so they have purged their sentences in a very short time.[40] Only the eighth and last will stay on earth, will grow and will have a career —and what a career! His life-cycle will be longer than the one of the history which he will "enframe": it is Dyauḥ-Bhīṣma.

This epic transposition doubtless drops a hint on the birth of the god himself, of Dyauḥ, a mythical trait that the Veda hymns had no opportunity to mention,[41] and the cosmic significance of which is transparent (we are reminded of the close connection, in Greece, of Okéanos and Ouranos).[42] *The sky was born of a great aquatic goddess, the last and sole survivor of a series of eight brothers of whom all, as soon as they were born, vanished before him, drowning at once in the maternal waters.* The second epic version, the one that does not mention Dyauḥ, offers a more complete correspondence in numbers: the final survivor is not the eighth one but the ninth one, constituted by the synthesis of portions of each other which the eight drowned ones had agreed to give for this purpose.[43] In both of its forms, we feel how close this scene is in principle and within its limits, to the Scandinavian tradition, though different in the arrangement of facts. This applies to the birth of Dyauḥ's homologue, this Heimdall whom nine waves begot—or, to be exact, according to the analysis suggested

---

[40] *Mahābhārata*, I, 3907–3908.

[41] In the case of the Pāṇḍu (sickly pale; stricken with a sexual prohibition equal to impotence), ritual texts have kept the equivalent mythical traits of his prototype Varuṇa; as for the wheel of Karṇa's chariot, embedded in the earth, and "Kṛṣṇa's steps," the hymns allude at least to the adventures or acts of Sūrya and of Viṣṇu who are the prototypes of them; Dhṛtarāṣṭra has the blindness that some ritual texts attribute to Bhaga, his prototype (Dumézil, *Mythe et epopée* I, pp. 31–257). Here, by analogy, one could think that the mechanism of the transposition was the same, but there is no more any trace of the prototype myth; strictly speaking, neither the hymns nor the rituals use myths relative to Dyauḥ.

[42] The oldest attested form of these relations, the Homeric one, make of Okeanos the primordial father of everything, gods included, θεῶν γένεδις. Later (Hesiod, etc.) he will be one of the Titans, son of Ouranos and of Gaia.

[43] *Mahābhārata*, I, 3860–3862.

by Gwenhudwy's ram, whom the ninth wave begot, coming after eight others.[44]

"Remarques comparatives sur le dieu scandinave Heimdallr," *Études celtiques* 8 (1959), 263–283.

---

[44] The Celtic god *Lugu-*, as we can imagine him according to the Irish Lug and the Lleu Llawgyfes of the Mabinogi of Math is neither a "frame god" nor a "sky god." Nevertheless we find attached to his "childhood" the four themes that constitute the "childhoods" of Dyauḥ-Bhīṣma: (1) Like Bhīṣma, at birth he is the only survivor of a group of brothers (two in the Mabinogi, the other being *Dylan Ail Ton* "Dylan similar to the Wave" or "son of the Wave"; three in a folklore narrative about Lug, W. J. Gruffydd, *Math vab Mathonwy* [1928], p. 73, cf. p. 67) in which the others were immediately drowned in the sea and the other (Dylan) was received by the wave in which he threw himself and acquired the characteristics of an aquatic creature. (2) In connection with this theme, just as Bhīṣma and his older drowned brothers are the sons of the cosmic river, the Gangā, personified, just so Lleu and his older brother Dylan are the sons of Aranrot (Arianrhod), sea heroine, the stay of which is still marked by a reef (J. Rhŷs, *Celtic Folklore, Welsh and Manx* [1901], I, 207–209. The theme is found in the Irish legends about Lug, born of a princess imprisoned in the Tor Mor of the small island of Tory, "on a cliff jutting into the Ocean," Gruffydd, *Math*, p. 65. (3) The birth of Bhīṣma (*Mahābhārata*, I, 3924–3959) and of Lug (Gruffydd, *Math*, p. 65) are the direct and vengeful consequence of the theft of the marvelous cow, of the "Cow of Plenty" (the birth of Lleu is introduced, less directly, by the stealing of Pryderi's marvelous pigs, the first pigs known in the island of Brittany). (4) The young Lleu (traces of this theme on the Irish Lug: Gruffydd, *Math*, p. 71) is struck by three interdictions that if they were not "turned around" by the skill of his uncle the magician Gwydion, would inhibit his life: he must not receive a name, nor arms, nor a wife; Dyauḥ, incarnated in the young prince Devavrata, is struck by two interdictions: he must renounce being king and getting married. Since he accepts the interdictions heroically, gods and men give him a new name, "Bhīṣma" (*Mahābhārata*, I, 4039–4065). Taking into account the magic value of the name, well established in the Celtic domain as elsewhere, it will be noted that the three prohibitions that threaten Lleu are distributed among the three functions of magic, military force, and fecundity.

CHAPTER 8

Notes on the Cosmic Bestiary of the Edda and the Rig Veda (1959)

The animal kingdom that throngs the branches of the ash tree Yggdrasil suggests analogies with the fauna of similar trees in folklore. Although we are now recognizing increasing numbers of these analogies,[1] there are still many others left unnoticed. For example, the eagle in its branches and the serpents crouched at its roots suggest not the general animosity between birds and serpents, but the particular enmity between a certain bird and a serpent who, in some folk tales, occupy identical positions on a tree.[2]

In addition to Yggdrasil, a veritable *axis mundi* that climbs from the bowels of the earth to the sky, Nordic mythology recognizes a less pretentious tree named Lærad (ON Læráðr), which is located entirely in the upper world, specifically near or in the home of Odin. Most likely this corresponds in mythology either to the village tree[3] or to the tree that stands at the center of a house (probably as part of the original framework)[4] such as the oak in the great hall of the Volsungs. In any case, all of this derives from a central idea that appears again in the world tree,[5] and it is difficult, perhaps futile to try to determine whether this practice produced the myth or vice-versa.

The bestiary of Lærad is strikingly similar to that of Yggdrasil,

---

1 See the diligent collection of these analogies in de Vries, *AGR* 2 (1957), pars. 583–584.

2 For example, Dumézil, *Contes Lazes* (1937), pp. 100–101.

3 Birger Pering, *Heimdall, Religionsgeschichtliche Untersuchungen zum Verständnis der altnordischen Götterwelt* (Lund, 1941), p. 109.

4 De Vries, *AGR* 2 (1957), par. 586.

5 M. Eliade, *Traité d'histoire des religions* (1949), pp. 258–259 (par. 112: "Arbre-axis mundi").

and hardly less varied. The ash tree, besides harboring the serpents and the eagle (the latter carrying a small, parasitic vulture between its eyes) also serves as a gymnasium for a perfidious squirrel and as pasture land for four stags. Of Lærad the *Grímnismál* tells the following in stanzas 25 and 26 (*Edda* [*Kuhn*], p. 62; *Edda* [Bellows], p. 94):

25 Heiðrún heitir geit, er stendr hǫllo á Heriafǫðrs
oc bítr af Læraðs limom;
scapker fylla hon scal ins scíra miaðar,
knáat sú veig vanaz.

26 Eicþyrnir heitir hiǫrtr, er stendr á hǫllo Heriafǫðrs
oc bítr af Læraðs limom;
enn af hans hornom drýpr í Hvergelmi,
þaðan eigo vǫtn ǫll vega.

Heithrun is the goat who stands by Heerfather's hall,
And the branches of Lærath she bites;
The pitcher she fills with the fair-clear mead,
Ne'er fails the foaming drink.

Eikthyrnir is the hart who stands by Heerfather's hall,
And the branches of Lærath he bites;
From his horns a stream into Hvergelmir drops,
Thence all the rivers run.

Thus, the source of the waters is Hvergelmir, literally "the boiling caldron."[6] Strophe 26 places it at the foot of Lærad, thereby being still in the upper world, in the territory of Odin, so the water dripping from the antlers of the Stag can reach the earth, and the terrestrial streams can have their source there. The strophes that follow[7] list the fantastic names of a number of streams, the last of which "fall" into the world of men and from there into the subterranean gulf of Hel (strs. 28–29), but the first of which seem not to leave the domain of the gods, *þær hverfa of hodd goða* (str. 27).[8] Snorri, however, places Hvergelmir in the subterranean world, at the roots of Yggdrasil, just above Niflheim. This reservoir is probably the home of the anonymous serpents, *ormar*, and definitely the home of Nid-

[6] De Vries, *AGR* 2 (1957), par. 577; Pering, *Heimdall*, pp. 104–114, whose chapter 4 ("die himmlische Welt," pp. 98–119) is an attentive discussion of the Eddic cosmography.

[7] There is no reason to consider these strophes as interpolated, despite, for example, H. Gering and B. Sijmons, *Kommentar zu den Liedern der Edda* (1927), I, 198.

[8] "They flow through the *hodd* of the gods." Since S. Bugge (*Norrœn fornkvædi* [Christiania, 1867], p. 81), we give *hodd* here the meaning of "home, dwelling-place."

hogg, that serpent or dragon who gnaws respectively the roots and the base of the trunk of Yggdrasil.[9] Because the two trees are mythical equivalents, Snorri's choice in placing Hvergelmir is understandable; no doubt others before him had questioned to which tree it belonged.

U. Holmberg has given us a satisfying interpretation of one of the quadrupeds that lives near the top of both trees.[10] Just as the trees seem to correspond to the axis of the world, so the eagle at the top of Yggdrasil might represent the polar star,[11] and the nearby stags in the branches might represent one or more constellations adjoining the polar star. Other peoples of the north offer similar images: that which we call "Ursa Major" the Lapps of Scandinavia still call *sarw, sarva,* "Reindeer" or "Moose," names also used by several peoples in Siberia (Samoyeds, Ostyaks) and in Greenland. The same analysis can be used for the goat, who is another quadruped at the same level of the tree, but is distinct from the stag because of his different, but equally useful, cosmic functions.[12] These two animals of Lærad must therefore represent two rather stationary constellations, located in the extreme north of the sky. We have mythical traces of an astral imagery created by those hardy navigators of ancient Scandinavia, especially those of Norway, despite the fact that the more prestigious astronomy of the Mediterranean has mostly obliterated it. Examples of these traces, besides the above, are the "Eyes of Thjazi"[13] and the "Toe of Aurvandill," the latter apparently being the morning star of the Germanic community,[14] judging from the meanings of *ēarendel* in Old English.

---

9 *Snorra Edda* (Jónsson), p. 22 (*Gylfaginning,* chap. 15, utilizing *Grímnismál* strs. 34–35). The presence of Nidhogg in Hvergelmir appears from the expression of Snorri, who mentions Nidhogg in connection with Hvergelmir as its main peculiarity.

10 U. Holmberg, "Valhall och världsträdet," *Finsk tidskrift för viterhet* (*sic*) 83 (1917), 347–348; cf. H. Pipping, "Eddastudier, I," *Studier i nordisk filologi* 16 (1925), 33. Opposed with feeble arguments by Pering, *Heimdall,* p. 108.

11 Cf. the eagle (on one foot!) sculpted at the top of the perches, representing the axis of the world among the Dolgan Siberians, U. Holmberg, *Der Baum des Lebens* (1922), p. 16.

12 Despite Holmberg "Valhall" (see above, note 10), p. 345, who says of the goat, "Bilden är en stereotyp efterbildning af hjortmyten, som oftare förekommer, och det är mycket sannolikt, att myten om hjorten och myten om geten äro grenar af samma stam." M. H. Güntert, after S. Bugge, R. Meyer, and others, but without proposing a borrowing, has compared the foster mother goat of the *Edda* with the goat Amalthée, *Der arische Weltkönig und Heiland* (1923), p. 369.

13 *Snorra Edda* (Jónsson), p. 81 (*Skaldskaparmál,* chap. 4).

14 De Vries, *AGR* 2 (1957), par. 432. Some attempts at identification with stars of the "Eyes of Þjazi" were made by N. Beckman (alpha of the Lyre, and alpha of the Stork) and by I. F. Schroeter (Castor and Pollux) in *Maal og Minne* (1919), pp. 44–45, 120–121, respectively.

Crouching in the waters of Hvergelmir (as he does when the cauldron is placed under Yggdrasil) the serpent or dragon Nidhogg is not susceptible to astrological explanation: he is a subterranean being, a being of the deep, a wretch who will be on the side of the demons and monsters in that final battle when land and gods will perish.

* * *

No doubt it is conceptions of this sort which gave rise to the two enigmatic figures of the *Rig Veda*, the "one-legged Billy-goat" (Ajá ékapād),[15] mentioned five times, and the "Serpent (or Dragon) of the deep," (*Ahi budhnyà*), mentioned twelve times.[16] The first is never mentioned without the second (usually listed directly before or after him), except in X, 65, 13, as follows:

> May the daughter of Parvīru (the lightning?), the thunder, the one-legged Billy-goat, the bearer of the Sky, the Sindhu (or the river), the ocean waters, may all the gods heed my words, (just as) Sarasvatī (river-goddess), with pious thoughts, with Puramdhi (the deified Abundance).

But the text closely recalls X, 66, 11, where the two figures are found together as usual:

> May the Ocean, the Sindhu (or the river), space, the mid-earth-and-sky, the one-legged Billy-goat, the thunder, the sea, the Serpent of the deep, heed my words, (just as) all the gods and my generous patrons.

Thus the association is basic. The second text, because of the concepts that precede each of the two animals, and the first, because of the concepts that surround the billy-goat, suggest a specific geographic relation of the billy-goat with the air and sky, and of the serpent with the waters. The little that we know from elsewhere confirms this distribution.[17]

Concerning the "Serpent of the deep," we notice that there seems to be no distinction between the conception of terrestrial waters and that of atmospheric waters; that is, between ocean and cloud. (This is

---

[15] Very early the Indians speculated on this name of the goat, interpreting *a-já* "the not born"; many substantial Indianists have been engaged in turn: A. Ludwig, A. Bergaigne, K. Geldner, and others. See A. Minard, *Trois énigmes sur les cent chemins*, II (1956), par. 742, b.

[16] As often happens, the most objective statement of the facts remains that of A. A. MacDonell, *Vedic Mythology* (Strassburg, 1897), pars. 26, 27.

[17] ["Billy-goat" and "serpent," indicating the two animals:] VII, 35, 13 (hymn of çám): billy-goat (qualified as *deváḥ*), serpent, the ocean, Apām Napāt, Pṛṣṇi; but VI, 50, 14: billy-goat, serpent, the earth, the ocean, the pantheon; II, 31, 6, gives nothing in this regard: serpent, billy-goat, Trita, Rbhukṣan, Savitṛ, Apāṃ Napāt.

has supported, cannot any more easily be transported into the *Rig Veda*. In a text of the *Mahābhārata*, the sun is described as a luminary that for eight months pumps water by means of a black *pāda* (foot? ray?), water that it will turn into rain during the other four months. If this image has a connection with our billy-goat (which is not certain), it must be the effect of a later adaptation, since it seems overly difficult to attribute to the hymn poets a myth that Przyluski thinks "suggests to the peoples of Asia the monsoons by means of the spectacle of the whirlwinds." None of the numerous passages of the *Rig Veda* concerning the sun makes the least allusion to this process of seasonal "pumping."

Thus, diverse reasons convince us not to equate the one-legged goat with the sun, despite his being luminous and lodged in the sky. This is the humble and limited conclusion we can draw from an obscure strophe of one of the "Rohita Hymns" (*Atharva Veda*, XIII, 1, 6),[28] the only text of the *Atharva Veda* where he is named. This conclusion also proceeds from the almost unique[29] survival of our goat and serpent (henceforth inseparable companions) in the list of the twenty-eight patrons of constellations of the lunar zodiac. Granted, these two consort there with many other divinities, including some of the greatest, which had no special reason to fill this role. But that in itself may be the main point: if two such insignificant figures of the *Rig Veda* were included and preserved in the company of Varuṇa, Mitra, Indra, Viṣṇu, and the rest, it is possible that the very juxtaposition with these notorious, omnipresent gods gives them (or at least one of them, who then brings the other along) a direct and traditional connection with the luminaries of the sky.

Can one be more precise? Fifty years ago, in a book that did not enjoy a good reputation, H. Brunnhofer thought he had shown that the one-legged billy-goat was the name of the fixed polar star *dhruvá*

Oriental Studies VII, pp. 457–460, utilizing *Mahābhārata*, XII, 13.906–13.908. Dumont has compared an account from the collection *Vikramādityacarita*, which is in effect a beauteous solar fairyland—but wholly literary.

28 "Rohita a engendré le ciel et la terre; Parameṣṭin y a tendu son fil; à ce [fil] s'est appuyé Aja Ekapada, il a affermi le ciel et la terre par sa vigueur" (V. Henry, trans. [Paris, 1892–1896]). "Róhíta produced heaven and earth; there Parameṣṭin (the lord on high) extended the thread (of the sacrifice). There Aja Ekapāda (the one-footed goat, the sun) did fix himself; he made firm the heavens and earth with his strength" (M. Bloomfield, trans. [Oxford, 1897]). "The ruddy one generated heaven-and-earth; there the most exalted one stretched the line; there was supported the one-footed goat; by strength he made firm heaven-and-earth" (W. D. Whitney, trans. [Cambridge, Mass., 1905]).

29 The two names were also given to two Rudra and, as surnames, applied to Çiva.

(which played a heroic role in the nineteenth-century discussions on the date of the *Rig Veda.*)[30] He interpreted the epithet "uniped" as expressing the fact "that the North Star, that is the Billy-goat, always remains standing immovably on one and the same spot, as if it lacked feet for walking, or as if, like a stork, it remained forever standing on one leg." He is clearly wrong, even though his arguments have influenced as critical a spirit as A. Hillebrandt.[31] One may question the justification that adduces a certain mythical *ajá* (lacking the specific "one legged"), a sort of Urgott (already understood as *a-já*, "not born"?) whose principal service is to have fixed or established (*dhṛ-, ṣkambh-*) the earth and especially the sky.[32] We must recall, however, that in X, 65, 13 the one-legged billy-goat is followed immediately by the "bearer (or maintainer)[33] of the sky," *divó dhartā́*, as if one of the two concepts suggested the other. Thus, this "bearer (or maintainer) of the sky" is close to the image of an animated "Himmelsstütze" (*dhárman divó dharúne*, X, 170, 2, in speaking of the light of the sun), and of an inanimate "Himmelssäule" (*divó . . . skambhó dharúnaḥ*, IX, 74, 2, or *viṣṭambhó dharúṇo diváḥ*, IX, 2, 5, mystically applied to Soma).[34] Instead of being the polar star, the one-legged billy-goat might be a neighboring constellation, and consequently nearly stationary.

This conception could be confirmed by the fact that the one-legged goat and the serpent of the deep (under names hardly altered) are linked by their functions as regents over the twenty-sixth and twenty-seventh lunar asterisms[35] to Kubera, god of wealth. As such, they keep

---

30 H. Brunnhofer, *Arische Urzeit* (1910), pp. 147–163 ("Der Polarstern").

31 A. Hillebrandt, *Vedische Mythologie*, 2d ed. (1929), II, 306–307: "Auffallend ist, dass er [=Aja ekapād] öfter unter dem Ahi budhnya angerufen wird. Ist er ein Gegensatz zu ihm? Brunnhofer's Ansicht, dass er der Polarstern sei, scheint mir noch nicht so von vornherein abzuweisen, wie es geschehen ist."

32 *Atharva Veda*, I, 67, 5; VIII, 41, 10; X, 82, 6.

33 Träger" or "Stützer" or "Bewahrer." See the text at n. 19 above. This qualification is applied to two separate gods, considered as creators or maintainers of the world; three times to Soma (in the ninth book; cf. three times the synonymous expression *dharúṇo diváḥ*, qualifying Soma), twice to Savitṛ, once to Indra, once (in the plural) to Aditya. Twice (here, and in the plural, X, 60, 10) the expression is linked to no special god and must therefore have a more literal value. In these two cases, consisting of lists of divine names, one could think of construing "bearer(s) of the sky" in apposition with the name that precedes or follows (here with Ajá ékapād, there with Ṛbhu): but it seems that, in these lists, each term forms an autonomous unit.

34 Cf. again, concerning Indra and Soma, *Atharva Veda*, VI, 72, 2: "You have sustained the heaven with a prop (*úpa dyā́ṃ skambháthu skámbhanena*), you have greatly extended mother earth."

35 The asterism of the Billy-goat is formed from α, and without doubt from ζ of Pegasus; that of the Serpent from α of Andromeda and the γ of Pegasus: E.

with them gold "made by Fire on earth and increased by Wind,"[36] for Kubera is that one of the four *lokapāla* (the masters of the cardinal directions) whose headquarters are in the *north.*

Thus, through fleeting allusions in the hymns, one catches a glimpse of a pre-Vedic conception similar to the more realistic image that the Scandinavian cosmography supplied two thousand years later: to a serpent of the deep at the bottom of the world's axis corresponds an almost stationary billy-goat at the top, no doubt represented by some group of stars.[37]

This conception also accounts for a mythical conception of the aberrant Indians of Hindukush (Nuristan, formerly Kafiristan), whose amazingly archaic traditions our comparative research has not yet exploited. In the impassioned account of his voyage of 1889, Sir George Scott Robertson wrote the following:[38]

> A good story was told me about the sacred tree, whose branches were seven families of brothers, each seven in number, while the trunk was Dizane (goddess of Agricultural prosperity: cf. Vedic *Dhiṣáṇā* [Morgenstierne])[39] and the roots Nirmali (goddess of births); but the record of this story was lost in a mountain torrent.

Nevertheless, on the subject of the birth of the god Bagišt, Robertson reports some other details about this strange tree; he got them from a high priest of the Valley of Kám:[40]

> In a distant land, unknown to living men, a large tree grew in the middle of a lake. The tree was so big that if anyone had attempted to climb it, he would have taken nine years to accomplish the feat; while the spread of its branches was so great that it would occupy eighteen years to travel

---

Burgess, "Translation of the Sûrya-Siddhânta," *Journal of the American Oriental Society* 6 (1860), 342–343; already identified (1807) by H. Colebrooke, "On the Indian and Arabian divisions of the Zodiac," *Miscellaneous Essays* (1837), II, 343.

36 *Mahābhārata*, V, 3896–3899; the two regents are here called, in one word in the instrumental plural, *ajaikapādahirbradhnaiḥ*.

37 "This is how the Ostyaks of the Jenisei perceive the moose in our Ursa Major: the four main stars are the feet; the three others are three hunters, one Tungus, one Ostyak, one Russian; they also add three stars in front of the constellation to form the nose and the ears of the animal" (Holmberg, "Valhall," p. 348 n. 1, after V. J. Anučin). The "one foot" of the Vedic Billy-goat can be the interpretation of an alignment of stars in the constellation which it designates; but the Siberian configuration of the polar eagle-star designated above, n. 11, can also suggest a very simple explanation of this "one foot," if, as is probable, the Vedic and pre-Vedic Indians materialized, i.e., hewed in wood the "support of the world" and its higher accessories.

38 Sir George Scott Robertson, *The Kafirs of the Hindu-Kush* (1896), p. 386.

39 The dialect forms of this name are Kati *Disäri, Dissaune*, Prasun *Disnī*; cf. Ashkun *däsäṇi* "ogress": G. Morgenstierne, "The Language of the Prasun Kafirs," *Norsk Tidsskrift for Sprogvidenskap* 15 (1949), 283.

40 Robertson, *The Kafirs*, pp. 382–383.

from one side of it to the other. Satarám (god of the atmosphere, regulator of the rain, cf. Sk. *sudharma* [Morgenstierne][41] or Indra *Sutrāman*?) became enamoured of the tree, and journeyed towards it. On his near approach he was suddenly seized with a mighty trembling, and the huge tree burst assunder disclosing the goddess Dizane in the center of its trunk. Satarám had, however, seen enough; he turned round and fled in consternation.

Dizane began to milk goats (a question as to where the goats were, in the water or in the tree, was thrust aside with a wave of the hand). While she was engaged in this occupation, a devil observed her. He had four eyes, two in front and two behind. Rushing forward, he seized Dizane, while she bent her head to her knees, quaking with terror. The fiend tried to reassure her, saying, "It is for you I have come." She afterwards wandered into the Presungul, and stepping into the swift-flowing river, gave birth to an infant, who at once, unaided, stepped ashore, the turbulent waters becoming quiet and piling themselves up on either hand, to allow the child to do so.[42]

Thus was the birth of Bagišt, god of the waters and distributor of wealth (cf. Vedic Bhaga, of which his name seems to be a barbaric superlative): how we regret that Robertson could not obtain from his imperious informant the assurance that the goats Dizane immediately began milking were, as seems probable, *on the tree*!

"Notes sur le bestiaire cosmique de l'Edda et du Rg Veda," *Mélanges de linguistique et de philologie, Fernand Mossé, In Memoriam* (Paris: Librarie Marcel Didier, 1959), pp. 104–112.

[41] Morgenstierne, "Language," p. 283.

[42] Morgenstierne, "Some Kati Myths and Hymns," *Acta Orientalia* 15 (1956), 161–189, gives a somewhat different variation, both without the prologue of the tree and of the birth of Bagišt (pp. 167–168), and a brief description of Nirmalī (pp. 175–176); Sudrem and Dizäri also appear in these very precious texts. Another myth summarized by Robertson, *The Kafirs*, p. 388, speaks of a large, evil-doing serpent, but without connection with the Tree.

Index

Achaeans, xiii
Adam of Bremen, 4, 36, 42, 66, 72, 74, 123
Aditi, 127
Āditya, 49, 145
Adonis, 62
Ægir, 97, 116, 133
Æneid, 17
Æsir, xiii, xxiii, xxx, xxxi, 3–25, 28, 34, 36, 58–61, 66–68, 78, 103, 131, 133
Agni, xv
Agricola, Michael, 107, 109, 113
Ahi budhnyà, 144
Ahura Mazdā, 43, 52
Ajá ékapād, 144
Allan Mault, 93, 97
Amalians, 33
Anglii, 75
Anna Perenna, 19
Aṇra-Mainyu, xxviii, 62
Apām Napāt, 145
Arinbjǫrn, 77
Arjuna, 52, 54, 78
Arya, xiv, 49, 57
Aryaman, xiv, xxxiii, xxxvii, 49, 50, 51, 56, 58, 62, 63
Aryan, x, 16, 41, 49, 50
Aša, 49, 52
Asgard, 9, 10, 61, 90
Aši, 49, 50
Asia, etymology, 13, 15
Askr, 101
Aśvin, xii, 16, 53, 54
Atharva Veda, 146, 147
Attis, 62
Aurvandill, 143
Avesta, xx, xxviii, 43, 52
Aviones, 75
Aztecs, xvii

Baetke, Walter, 44
Bagišt, 149, 150
Balder, xxviii, xxx, xlvi, 11, 26, 48, 49, 58–65
Balderus, xl
Baldrs draumar, 133
Baltic, xxv, xxxvi
Basilius, 32
Battle Axe people, 12
Beli, 78
Benveniste, Émile, xv
Beowulf, 105, 106
Berserks, xxvi, 29, 41
Bestla, 101
Betz, Werner, xxx, xxxii, xliii, xlv, 12
Beyla, xxxi, 89–116
Bhaga, xiv, 49, 51, 56, 57, 62, 150
Bharata, 54
Bhīma, 54, 55, 78
Bhīṣma, 129, 130, 138, 139
Bhṛgu, 39
Bieka Galles, 76
Bloomfield, Maurice, 146
bō airìg, 16, 118
Boðn, 8
Bodvar, 70
Boiorix, 44
Bragi, 8, 10, 90
brāhmaṇa, 16, 40, 51, 120, 145
Brahmins, 18
Brate, Erik, 79
Breithablik, 11, 59
Brimir, 97
Brot af Sigurðarkviða, 40

Brunnhofer, H., 147
Brynhild, 40
Bugge, Sophus, 100
Byggvir, xxxi, 89–117

Caesar, 19, 32, 42, 118
Cahen, Maurice, 72, 111
Caucasian, 64
Celtic, xxv, 16, 34, 118
Chambers, R. W., 106
Charat, Francis, vii
Closs, Alois, xxii, xxxv
Cocles, 45. *See also* Horatius
Collinder, Björn, 111
Colosseum, 32
Comparative mythology, xx
Comte, Auguste, xxii
Constantine, 36
Coriolanus, xv
Cothi, Lewis Glyn, 137
Couchoud, Paul-Louis, xlv
Cu Chulainn, 70, 71
Cult, 5
Curiaces, 71
Curiatii, xiv
Cyavana, 25

Daksa, 127
Davidson, H. R. Ellis, xxxiii
Derolez, René, xxxviii
Dharma, 53, 56, 63
Dhṛtarāṣṭra, 54–64
Dionysius, 21
Dioscuri, xii, xxix, 77
Dius Fidius, xi, xxvi, 39, 47
Dizane, 149, 150
Drudj, 52
Druids, 16
Duchesne-Guillemin, Jacques, xvi
Dumézil, Georges, ix, x, xix, xx, xxiv, *passim*
Dumont, P. E., 146
Dundes, Alan, xviii
Durkheim, Émile, x
Duryodhana, 54–64
Dyauḥ, Dyaus, 35, 37, 128–130, 138, 139
Dyu, 128

Edda(s), xxiii, xxxi, 19, 26, 32, 42, 64, 72, 78, 97, 104, 105, 110, 126, 141. See also *Poetic Edda; Prose Edda*
Egill Skallagrímsson, 5, 77
Eikthyrnir, 142
Eisen, M. J., 106, 109, 110
Eldir, 97, 103, 116
Eliade, Mircea, xxxiv

Elves, 3
Embla, 101
Eschatology, 51, 52, 58, 64
Etruscans, 45
Evans, David, xvi

Fantastic Hunt, 30
Fardd, Myrddin, 134–137
*Felþinaz, 110
Fenrir, xli, 43, 45, 58, 61
Fensalir, 59
Feretrius, 36
Feridūn, 71
Fides, 39, 47, 48
Finnish, 34, 109
First function, xi, 36, 124
Fjalar, 8
flaith, 16, 118
Folklore Fellows, xxii
Folkvangar, 73
Forseti, 59
Fortuna, 51
Franks, xxxiii
Frey, xii, xiii, xxiii, xxv, xxviii, xxxviii, xxxix, xl, 3–11, 17, 18, 20, 24, 31, 33, 61, 66, 72, 73, 77–79, 90, 93, 94, 96, 102, 105, 110, 115, 119, 123
Freya, xii, xxiii, xxxi, xlvi, 3, 4, 6, 7, 10, 17, 18, 66–68, 73, 74, 79, 90, 103, 117
Fricco, 4, 5, 72, 123
Frigg, 6, 59, 90
Frisians, 43
Frodi, xxxix, xl, 73
Frösö, 79
Frotho, xxviii
Function, xi, 36. *See also* First function; Second function; Third function; Sovereign function

Galar, 8
Gandharvas, xxvi
Ganges, 139
Gapt, 33
Garm, 61
Garthríki, 10
Gautr, 33
Gefjon, 10, 90
Geiger, Bernhard, 52
Gerd, 5, 78
Gering, Hugo, 94
Germania, 32, 34, 35, 43, 47, 75
Germanic, xxii, xxv, xxix, xxx, xxxiii, xxxvi, 32, 48, 62
Germanic mythology, xx, xliii
Gerschel, Lucien, xv, xxxv

Gēryon, 71
Gesta Danorum, 7, 11. *See also* Saxo
Giantland (Jotunheim), 67, 68
Glitnir, 59
Golther, Wolfgang, 93
Gopen, George, vii
Gothic, 34
Goths, 19, 32, 33
Götterdämmerung, 61
Grand Bundahišn, 52
Greek, xxv
Grettir, 45
Grimm, Brothers, xx, xxii, xxiii
Grimm, Jacob, xxiv
Grímnismál, 29, 40, 127
Grjóttúnagarðar, 69
Grönbech, Vilhelm, xxi
Grundtvig, Svend, 93, 97, 98
Gullinhjalti, 70
Gullintanni, 131
Gullveig, 8, 24
Gunnar, 40
Güntert, Herman, xxii, 11
Gunther, xli
Gwenhidwy, 134–139
Gylfaginning, 73
Gylfi, 10

Hadingus, xxviii, xxxviii, xxxix, xlvi, 7, 30
Hagen, xli
Hallfreðr Vandræðaskáld, 6
Hallinskíði, 131
Hárbarðsljóð, 30, 40, 71, 123
Hārut-Mārut, 22
Hatherus, 62
Haugen, Einar, vii, ix, xvi, xix, xx, xxxi
Hávamál, 27
Heiðrek, 133
Heimdall, xv, xxxi, xxxv, xlvi, 11, 61, 67, 91, 105, 119, 126–133, 138, 139
Heimdallargaldr, 132
Heimskringla, 8, 31
Heinzel, Rudolf, 21
Heithrun, 142
Hel, 58, 60, 61, 63, 142
Helm, Karl, xxiv, xxvii, xxxiii, xxxiv, xxxvii, 31
Hengist, xxxvii
Henry, V., 146
Herakles, xiii, xxix, xxxv, xl. *See also* Hercules
Hercules, xiv, xxix, 19, 30, 35, 43, 47, 66, 71. *See also* Herakles
Herfjǫtur, 40
Hermunduri, 42
Herodotus, 65
Hillebrandt, A., 148
Himinbjorg, 11, 130
Hindukush, 149
Historical-evolutionist school, xxii, xxvii, xxxiv, 12, 17
Hittites, 124
Hleithrar, 10
Hlorridi, 91
Hoder, xl, 49, 58–61, 63, 64. *See also* Hatherus; Hotherus
Hoenir, 9, 25
Höfler, Otto, xxi, xxvi, xxx, xxxv, 12
Holmberg, Uno, 112, 113, 143
Hora Galles, 72, 96, 124
Horatius Cocles, xiv, xli, 46, 47, 71
Horsa, xxxvii
Horwendillus, xl
Hotherus, Høtherus, xl. *See also* Hatherus
Hott, 70
Hrolf Kraki, 70
Hrungnir, 68–70
Húsdrápa, 132, 135
Hvergelmir, 142–144
Hyndla, 74, 101
Hyndluljóð, 74, 127, 132

Idun, 90
Iliad, xiii
Indo-European, xi, xvi, xvii, xx, xxi, xxii, xxx, xxxv, xxxvi, xliii, 12, 15, 16, 18, 20, 23, 25, 35, 37, 39, 45, 48, 64, 71, 77
Indo-Iranian, xxv, 16, 18, 22, 25, 34, 39, 42, 49, 52, 56, 62
Indra, xii, xiv, xv, xxv, xxix, xxxv, xl, xli, 16, 17, 20, 22, 24, 25, 34, 37, 38, 41–43, 53, 54, 66, 71, 118, 147, 150
Ingunar-Freyr, 90
Iranian, 20, 61, 62, 64–66
Irish, 135
Irmin, xxxiii, xxxvii
Isis, 19, 74
Italic, xxv, 16, 25

Janus, xv, 126, 127
Jataka, 58
John Barleycorn, 93, 97
Jones, Francis, 137
Jones, G. Hartwell, 137
Jones, J., 134
Jones, T. Gwyn, 136
Jónsson, Finnur, 5, 100

Jordanes, 33
Jung, C. G., xxxiv
Jupiter, xi, xxvi, 16, 17, 24, 35, 36, 37, 39, 47, 50, 96
Juventas, xiv, 50

Kali, 56
Karsten, T., 79
Kaurava, 129
kenning, 74, 78
Kentauroi, xxvi
Kerényi, Carl, xxxiv
Konr, 119, 124
Krohn, Kaarle, 113
kṣatra, 40
kṣatriya, xii, 2, 16, 18, 120, 121
Kubera, 148, 149
Kudrun, xxxvi
Kummer, Bernhard, xxi
Kvas, 22
Kvasir, 8, 9, 11, 21, 62

Lærad, 141, 142
Lapp, 29, 71–73, 76, 95, 96, 111, 123, 124, 143
Le Roux, Françoise, xvi
Lévi-Strauss, Claude, xvi, xvii, xxxiv
Lid, Nils, 94, 95, 100, 116
Littleton, C. Scott, vii, xix, xxxv, xxxvi, xxxviii
Livy, xiv, 46, 47
Lokasenna, 30, 74, 89–117, 127, 132
Loki, xxviii, xxxii, xxxix, xlvi, 6, 22, 30, 40, 49, 58–68, 74, 89–92, 95, 100, 103, 105, 115, 129, 132
Lug, xli

Mac Cecht, 71
Mada, 22, 62
Mælaren, 10
Magni, 69
Mahābhārata, xiii, xv, xl, 21, 22, 23, 53, 58, 62–64, 78, 128, 129, 138, 147
Mannhardt, Karl, 61, 115, 117
Mannhardt, Wilhelm, xxiii
Marius, 54
Mars, xii, xxxviii, 17, 19, 30, 35, 42, 43, 47
Marut, 42
Mauss, x
Maximus, 50
Mazdaism, 58, 129
Meche, 71
Megalith people, 12
Meic Nechtain, 71
Meillet, Antoine, 39
Menasce, Jean de, 22
Mercurius, Mercury, 19, 30, 32, 35, 40, 42, 43, 47
Mermaid, 134
Middle High German, xxxvi
Mímir, 9, 25, 27, 28
Mitani, 16
Mithra, 43, 66
Mitothyn, xxv
Mitra, xi, xiv, xv, xxvi, 16, 20, 34, 37–40, 46–49, 53, 56–59, 62, 63, 118, 145, 147
Mjollnir, 66, 67
Mogk, Eugen, xxiii, xxviii, 7, 11, 21, 131
Montelius, Oscar, 34
Morforwyn, 134
Morganwy, Iolo, 137
Morgenstierne, Georg, 150
Mucius Scaevola, xli, 46, 47
Müllenhoff, Karl, 92
Müller, Max, x, xxii, xxiv, 35, 92, 98, 145
Müller, W., 133

nakṣatra, 145
Nakula, 54, 78
Nartes, 65
Nāsatya, xxix, 16, 18, 20, 22–25, 38, 53, 54, 77, 118
Nerthus, xxxvi, xl, 18, 75, 76
Nibelungen, 29
Nidhogg, 142, 144
Niflhel, 67
Ninck, Martin, xxi
Nirmali, 149
Njord, xii, xiii, xxiii, xxv, xxviii, xxxvi, xxxviii, xxxix, xl, 3–11, 17, 18, 31, 33, 66, 73–79, 90, 117, 119
Nóatún, 11, 73, 77
Norns, 104
Nuader, xli
Numa, 39

Odin, xi, xiii, xxi, xxiii, xxv, xxvi, xxix, xxx, xxxi, xxxiii, xxxvi, xxxviii, xli, 3–10, 14, 17–19, 23, 24, 26, 28–31, 33, 40, 41, 45, 46, 48, 51, 58, 60–62, 67, 69, 71–73, 78, 118, 122–125, 141. *See also* Wodan
Óðrörir, 8
Ohlmarks, Åke, xxxii
Okéanos, 139
Old Irish, 34
Olo, xxix

Olrik, Axel, 71, 72, 93, 97, 98, 106, 111
Olsen, Magnus, 32, 76, 94, 100, 106, 109–111, 116
Opedal, Halvor, 76
Optimus, 50
Ornir, 97
Ossetic, xxviii, 64, 65
Ostyaks, 143
Ouranos, xxv, 37, 139
Ovid, xiv, 19

Paiute, xvii
Pāṇḍava, xiii, 53–58, 64, 128, 129
Pāṇḍu, 53–57, 62, 130
Paul, Hermann, xlv
Pedersö, 79
Peko, Pekko, 105–115
Pellon, 110
Pellonpecko, 107, 109, 113, 114, 115
Pering, Birger, 126, 131, 132, 133
Petersen, Karl Nikolai Henry, 31
Philippson, Ernst Alfred, xxxvii, xxxviii, 11, 12, 14
Picts, 13
Pipping, Rolf, 27
pišṭhra, 124
Pliny the Elder, 103
Plutarch, 44
Poetic Edda, 30
Polomé, Edgar, xvi, xxxvi
Porsenna, 45
Positivism, xxi
Prajāpati, 146
Propp, Vladimir, xxxiv
Prose Edda, xxiii, 8, 73
Przyluski, J., 146, 147
Puhvel, Jaan, xvi, xxxv, xxxvi
Pūšan, 51

Quirinus, xii, xxxviii, 17, 20
Quirites, 50

Ragnarok, 58, 61, 64, 129
Randulf, Johann, 96
Rees, Brinley, 137
Reinach, Solomon, 100
Reudigni, 75
Rhŷs, John, 134
Rig, 119, 130
Rigsþula, xxxi, 118–120, 122, 124, 125, 127, 129, 130
Rig Veda, xv, xxxi, 38, 39, 41, 47, 52, 71, 127, 141, 144–148
Robertson, George Scott, 149, 150
Rohinī, 145
Rohita Hymns, 147
Romulus, 24, 39
Rota, 33
Runes, 27, 34

Sabines, xiii, 24
Sæmundar Edda, 93
Sahadeva, 54, 78
Sahlgren, Jöran, 111
Salin, Bernhard, 11, 12, 31
Samoyeds, 143
Sanskrit, 16
Sarasvati, xii
Śatapatha Brāhmaṇa, 40
Satarám, 150
Savītṛ, 51, 127
Saxland, xxiii, 10
Saxnot, 19
Saxo (Grammaticus), xxviii, xxix, xxxi, xxxviii, xxxix, xl, xlvi, 7, 11, 13, 26, 120
Saxons, xxxiii, 19
Scaevola, 45. *See also* Mucius
Schröder, Franz Rolf, xxxv
Schück, Henrik, 11
Scots, 13
Scythian, 65
Seaxnēat, 19
Sebillot, 135
Second function, 124
Semele, 19
Semnones, 32
Setälä, E. N., 109
Setukesians, 107
Shah Nameh, 128
Shamanism, 27
Sievers, Eduard, 98, 99, 101
Sif, 68, 91
Sigrdrifumdl, 103
Sigurd, 29, 40, 41
Sijmons, Bernhard, 99
Simrock, Karl, 21
Sino-Tibetan, xvii
Siouan, xvii
Śiśupāla, xl
Sjoestedt, Marie-Louise, xvi
Skadi, 76, 77, 91
Skáldskaparmál, 7, 8, 11, 13, 14, 21
Skanke, 72
Skírnir, 78
Skírnismál, xl, 5, 20, 78
Skithblathnir, 28
Skjold, 10
Slavic, xxv
Sleipnir, 30

Snæbjǫrn, 133
Snorri (Sturluson), xxiii, xxviii, xxxi, xxxix, xlvi, 8, 13, 15, 16, 21, 23, 25, 26, 31, 45, 59, 67, 68, 70, 73, 78, 126, 131, 132, 142, 143
Solar mythology, x, xx, xxi
Soma, 21, 38, 39, 148
Són, 8
Sovereign function, xxvi, xxxviii
Sozryko, 64, 65
Sraoša, 49, 50, 52
Stammler, Wolfgang, xlvi
Starcatherus, xxix, 62
Starkad, xiv, xxxi, xl, 29. *See also* Starcatherus
Stator, 36
Structuralism, xvi, xxxiv
Strutynski, Udo, xix
śūdra, 120, 124, 125
Suevians, 19
Suiones, 75
Surt, 61
Sūrya, 146
Syrdon, xxviii, 64, 65

Tacitus, 18, 19, 30, 32, 35, 40, 43, 66, 74, 75
Tarpeia, 24
Tcherkessian, 65
Terminus, xiv, 50
Thing, 43
Thingsus, 43
Third function, xii, 53, 124
Thjalfi, 66, 69
Thjazi, 143
Thökk, 60, 61
Thomsen, Vilhelm, 109
Thor, xii, xiii, xxiii, xxv, xxxv, xxxvii, xli, 3–6, 11, 17–19, 23, 30, 33, 42, 43, 47, 61, 66–69, 71–73, 78, 79, 91, 96, 118, 123–125
Thruthvang, 11
Thrym, 67, 68
Thunar, 19
Tislund, 43
Titus Tatius, 24
*Tiwaz, *Tiuz, xxv, 37, 38, 43
Torsö, 79
Toth, Alan, vii
Trajan, 36
Tripartite, x, xxiv, xxxi, xxxv, xxxviii, xlv, 5, 119
Trita Āptya, xiv
Trojans, xiii
Tuesday, 44
Turville-Petre, Gabriel, xxiv, xxxiii, xlvi
Tvaṣṭar, xiv, 128
Tychè, 51
Tyr, xi, xiii, xxv, xxvi, xxx, xxxi, xxxiii, xxxvii, xli, 3, 19, 26, 35, 37, 40, 43, 44–48, 51, 59, 61, 63, 78, 90, 95, 130

ubhe virye, 18
Uhland, Ludwig, xxiii, 92
Ullr, xxv, 78
Umbrians, 17
Unwerth, W. von, 33
Uppland, 4, 14, 72
Uppsala, 4, 42, 66, 72–74
Urth, 104
Uṣas, 127
Uto-Aztecan, xvii
Uuōten, 19. *See also* Wodan

Vafþruðnismál, 27
Vaiśya, 16, 120, 124
vajra, 17, 66
Valerius Publiola, 47
Valhalla, 29, 30, 32, 40, 42, 58, 60, 68
Vali, 78
Valkyries, 29, 40, 42, 123
Vanaheim, 9
Vanir, xiii, xxiii, xxvi, xxx, xxxi, 3, 4, 7–14, 16, 18, 20, 24, 25, 34, 73, 78
Varini, 75
varṇa, 16, 120, 124
Varuṇa, xi, xv, 16, 20, 34, 36–39, 41, 46, 49, 53, 56, 62, 71, 118, 129, 147
Vayu, xv, 53, 54, 128
vazra, 66
Ve, 10
Veda(s), Vedic, xx, 16–18, 20, 35, 42, 49, 50–53, 56, 62, 63, 77, 128, 138, 139
Veralden Olmay, 96
Verethragna, 43
Vesta, xv
Vian, Francis, xvi
Vidar, xli, 61
Vidura, Vidhura, 54, 55, 56, 57, 58, 62, 63, 64
Vienna School, xxi
Víkarr, 30. *See also* Wicarus
Vili, 10
Vindhlér, 136
Viṣṇu, xli, 147
Vohu Manah, 49
Volsunga Saga, 30, 103
Volsungs, 141

Vǫluspá, 6, 7, 11, 13–15, 24, 27, 60, 104, 127
Vries, Jan de, xvi, xxvii, xxx, xxxii, xxxiii, xlv, 12, 31, 36, 44, 71, 126–128, 130–132
Vṛtra, 39, 129
Vulcan, 19

Walther, xli
Walther von der Vogelweide, 99
Ward, Donald, xvi, xxxvi, xxxviii
Warrior, xiii
Welsh, 134, 135
Wentz, W. Y. E., 137
West Germanic, 18, 19, 32
Westen, Thomas von, 72
Wicarus, xxix. *See also* Víkarr
Wikander, Stig, xv, 53, 128, 129
Wodan, *Wōðanaz, Woden, xxi, xxiv, 4, 5, 30, 32, 33, 35, 40, 42, 43, 72, 123. *See also* Odin
Wode, xxiv
World serpent, 61

Yama, 36, 41
Yggdrasill, 104, 141, 143, 144
Ynglingar, 7, 30
Ynglingasaga, 7, 8, 11, 13, 14, 41, 73
Yoshida, Atsuhiko, xvi
Young, Jean I., 134
Yudhiṣṭhira, 54–58, 62–64

Zagreus, 21
Zelenin, 113
Zeus, 35, 37
Zio, 35, 37
Zoroastrian, 16, 38, 43, 49–52, 58, 61, 62, 65

Þrymskviða, 67, 127
*Þunraz, 66